Advances in
MATHEMATICAL ECONOMICS

AF881860

Aims and Scope. The project is to publish *Advances in Mathematical Economics* once a year under the auspices of the Research Center for Mathematical Economics. It is designed to bring together those mathematicians who are seriously interested in obtaining new challenging stimuli from economic theories and those economists who are seeking effective mathematical tools for their research.

The scope of *Advances in Mathematical Economics* includes, but is not limited to, the following fields:

- Economic theories in various fields based on rigorous mathematical reasoning.
- Mathematical methods (e.g., analysis, algebra, geometry, probability) motivated by economic theories.
- Mathematical results of potential relevance to economic theory.
- Historical study of mathematical economics.

Authors are asked to develop their original results as fully as possible and also to give a clear-cut expository overview of the problem under discussion. Consequently, we will also invite articles which might be considered too long for publication in journals.

S. Kusuoka, T. Maruyama (Eds.)

Advances in Mathematical Economics

Volume 12

Springer

Shigeo Kusuoka
Professor
Graduate School of Mathematical Sciences
University of Tokyo
3-8-1 Komaba, Meguro-ku
Tokyo, 153-0041 Japan

Toru Maruyama
Professor
Department of Economics
Keio University
2-15-45 Mita, Minato-ku
Tokyo, 108-8345 Japan

ISSN 1866-2226 e-ISSN 1866-2234
ISBN 978-4-431-99865-5 e-ISBN 978-4-431-92935-2
DOI 10.1007/978-4-431-92935-2
Springer Tokyo Berlin Heidelberg New York

Printed on acid-free paper

Springer is part of Springer Science+Business Media (www.springer.com)

Table of Contents

Research Articles

Adv. Math. Econ. 12, 1–21 (2009)

Advances in
MATHEMATICAL
ECONOMICS

Unemployment and income distribution in the medium-run growth model

Hideyuki Adachi*

Onomichi University, Onomichi, Hiroshima, Japan
(e-mail: adachih@onomichi-u.ac.jp)

Received: June 15, 2008
Revised: October 17, 2008

JEL classification: E10, E24, E25, O41

Mathematics Subject Classification (2000): 34D23

Abstract. By extending the Solow growth model so as to include the unemployment rate as an endogenous variable, I construct a medium-run growth model and explore evolutions of major macroeconomic variables in the medium-run. Instead of assuming that the real wage rate is perfectly flexible to assure always full-employment in the labor market, I introduce a wage-setting equation a la Blanchard (Brooking Pap. Econ. Act. 2:89–158, 1997) that assumes a negative relation between the level of real wage and the unemployment rate. An important characteristic of this model is that it includes unemployment even in the steady growth equilibrium. This model can analyze the theoretical relationships among the main macroeconomic variables including the rate of growth, the rate of unemployment, and the labor share of income in the medium-run. Applying this model to the Japanese economy, we attempt to explain the trend of major macroeconomic variables during the last 50 years; as the growth rate of real GDP tended to decline over last 50 years, the unemployment rate, the capital coefficient and the labor share had tendencies to rise over time. The trends of these macroeconomic variables are shown to be explained consistently with our model under certain conditions on parameters of the model.

Key words: capital coefficient, labor share, medium-run growth model, the rate of unemployment

* The author would like thank Ichiro Tokutsu, Taiji Hagiwara, and Hidefumi Kawakatsu for help with data and diagrams. He is also grateful to an anonymous referee for valuable comments.

S. Kusuoka, T. Maruyama (eds.), *Advances in Mathematical Economics Volume 12*,
DOI: 10.1007/978-4-431-92935-2_1,

1. Introduction

Macroeconomic theory is broadly divided into two sub-areas: the long-run theory and the short-run theory. The former focuses on growth and its determinants, and the latter on the study of business cycles. In standard textbooks of macroeconomics, the key difference between the short-run and the long-run is considered to lie in the behavior of prices and wages. In the long-run, prices and wages are flexible and respond to excess supply or demand to clear any market. In the short-run, many prices and wages are sticky at some predetermined level. The short-run theory deals with macroeconomic fluctuations that reoccur every 5–10 years, while the long-run theory analyzes the patterns of growth that arise over periods of several decades.

Recently, there has been substantial interest in macroeconomic problems that do not easily fit into either of these two sub-areas. As examples of such problems, we may mention divergent trends in unemployment in Europe in 1980s and 1990s, persistent stagnation in Japan in 1990s, and the long lasting boom in the US from 1991 to 2001. Each of these phenomena is not easily categorized as a business cycle or a growth phenomenon. Neither the short-run theory nor the long-run theory can provide an appropriate framework to analyze those phenomena, so that different tools for analysis may be required to understand them. Blanchard [2] calls macroeconomic changes that extend over periods of 10–20 years as medium-run phenomena, and suggests the importance of developing macroeconomics of the medium-run.[1] This area of research is developed also by Malinvaud [5,6], Solow [8,9], Beaudry [1], and so on.

In this paper, we construct a medium-run growth model, which can explain the persistent unemployment, by introducing the wage-setting equation into the Solow growth model. If the rate of technological progress is constant and labor-augmenting, this model has a unique steady growth equilibrium that satisfies the stability condition as is the same in the Solow model. In contrast to the Solow model, however, our model includes a constant rate of unemployment even in the steady growth equilibrium. This is due to the imperfect flexibility of wages that is implied by the wage-setting equation.

---

[1] The definition of the medium-run, especially about its span, is different depending on the authors. Blanchard [2] has suggested naming macroeconomic changes that spread over periods of 15–30 years. Solow [8] defined the medium-run as "five-to-ten-year time scale at which some sort of hybrid transitional model is appropriate." Beaudry [1] says "medium-run macroeconomics refers to aggregate economic phenomena that manifest over periods of 10–25 years." In spite of some differences in their view of the time span, all of them agree in the point that this area of research deals with the phenomena that are not dealt with either by short-run or long-run macroeconomics.

Thus, our model may be characterized as a medium-run growth model since it deals with the time horizon over which the labor market is not cleared completely. Using this model, we will analyze how the rate of economic growth, the rate of unemployment and the labor share are related each other in the medium-run.

As an application of this model, we attempt to explain the trend of major macroeconomic variables in Japan during the last 50 years. As the growth rate of real GDP tended to decline over last 50 years in Japan, the unemployment rate, the capital coefficient and the labor share tended to rise over time. The trend of these macroeconomic variables are shown to be explained consistently, according to our model, if parameters in the model such as the rate of labor-augmenting technological progress, the capital efficiency coefficient, the rate of saving, and the elasticity of substitution between labor and capital satisfy certain conditions. These conditions, we argue, seem to conform to what happened in the Japanese economy during the last 50 years. The framework of our model is so simple and general that it may provide interpretations of medium-run evolutions not only in Japan but also in other countries.

2. The medium-run growth model

In this section, we construct a medium-run macroeconomic model that can explain changes in unemployment in the evolution of the growth path. The model developed below basically adopts the framework of the Solow growth model,[2] but extends it so as to include unemployment as an endogenous variable. The model may be called "the medium-run growth model" since it deals with the time horizon over which the labor market is not yet perfectly adjusted. In other words, it deals with the period that is not as short as prices are considered to be rigid, but is not so long as prices are considered to be flexible enough to attain full-employment. Thus, the model developed below is able to analyze the determination of the unemployment rate in the growth process.

The production function is assumed to include factor augmenting technological progress to be represented as follows:

$$Y = F(AN, BK), \tag{2.1}$$

where Y is output, N is labor employment, K is the stock of capital, A is the efficiency of labor, and B is the efficiency of capital. Assuming that the production function is subject to the constant returns to scale, we can rewrite it as

$$y = Bf(n). \tag{2.2}$$

[2] As for the Solow growth model, see [7].

Here, y is output per unit of capital and n is the efficiency labor per unit of efficiency capital, i.e.

$$y \equiv \frac{Y}{K}, \qquad n \equiv \frac{AN}{BK}. \tag{2.3}$$

The production function rewritten in the ratio form as $f(n)$ is assumed to be concave in the strong sense and satisfy the following conditions:

$$f(0) = 0, \quad \lim_{n \to 0} f'(n) = \infty, \quad \lim_{n \to \infty} f'(n) = 0. \tag{2.4}$$

We assume, as with the Solow model, that a constant proportion of income is saved and invested. Then, the growth rate of capital is given by the following equation:

$$\frac{\dot{K}}{K} = sBf(n), \tag{2.5}$$

where s represents the saving rate. It is assumed, for simplicity, that there is no depletion of capital.

The structure of the model formulated so far is the same as that of the Solow model. However, the formulation of the labor market in our model is different from that of the Solow model. Instead of assuming that wages and prices are always market-clearing, our medium-run growth model assumes that prices and wages are more or less sticky due to the behavior of monopolistically competitive firms and the bargaining between firms and laborers. The price-setting equation together with the wage-setting equation determines the real wage rate and the employment rate (i.e., one minus the unemployment rate). The employment rate thus determined is normally less than unity, meaning that there exists unemployment.

At each point in time, a firm with given stock of capital faces the problem of determining employment and output. For simplicity, let all firms be homogeneous. Then, n that is defined by the second equation in (2.3), is both employment of a firm with given stock of capital and the ratio of labor to capital for the economy as a whole. As each firm is monopolistically competitive in the goods market, it faces the downward sloping demand curve. The demand for its goods is assumed to be given, in the inverse form, by

$$p = \left(\frac{y}{\bar{y}}\right)^{-\eta}, \quad 0 \leq \eta < 1. \tag{2.6}$$

Here, p is the price charged by the firm relative to the price level, $\bar{y}$ is the average output of all firms, and η is the inverse of the elasticity of demand. At each point in time, a firm determines the amount of labor for given capital stock n to maximize profit per unit of capital π which is expressed as

$$\pi = py - \left(\frac{B}{A}\right) wn. \tag{2.7}$$

Here, w is the real wage rate in terms of the price level. The first order condition of the profit maximization and the symmetry condition that all firms must charge the same price (i.e., $p = 1$) imply that

$$\left(\frac{1}{\mu}\right) f'(n) = \frac{w}{A}, \tag{2.8}$$

where $\mu = 1/(1 - \eta)$ is the markup of price over marginal cost. For any given real wage rate, this equation determines the demand for labor per unit of capital for each firm. Then the aggregate demand for labor becomes as $N = (B/A)nK$.

Let us next consider the supply side of the labor market. The Solow model assumes that the supply of labor grows at a constant rate independently of the wage rate, and that it is fully employed through the adjustment of flexible wages and prices. In our medium-run growth model, by contrast, the supply side of the labor market is represented by a wage-setting equation, which makes wages tend to exceed the market-clearing level. The wage-setting equation can be derived from bargaining or efficiency wage models.[3] Those theoretical models of wage-setting generate a strong core implication that the tighter the labor market, the higher the real wage, given the workers' reservation wage. The simplest formulation of the wage-setting is given by the following equation which was proposed by Blanchard[4]

$$\frac{w}{A} = \gamma \left(\frac{N}{N_s}\right)^{\varepsilon}, \tag{2.9}$$

where N_s is the population of labor, so that N/N_s is the employment rate. The parameter γ reflects reservation wages, and ε represents the sensitivity of the real wage rate to the tightness of the labor market.

Denote the ratio of labor population in efficiency unit AN_s to capital in efficiency unit BK by n_s, i.e.

$$n_s \equiv \frac{AN_s}{BK}. \tag{2.10}$$

Then, equation (2.9) is rewritten, by using this and the definition of n in (2.3), as

$$\frac{w}{A} = \gamma \left(\frac{n}{n_s}\right)^{\varepsilon}. \tag{2.11}$$

---

[3] See [4, Chaps. 2 and 3].

[4] See [2, p. 108].

From (2.8) and (2.11), the equilibrium of the labor market is expressed by the following equation:

$$\left(\frac{1}{\mu}\right) f'(n) = \gamma \left(\frac{n}{n_s}\right)^{\varepsilon}. \tag{2.12}$$

At a given point in time, n_s is constant since the population of labor in efficiency unit AN_s and capital stock in efficiency unit BK are given. Thus, this equation determines the value of n. It must satisfy the inequality $n \leq n_s$ in order for this solution to be economically meaningful. In the following, we assume that this condition is satisfied.[5] Then labor employment is determined by $N = (B/A)nK$.

As with the Solow model, labor population N_s is assumed to grow at a constant rate λ, i.e.

$$\frac{\dot{N}_s}{N_s} = \lambda. \tag{2.13}$$

The rate of labor-augmenting technological progress denoted by α and the rate of capital-augmenting technological progress denoted by β are also given constant, i.e.

$$\frac{\dot{A}}{A} = \alpha, \quad \frac{\dot{B}}{B} = \beta. \tag{2.14}$$

Taking the time derivative of (2.10) and considering (2.13) and (2.14), we have

$$\frac{\dot{n}_s}{n_s} = (\alpha - \beta + \lambda) - sBf(n). \tag{2.15}$$

This equation and (2.12) constitute a complete system to determine the paths of n and n_s. Then, the path of the employment rate n/n_s is also determined.

We include capital-augmenting technological progress as well as labor-augmenting technological progress at the start of the discussion, in order to consider the role of biased technological progress in our model. It will be shown below that the steady growth equilibrium is not consistent with steady capital-augmenting technical progress (i.e., with $\beta > 0$ or $\beta < 0$). However, occasional changes in the level of capital efficiency B are consistent with steady growth equilibrium. By including the capital efficiency coefficient explicitly in our model, we can analyze the effects of biased technological changes on unemployment and income distribution as will be shown below.

As is mentioned above, the employment-capital ratio n that is determined by (2.12) is normally less than n_s, meaning that there always exists some

---

[5] We may replace the wage-setting function (2.11) by a more general function such that $w/A = g(n/n_s)$, where $g' > 0$ for $0 < n/n_s < 0$ and $g(n/n_s) \rightarrow \infty$ as $n/n_s \rightarrow 1$. Then, any solution of n for equation $(1/\mu) f'(n) = g(n/n_s)$ satisfies the condition $0 < n/n_s < 1$.

unemployment in our model. However, when parameter ε tends to infinity in equation (2.12), which means that the real wage rate becomes completely flexible, we must have $n = n_s$. In other words, the continuous full-employment is ensured when $\varepsilon \to \infty$. In addition, let us set $\beta = 0$ and $B = 1$ in equation (2.15), which means that technological progress is purely labor-augmenting. Then, it becomes as

$$\frac{\dot{n}}{n} = (\alpha + \lambda) - sf(n). \tag{2.16}$$

This equation is the same as the dynamic equation in the Solow model. Moreover, if we put μ=1 (i.e., $\eta \to \infty$) in (2.8), the commodity market of the model becomes perfectly competitive. Then, this model agrees with the Solow model. Thus, the Solow model is interpreted as an extreme case of our model.

3. The steady growth equilibrium and its stability

Turning back to the complete system of the medium-run growth model consisting of (2.12) and (2.15), let us focus on the case where this system has the steady growth equilibrium. If we denote the steady state values of (n, n_s) by (n^*, n_s^*), they must satisfy the following equations:

$$\frac{1}{\mu} f'(n^*) = \gamma \left(\frac{n^*}{n_s^*} \right)^{\varepsilon}, \tag{3.1a}$$

$$f(n^*) = \frac{\alpha - \beta + \lambda}{sB}. \tag{3.1b}$$

Thus, the steady state equilibrium requires that the right-hand side expression of equation (3.1b) to be constant. This condition implies $\beta = \dot{B}/B = 0$, so that there is no capital-augmenting technological progress. In other words, technological progress must be purely labor-augmenting for the steady growth equilibrium to exist. It should be noted, however, that the steady growth is consistent with once for all change in the efficiency coefficient of capital, B. A change in B brings about a shift in the steady growth equilibrium. In order to examine this effect, we will make parameter B explicit in the following model.

Thus, the complete system that is consistent with the steady growth equilibrium is represented by the following equation system:

$$\frac{1}{\mu} f'(n) = \gamma \left(\frac{n}{n_s} \right)^{\varepsilon}, \tag{3.2a}$$

$$\frac{\dot{n}_s}{n_s} = (\alpha + \lambda) - sBf(n). \tag{3.2b}$$

The steady growth equilibrium of this system is attained at $(n^*, \; n_s^*)$ such that

$$\frac{1}{\mu} f'(n^*) = \gamma \left(\frac{n^*}{n_s^*} \right)^{\varepsilon}, \tag{3.3a}$$

$$f(n^*) = \frac{\alpha + \lambda}{sB}. \tag{3.3b}$$

This steady growth equilibrium is stable if the dynamic equation (3.2b) decreases with n_s, i.e.

$$\frac{d(\dot{n}_s/n_s)}{dn_s} = -sBf'(n)\frac{dn}{dn_s} < 0. \tag{3.4}$$

Here, in view of (3.2a),

$$\frac{dn}{dn_s} = \frac{\gamma\varepsilon(n/n_s)^{\varepsilon}}{\gamma\varepsilon(n/n_s)^{\varepsilon-1} - nf''(n)} > 0. \tag{3.5}$$

Therefore, the system converges to the steady state starting from any initial conditions.

In contrast to the Solow model in which the labor force is always fully employed, the steady state in our model includes a constant rate of unemployment. It is caused by the imperfect adjustment of the labor market due to inflexibility of real wages. This means that the time horizon over which the steady state is attained in our model is not so long as that in the Solow model in which wages and prices are assumed to be flexible to clear all markets. In this sense our model may be interpreted as dealing with the medium-run in which prices and wages are not as sticky as in the short-run but not as flexible as in the long-run. In the following, this medium-run growth model is used to analyze the relationship among the rate of growth, the rate of unemployment and income distribution.

4. Growth and the employment rate in the medium-run

In this section, we discuss the relationship between growth and unemployment in the medium-run. In view of (2.2), (2.5), and (3.3b), the growth rate of output Y and that of capital K in the steady state are the same and given as follows:

$$\left(\frac{\Delta Y}{Y}\right)^* = \left(\frac{\Delta K}{K}\right)^* = \alpha + \lambda. \tag{4.1}$$

Thus, the steady growth rate in our model is determined as the sum of the rate of technological progress α and the rate of population growth λ, so that it is independent of the saving rate s. Thus, the determinants of the steady growth rate in our model are the same as that in the Solow model.

Let us next examine how the employment rate is determined in our model. Denoting the employment rate (i.e., 1 minus the unemployment rate) by z, we have

$$z \equiv \frac{n}{n_S}. \tag{4.2}$$

Taking its derivative with respect to time, we have

$$\frac{\dot{z}}{z} = \frac{\dot{n}}{n} - \frac{\dot{n}_S}{n_S}. \tag{4.3}$$

By using this relationship, the complete system consisting of (3.2a) and (3.2b) is reduced to a system of a single variable z.

First, equation (3.1a) is rewritten as follows:

$$\frac{1}{\mu} f'(n) = \gamma z^{\varepsilon}. \tag{4.4}$$

Taking logarithm of this equation and differentiate it with respect to time, we have

$$\frac{\dot{n}}{n} = -\frac{\varepsilon\sigma}{1-\theta}\frac{\dot{z}}{z}. \tag{4.5}$$

Here θ is the elasticity of output with respect to labor employment and σ is the elasticity of substitution between labor and capital, which are defined as follows:

$$\theta \equiv \frac{nf'(n)}{f(n)}, \qquad \sigma \equiv -\frac{f'(n)[f(n) - nf'(n)]}{nf''(n)f(n)}. \tag{4.6}$$

When the production function $f(n)$ has well-behaved properties, the values of these parameters must be $0 < \theta < 1$ and $\sigma > 0$. Substituting (4.5) and (3.2b) into (4.3), we get the following equation:

$$\frac{\dot{z}}{z} = \frac{1-\theta}{1-\theta+\varepsilon\sigma}[sBf(n) - (\alpha+\lambda)]. \tag{4.7}$$

The right-hand side of this equation still includes n. If it is expressed as a function of z, we get a complete dynamic system in terms of a single variable z.

For this purpose, we solve equation (4.4) with respect to n, and get

$$n = f'^{-1}(\mu \gamma z^{\varepsilon}). \tag{4.8}$$

Since $f'(n)$ is a monotonic decreasing function, n is monotonically decreasing with respect to z. Therefore, $f(n)$ can be transformed into a function of z as follows:

$$f(n) = f(f'^{-1}(\mu \gamma z^{\varepsilon})) = \phi(z). \tag{4.9}$$

Since $f(n)$ is a monotonic increasing and $f'(n)$ is a monotonic decreasing function, $\phi(z)$ becomes a monotonic decreasing function. Substituting (4.9) into (4.7), we obtain a dynamic equation of z as follows:

$$\frac{\dot{z}}{z} = \frac{1-\theta}{1-\theta+\varepsilon\sigma}[sB\phi(z) - (\alpha+\lambda)]. \tag{4.10}$$

The steady growth equilibrium of this dynamic equation is attained at z^* which satisfy

$$\phi(z^*) = \frac{\alpha+\lambda}{sB}. \tag{4.11}$$

Figure 1 describes the dynamics of z in the diagram, taking $\dot{z}/z$ in the vertical axis and z in the horizontal axis. Equation (4.10) is represented by the downward sloping curve which intersects the horizontal axis at z^*, the steady state value of the employment rate. If the employment rate is initially at z_0 that is less than z^*, the actual z tends to increase, because $\dot{z}/z < 0$ at $z = z_0$. The opposite holds if the employment rate is initially at z_1 that is less than z^*. Thus, the steady growth equilibrium is stable, so that the system tends to the steady state from any initial conditions.

As is obvious from equation (4.11), the steady state employment rate z^* depends on the steady growth rate $\alpha + \lambda$, the savings rate s and the capital efficiency B. Since $\phi(z)$ is a decreasing function, z^* depends negatively on $\alpha + \lambda$, and positively both on s and on B. More strictly, shifts in the steady state employment rate in response to these parameters are represented by the following equation that is obtained by taking the difference of both sides of equation (4.11)

$$\Delta z^* = \frac{\phi}{\phi'}\left[\frac{\Delta(\alpha+\lambda)}{\alpha+\lambda} - \frac{\Delta B}{B} - \frac{\Delta s}{s}\right]. \tag{4.12}$$

Here, $\phi/\phi' < 0$. It follows from this equation that

$$\Delta z^* \leq 0 \text{ or } \geq 0, \quad \text{according as whether} \quad \frac{\Delta(\alpha+\lambda)}{\alpha+\lambda} - \frac{\Delta B}{B} - \frac{\Delta s}{s} \geq 0 \text{ or } \leq 0. \tag{4.13}$$

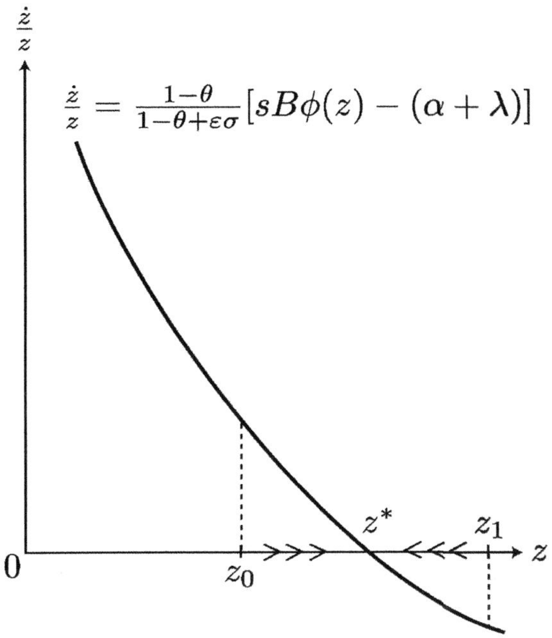

Fig. 1 Dynamics of the medium-run growth model

This result implies that the steady state employment rate (z^*) is decreased when any one of the following changes in the parameters occurs: (1) an increase in the rate of steady growth ($\alpha + \lambda$), (2) a decrease in the capital efficiency (B), (3) a decrease in the rate of savings (s). The transitional process to the new steady state is depicted by Fig. 2. When any one of these changes occurs, the downward sloping curve which represent equation (4.10) shifts downward (or to the left). Then, the rate of changes in the employment rate $\dot{z}/z$ at $z = z^*$ becomes negative, so that the employment rate z begins to decrease. The decreases in z continue until it reaches the new steady state z^{**}.

The above result that the steady state employment rate is negatively related to the steady state growth rate may seem contrary to what is normally expected. This result may be interpreted in the following way. The steady growth rate, $\alpha + \lambda$, represents the rate of population growth in efficiency unit. When $\alpha + \lambda$ increases, the steady state employment-capital ratio in efficiency unit, n^*, increases in view of equation (3.3b). But when n^* increases, the marginal product of labor in efficiency unit, $f'(n^*)$, decreases, and so does the real wage rate for the efficiency unit of labor. Then, the steady state employment rate, $z^* = n^*/n_s^*$, decreases as is obvious from (3.3a).

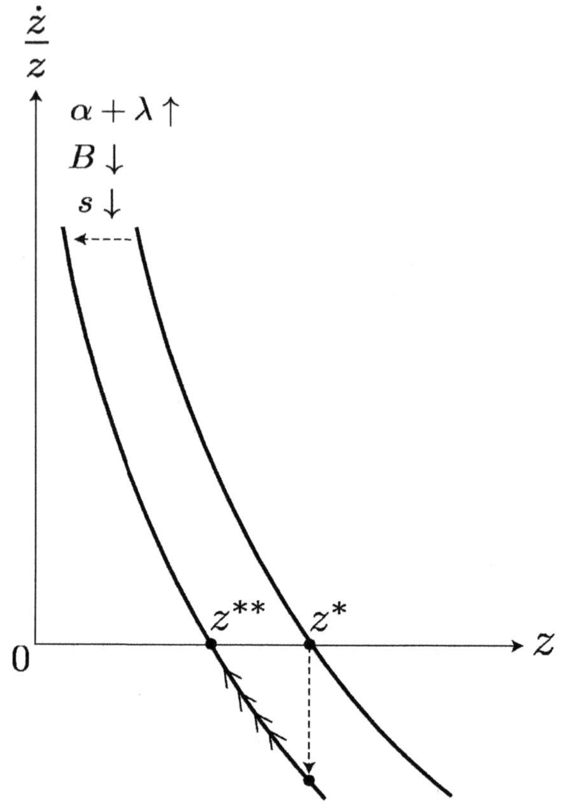

Fig. 2 Effects of changes in parameters

5. The labor share and capital coefficient in the medium-run

Let us next examine the relationship between growth and income distribution. By using (2.2), (2.3), and (2.8), the labor share wN/Y in our model is expressed as a function of n as follows:

$$\frac{wN}{Y} = \frac{1}{\mu}\frac{nf'(n)}{f(n)}. \tag{5.1}$$

Then, the rate of change of the labor share is given by

$$\frac{\Delta(wN/Y)}{wN/Y} = (1-\theta)\frac{\sigma-1}{\sigma}\frac{\Delta n}{n}. \tag{5.2}$$

Here, θ and σ are as defined by (4.6). We are examining here how the labor share in the steady state equilibrium shifts in response to changes in the parameters on which the steady state equilibrium depends. Notice that the steady state values of n is determined by (3.2b). Calculating $\Delta n/n$ from this equation and substituting it into (5.2), we can rewrite (5.2) as follows:

$$\frac{\Delta(wN/Y)}{wN/Y} = (1-\theta)\frac{\sigma-1}{\sigma}\left[\frac{\Delta(\alpha+\lambda)}{\alpha+\lambda} + \frac{\Delta B}{B} - \frac{\Delta s}{s}\right]. \tag{5.3}$$

As this equation shows, shifts in the labor share are caused by changes in technological progress, the growth rate of labor population and the savings rate. Notice that the expression in the bracket on the right-hand side of this equation is the same as that on the right-hand side of (4.12). Therefore, changes in those parameters influence on the labor share and the employment rate in the same direction if $\sigma < 1$, and in the opposite direction if $\sigma > 1$.

Finally, let us see the relationship between the capital coefficient and growth. The output-capital ratio in the steady growth equilibrium is derived from (2.2) and (3.2b) as follows:

$$\left(\frac{Y}{K}\right)^{*} = \frac{\alpha+\lambda}{s}. \tag{5.4}$$

Thus, the capital coefficient, which is the reciprocal of this output-capital ratio, depends negatively on the steady growth rate $\alpha+\lambda$ and positively on the savings rate s. In other words, the capital coefficient increases as the steady growth rate decreases or as the saving rate increases.

6. Evolutions of main macroeconomic variables in Japan

In this section, we apply the medium-run growth model developed above to the post-war Japanese economy, and examine whether it can consistently explain the evolutions of the main macroeconomic variables such as the rate of GDP growth, the rate of unemployment, the share of labor in national income and the capital coefficient. As we will see below, the tendencies of these variables in the post-war Japanese economy have distinctive features: as the rate of GDP growth tended to decline in the last 50 years, the rate of unemployment, the labor share and the capital coefficient all tended to rise. Why did this happen? As is shown below, our medium-run growth model can explain those tendencies of the main macro variables under certain conditions on the parameters of the model.

Let us first look at the evolutions of main macroeconomic variables in Japan in the last 50 years: from 1956 to 2005. We choose 1956 as the starting

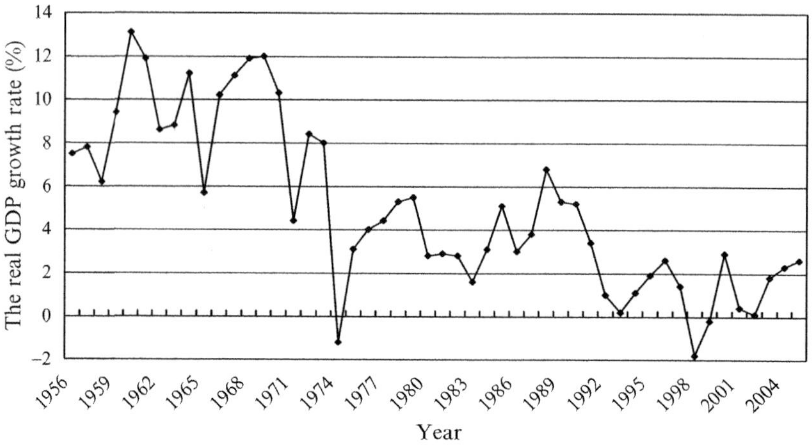

Fig. 3 Changes in the real GDP growth rate
Source: Long-term economic statistics in *Economic and Fiscal Policy White Paper*

point, because the Japanese economy recovered to the pre-war level in that year from the damage by the Second World War. As the terminal year, we choose 2005 due to the availability of the data. Figure 3 presents changes in the real GDP growth rate in the last 50 years. The real GDP growth rate shows a clear tendency to decline over time, though it also shows short-run changes with business cycles. From the point of view of the potential growth, the Japanese economy in the last 50 years can be divided broadly into three periods: the high growth period from 1956 to 1973, the stable growth period from 1974 to 1990 and the low growth period form 1991 to 2005. During the high growth period, the growth rate of real GDP was over or near 10% in most of the years and it was not less than 4% even in depressions. The high growth period came to an end in 1973 with the oil crisis. Though the growth rate declined abruptly after the oil crisis, it was about 4–5% in most of the years between 1974 and 1990. Compared with other countries during this period, GDP growth in Japan was rather high. This period, therefore, may be characterized as the stable growth period. The stable growth period ended in 1990 with the breakdown of the bubble boom that started in the middle of 1980s. After that, the Japanese economy fell into the long-run stagnation that lasted until quite recently. The growth rate during this period was between 1% and 2% in most of the years, and even minus in some years. The Japanese economy has begun to recover since 2002, but the growth rate is still around 2%. Thus, the growth rate of the Japanese economy has been declining over the last 50 years.

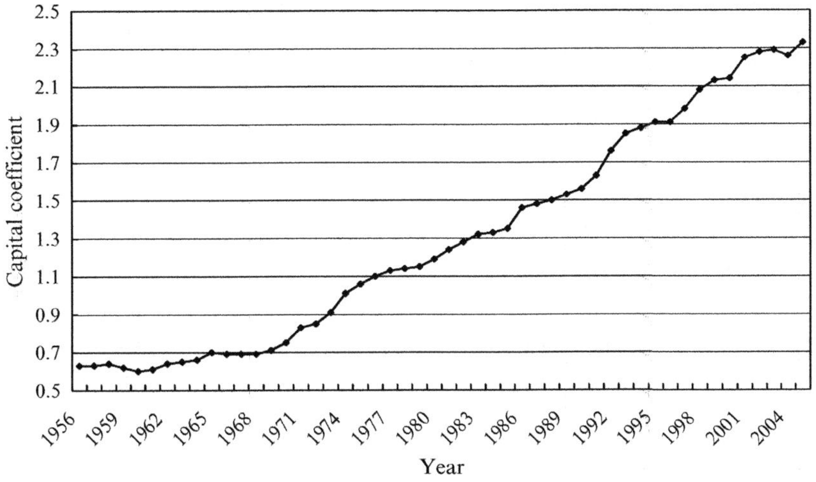

Fig. 4 Changes in capital coefficient
Source: Calculated based on *National Accounting Annual Report* and *Private Company's Capital Stack Annual Report*

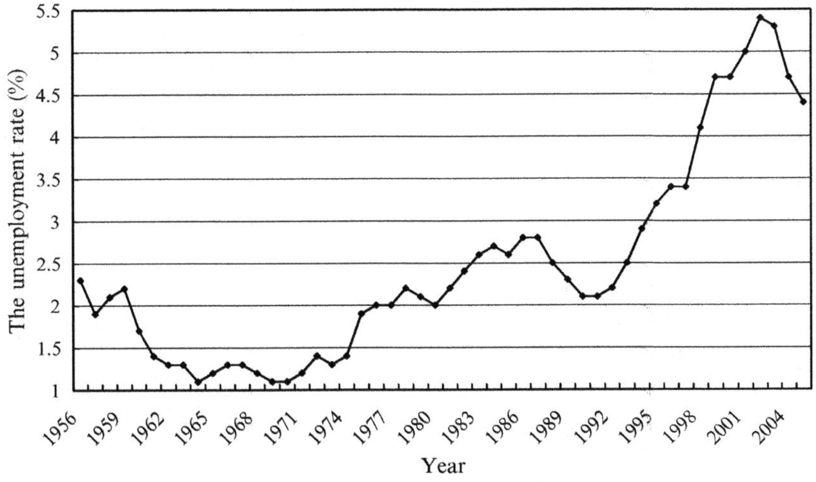

Fig. 5 Changes in the unemployment rate
Source: Long-term economic statistics in *Economic and Fiscal Policy White Paper*

Correspondingly, Figs. 4–6 show changes in the capital coefficient, the unemployment rate and the labor share over the same period. As Fig. 4 shows, the capital coefficient has risen consistently over time, starting from 0.6 in

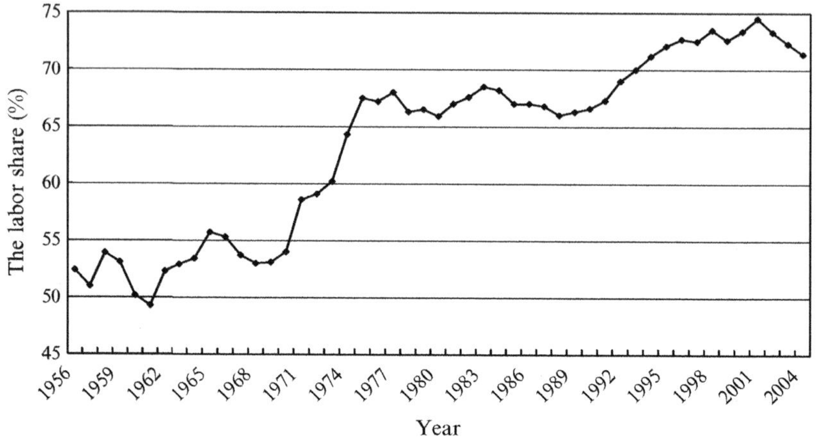

Fig. 6 Changes in the labor share
Source: Calculated based on data from long-term statistics in *Economic and Fiscal Policy White Paper*

1956 to 2.3 in 2005.[6] The rate of unemployment, as Fig. 5 shows, was in the 1–2% range through most of the high growth period. But it increased to the 2–3% range in the middle of 1970s, and then exceeded 3% in the middle of 1990s, reaching the peak at 5.6% in 2002. It has been decreasing recently as the Japanese economy has recovered from the stagnation since 2002, but it is still around the 4% level. Thus, the rate of unemployment has increased as a trend in the last 50 years, though it had some anti-cyclical fluctuations. Finally, Fig. 6 shows changes in the labor share. It was in the 50–60% range during the high growth period, and increased to the 60–70% range during the stable growth period, and then to 70–80% range in the low growth period. Thus, the labor share has increased as a trend, fluctuating procyclically within each period.

The Table 1 summarizes the above result by calculating the average values of those variables within each of the three periods. It clearly shows the characteristic of changes in those variables in the Japanese economy in the last 50 years: as the growth rate of real GDP decreased as a trend in the last 50 years, the capital coefficient, the unemployment rate and the labor share tended to rise together. In the following, we will attempt to explain these tendencies by using our medium-run growth model. The time span of each of the three periods lies between 14 and 17 years. The medium-run growth model

[6] I owe to Taiji Hagiwara, Kobe University, for data and calculation of the capital coefficients.

Table 1 Macroeconomic data for the three periods

	1956–1973 High growth period	1974–1990 Stable growth period	1991–2005 Low growth period
GDP growth rate (%)	9.3	3.7	1.3
Capital coefficient	0.69	1.28	2.05
Unemployment rate (%)	1.5	2.3	3.9
Labor share (%)	54.0	66.9	71.8
Savings rate (%)	18.5	16.2	10.9

developed above may suitably be applied to analyze economic changes with such time span. To be more concrete, the average values of the main macro variables may be interpreted as the steady state values of our model, while changes of those values from one period to another may be interpreted as a shift of the steady state.[7]

7. Explaining the trends of the post-war Japanese economy by our model

We shall now make an attempt to explain the trends of macroeconomic variables shown above based on our medium-run growth model. Let us start from the declining trend of the GDP growth rates shown by Fig. 3 or Table 1. As is mentioned above, the average value of the growth rates within each of the three periods given in Table 1 may be interpreted, due to our model, as the steady growth rate, $\alpha + \lambda$, prevailed in each period, since the number of years in each period seems to be appropriate length for attaining the medium-run equilibrium. If this is the case, the decreases in the average growth rates from one period to another mean that the steady growth rate, $\alpha + \lambda$, decreased over time. In Japan, as a matter of fact, the rate of technological progress, α, tended to decrease since the end of the high growth period, and the growth rate of labor population tended to decrease from around beginning of the low growth period.

Let us next see the capital coefficient. As is seen from Fig. 4 or Table 1, the capital coefficient in Japan in the last 50 years has a steadily rising trend. Since the steady state value of the capital coefficient is determined by (5.4) in our model, its rising trend is attributed either to decreases in $\alpha + \lambda$ or

[7] Table 1 also includes changes in the savings rate, which will be referred to in the next section.

to increases in s. As we have just seen, the potential growth rate, $\alpha + \lambda$, had a declining trend over last 50 years due to slowdown in technological progress and/or decreases in population growth, while the savings rate tended to decrease since around beginning of the 1980s. Thus, a rising tendency in capital coefficient in Japan may be interpreted to be caused by the declining trend in the potential growth rate $\alpha + \lambda$. On the other hand, the savings rate cannot give an appropriate account of this tendency.

We now turn to the rate of unemployment. The rate of unemployment in the last 50 years in Japan had a tendency to increase as Fig. 5 shows, while the rate of GDP growth tended to decrease in the same period as was seen before. So let us see what conditions are necessary to account for these two tendencies simultaneously based on our model. Equation (4.12) shows how the employment rate is affected by changes in parameters that are included in our model. Let us first focus on the term concerning technological progress. Since $\phi/\phi' < 0$ in equation (4.12), the employment rate is decreased ($\Delta z^* < 0$), i.e., the unemployment rate is increased, if the following condition is satisfied:

$$\frac{\Delta(\alpha + n)}{\alpha + n} > \frac{\Delta B}{B} + \frac{\Delta s}{s}. \tag{7.1}$$

Since the potential rate of growth tended to decline over the last 50 years, the left-hand side expression of the above inequality must be negative. Therefore, in order for this inequality to be satisfied, we must have

$$\frac{\Delta B}{B} + \frac{\Delta s}{s} < 0. \tag{7.2}$$

This condition implies that we must have either $\Delta B < 0$ or $\Delta s < 0$, or both of them.

The first condition ($\Delta B < 0$) means that the efficiency of capital must have decreased. In other words, technological progress must have a capital-using bias in order for the rate of unemployment to have a rising trend when the potential rate of growth is falling. Here, we are not prepared to present data for the efficiency of capital to verify that this condition is satisfied in the post-war Japanese economy. However, we can give some historical facts to support such a bias in technological progress. During the high growth period, Japanese economy suffered from serious environmental pollution as a by-product of rapid industrialization. To solve the pollution problems, the proportion of investment directed toward pollution control equipment or living related infrastructure was increased remarkably toward the end of the high growth period and thereafter. The efficiency of capital tended to decrease since then, because these capital equipments do not serve directly to increase output. Decreases in the efficiency of capital may also be explained

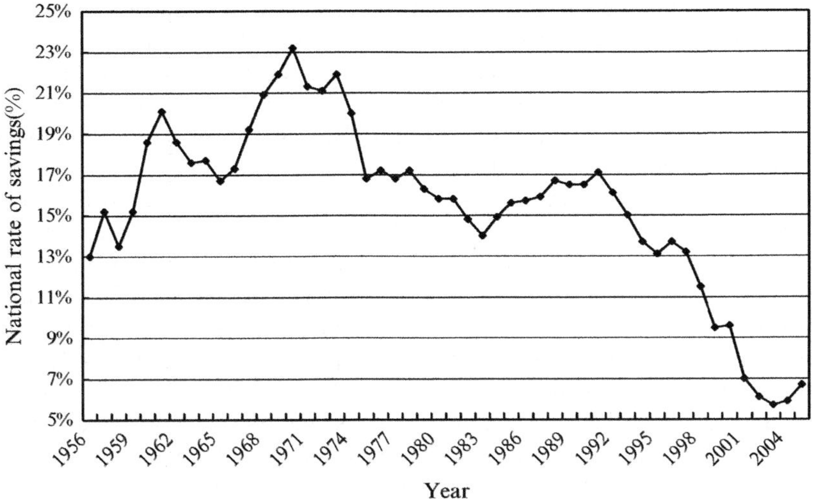

Fig. 7 Changes in the national savings rate
Source: Calculated based on long-term data from *National Accounting Report* (for 1956–1998) and data from *Economic Accounting* (for 1996–2005) in official homepage of Economic and Social Institute, Cabinet Office. The former data based on old SNA are recalculated so as to linked to the latter data that is based on 93 SNA

by decreases in the utilization of capital due to the long-run depression of the Japanese economy since the beginning of 1990s. This factor might have played more important role during the low growth period. From these reasons, it may safely be assumed that the first condition ($\Delta B < 0$) is satisfied in the post-war Japanese economy.

The second condition ($\Delta s < 0$) implies that the savings rate must have decreased. As is shown in Fig. 7, the savings rate tended to increase up to the end of the high growth period, and tended to decrease thereafter.[8] Especially, it has decreased remarkably since the beginning of 1990s. The last row of Table 1 shows the average savings rate in each of the three periods. It clearly shows that the savings rate tended to fall from one period to the next. Thus, the second condition is also satisfied. In Japan, the savings rate remained to be quite high compared with other countries throughout high growth period and the stable growth period. Since the beginning of the 1990s, however, Japan has experienced a marked decline in the savings rate. In view of our model, this decline in the savings rate explains consistently the increases in the unemployment rate during the low growth period.

[8] I owe to Ichiro Tokutsu, Kobe University, for data and calculation of the national savings rate.

To sum up, the condition (7.2) might plausibly be satisfied. It should be noticed, however, that the absolute value of $\Delta B/B + \Delta s/s$ must be large enough to satisfy (7.1) in order for our model to be consistent with the trends of the rate of unemployment and the potential rate of growth in the post-war Japanese economy. We will not check further into this matter quantitatively, since our concern here is to derive theoretical results.

Let us now turn to the labor share. Figure 6 plots the evolution of the labor share in Japan over last 50 years. This figure shows that the share tends to rise in the long-run, and fluctuates anti-cyclically in the short-run. We focus on the long-run tendency to see how it is explained with our model. According to our model, equation (5.3) shows how the labor share changes in response to changes in parameters. Compare this equation with equation (4.12) that represents changes in the employment rate. Then, we find that the expressions in the bracket of the two equations are the same. As we have just seen, (7.1) must be satisfied, since the unemployment rate had a rising trend in the last 50 years. In this case, in order for $\Delta(wN/Y)$ to be positive in (5.3), we must have

$$\sigma > 1. \tag{7.3}$$

In other words, the elasticity of substitution between labor and capital must be greater than unity. Is this condition plausible in real economy? Many econometric studies on production functions rather support the view that the value of σ is normally less than unity. This view may seem to contradict with the above condition (7.3) that is needed to support the validity of our model. I think, however, the magnitude of σ will depend on the time horizon that is taken into account in the model. The longer the time horizon, the larger will be the magnitude of σ, because the substitution between labor and capital for a given change in the wage-rental ratio takes time. Therefore, it might be quite plausible that σ exceeds unity when the time horizon is assumed to be more than 10 years as in our medium-run model.[9]

To summarize the results, the evolutions of macroeconomic variables shown in Table 1 are explained consistently by our model if the following conditions are satisfied:

$$\frac{\Delta B}{B} + \frac{\Delta s}{s} < \frac{\Delta(\alpha + \lambda)}{\alpha + \lambda} < 0, \quad \text{and} \quad \sigma > 1.$$

We also argued that these conditions might plausibly be satisfied. In order to prove this argument more exactly, we need some empirical studies.

[9] The referee pointed out that I had better present any reliable data to justify that $\sigma > 1$ in the long-run. Here, I just propose it as a theoretical hypothesis, leaving it to an econometrician for its test.

8. Conclusions

In this paper, I constructed a medium-run growth model that extended the Solow model by introducing the wage-setting equation of the Blanchard type. A special feature of this model is that it can explain unemployment in the growth process. Interpreting the steady state of this model as the medium-run equilibrium, we analyzed how the main macroeconomic variables such as the rate of growth, the rate of unemployment, the labor share and the capital coefficient change with changes in the parameters of the model. In order to test the plausibility of the model, we attempted to explain evolutions of the major macroeconomic variables during the last 50 years in Japan. The data show that the rate of unemployment, the capital coefficient and the labor share tend to rise as the rate of growth tends to decline over last 50 years. It has been shown that these macroeconomic tendencies can be explained consistently by the following factors: (1) a decreasing tendency in the rate of labor-augmenting technological progress, (2) decreases in the efficiency of capital, (3) a decreasing tendency in the savings rate, and (4) the elasticity of substitution between labor and capital being greater than unity.

In this paper, we have focused only on macroeconomic parameters (α, λ, B, s) to explain changes in the main macroeconomic variables. However, as is seen from (4.9), function ϕ that appear in equation (4.10) or (4.11) depends on μ, γ and ε. Thus, these microeconomic parameters will have influences on the rate of employment or the labor share. The next step is to analyze the effects of these parameters.

References

1. Beaudry, P.: Innis lecture: explorations in medium-run macroeconomics. Can. J. E. **38**(November) 1136–1159 (2005)
2. Blanchard, O.J.: The medium run. Brooking Pap. Econ. Act. **2**, 89–158 (1997)
3. Blanchard, O.J.: Macroeconomics, 2nd edn. New Jersey: Prentice-Hall 2000
4. Layard, R., Nickell, S., Jackman, R.: Unemployment. Oxford: Oxford University Press 1991
5. Malinvaud, E.: Notes on growth theory with imperfectly flexible prices. In: Fituossi J.P. (ed.): Modern macroeconomics. Oxford: Basil Blackwell, 1982 pp. 83–114
6. Malinvaud, E.: Medium-term employment equilibrium. In: Barnett W.A. et al. (eds.): Equilibrium theory and applications. Cambridge: Cambridge University Press 1991
7. Solow, R.M.: A contribution to the theory of economic growth. Q. J. Econ. 70 (February), 65–94 (1956)
8. Solow, R.M.: Towards a macroeconomics of the medium run. J. Econ. Perspect. 14(Winter), 151–158 (2000)
9. Solow, R.M.: Growth theory: an exposition, 2nd edn. New York: Oxford University Press 2000

Adv. Math. Econ. 12, 23–69 (2009)

Advances in
MATHEMATICAL
ECONOMICS

©Springer 2009

Convergences in a dual space with applications to Fatou lemma

Charles Castaing[1] **and Mohammed Saadoune**[2]

[1] Département de Mathématiques, Université Montpellier II, Place E. Bataillon, 34095 Montpellier cedex, France
(e-mail: castaing.charles@numericable.fr)

[2] Département de Mathématiques, Université Ibn Zohr, Lot. Addakhla, B.P. 8106, Agadir, Marocco
(e-mail: mohammed.saadoune@gmail.com)

Received: July 27, 2008
Revised: September 9, 2008

JEL classification: C01, C02, C62

Mathematics Subject Classification (2000): 29B20, 28A20

Abstract. We present new convergence results and new versions of Fatou lemma in Mathematical Economics based on various tightness conditions and the existence of scalarly integrable selections theorems for the (sequential)-weak-star upper limit of a sequence of measurable multifunctions taking values in the dual E' of a separable Banach space E. Existence of conditional expectation of weakly-star closed random sets in a non norm separable dual space is also provided.

Key words: Biting lemma, conditional expectation, Fatou lemma, Komlós convergence, sequential weak upper limit, Tightness

1. Introduction

Motivated by the study of Fatou lemma in Mathematical Economics, we present several types of convergence for multifunctions taking on convex weakly-star compact values in the topological dual E' of a separable Banach space E with specific applications to Fatou lemma in several dimensions. There has been a great deal of research on Fatou lemma when the multifunctions take values in the primal space E. See, e.g., [1, 3, 4, 6–9, 14, 18, 19, 22, 23, 25, 28] for references. For the case of a dual space, we

S. Kusuoka, T. Maruyama (eds.), *Advances in Mathematical Economics Volume 12*,
DOI: 10.1007/978-4-431-92935-2_2,

mention the recent contributions of Benabdellah and Castaing [6], Cornet and Martins da Rocha [18], Balder and Sambucini [5], Castaing Raynaud de Fitte and Valadier [13], Castaing, Hess and Saadoune [12], Castaing and Saadoune [15, 16]. In the present paper we provide, under new tightness conditions, several new convergence results for multifunctions with values in E' with sharp localizations of the limits and several new variants of Fatou lemma in the dual space E' via the integrability of the sequential-weak-star upper limit of a sequence of measurable multifunctions taking values in this space [12]. We also provide the existence of Conditional Expectations (CE) for weakly-star closed random sets in E'. See, e.g., [10, 11, 20, 21] for the problems of convergence of CE in Banach spaces. Since L^1-boundedness assumption is relaxed here, we obtain several significant generalizations in this study.

2. Notations and preliminaries

Throughout this paper the triple $(\Omega, \mathcal{F}, \mu)$ is a complete probability space, E is a separable Banach space and $D := (x_p)_{p\in \mathbb{N}}$ is a fixed dense sequence in the closed unit ball $\overline{B}_E$. We denote by E'_s (resp. E'_b) (resp. E'_{m^*}) the topological dual E' endowed with the topology $\sigma(E', E)$ of pointwise convergence, alias w^* topology (resp. topology of the norm) (resp. the topology $m^* = \sigma(E', H)$, where H is the linear space of E generated by D, that is the Hausdorff locally convex topology defined by the sequence of semi-norms

$$p_k(x') = \max\{| < x', x_p > | : p \leq k\}, \quad x' \in E', (k \geq 1)).$$

Recall that the topology m^* is metrizable, for instance, by the metric

$$d_{E'_{m^*}}(x'_1, x'_2) := \sum_{p=1}^{p=+\infty} \frac{1}{2^p} |\langle x_p, x'_1\rangle - \langle x_p, x'_2\rangle|, \quad x'_1, x'_2 \in E'.$$

We assume from now that $d_{E'_{m^*}}$ is held fixed. Further, we have $m^* \subseteq w^* \subseteq s^*$. When E is infinite dimensional these inclusions are strict. On the other hand, the restrictions of m^* and w^* to any bounded subset of E' coincide and $\mathcal{B}(E'_s) = \mathcal{B}(E'_{m^*})$ [12, Proposition 5.1], but the consideration of $\mathcal{B}(E'_b)$ is irrelevant here. Noting that E' is the countable union of closed balls, we deduce that the space E'_{w^*} is Suslin, as well as the metrizable topological space E'_{m^*}. A $2^{E'_s}$ valued multifunction $X : \Omega \rightrightarrows E'_s$ is measurable if its graph belongs to $\mathcal{F} \otimes \mathcal{B}(E'_s)$. Given a measurable multifunction $X : \Omega \rightrightarrows E'_s$ and a Borel set $G \in \mathcal{B}(E'_s)$, the set

$$X^- G = \{\omega \in \Omega : X(\omega) \cap G \neq \emptyset\}$$

is measurable, that is $X^{-}G \in \mathcal{F}$. In view of the completeness hypothesis on the probability space, this is a consequence of the Projection Theorem (see, e.g., Theorem III.23 of [17]) and of the equality

$$X^{-}G = \mathrm{proj}_{\Omega}\,\{Gr(X) \cap (\Omega \times G)\}.$$

In particular, if X is measurable, the *domain* of X, defined by

$$\mathrm{dom}\, X = \{\omega \in \Omega : X(\omega) \neq \emptyset\}$$

is measurable, because $\mathrm{dom}\, X = X^{-}E$. Further if $u : \Omega \to E'_s$ is a scalarly measurable mapping, that is, for every $x \in E$, the scalar function $\omega \mapsto \langle x, u(\omega)\rangle$ is $\mathcal{F}$-measurable, then the function $f : (\omega, x') \mapsto ||x' - u(\omega)||_{E'_b}$ is $\mathcal{F} \otimes \mathcal{B}(E'_s)$-measurable, and for every fixed $\omega \in \Omega$, $f(\omega, .)$ is lower semicontinuous on E'_s, shortly, f is a normal integrand, indeed, we have

$$||x' - u(\omega)||_{E'_b} = \sup_{p \in \mathbb{N}} \langle x_p, x' - u(\omega)\rangle.$$

As each function $(\omega, x') \mapsto \langle x_p, x' - u(\omega)\rangle$ is $\mathcal{F} \otimes \mathcal{B}(E'_s)$-measurable and continuous on E'_s for each $\omega \in \Omega$, it follows that f is a normal integrand. Consequently, the graph of u belongs to $\mathcal{F} \otimes \mathcal{B}(E'_s)$. Besides these facts, let us mention that the function distance $d_{E'_b}(x', y') = ||x' - y'||_{E'_b}$ is lower semicontinuous on $E'_s \times E'_s$, being the supremum of continuous functions. If X is a measurable multifunction, the distance function $\omega \mapsto d_{E'_b}(x', X(\omega))$ is measurable, by using the lower semicontinuity of the function $d_{E'_b}(x', .)$ on E'_s and measurable projection theorem [17, Theorem III.23], and recalling that E'_s is a Suslin space. A mapping $u : \Omega \Rightarrow E'_s$ is said to be scalarly integrable, alias Gelfand integrable, if, for every $x \in E$, the scalar function $\omega \mapsto \langle x, u(\omega)\rangle$ is integrable. We denoted by $G^1_{E'}[E](\Omega, \mathcal{F}, \mu)$ ($G^1_{E'}[E](\mu)$ for short) the space of all scalarly integrable (classes of) mappings $u : \Omega \Rightarrow E'_s$. The subspace of $G^1_{E'}[E](\mu)$ of all mappings u such that the function $|u| : \omega \mapsto ||u(\omega)||_{E'_b}$ is integrable is denoted by $L^1_{E'}[E](\mu)$. The measurability of $|u|$ follows easily from the above considerations and holds even E is an arbitrary Banach space, we refer to [6] for details. For any $2^{E'_s}$ valued multifunction $X : \Omega \Rightarrow E'_s$, we denote by $G\text{-}\mathcal{S}^1_X$ (resp. $\mathcal{S}^1_X$) the set of all $G^1_{E'}[E](\mu)$-selections (resp. $L^1_{E'}[E](\mu)$-selections) of X. The G-integral (resp. integral) of X over a set $A \in \mathcal{F}$ is defined by

$$G\text{-}\int_A X\, d\mu := \left\{ \int_A f\, d\mu : f \in G\text{-}\mathcal{S}^1_X \right\}$$

and

$$\int_A X\,d\mu := \left\{\int_A f\,d\mu : f \in \mathcal{S}^1_X\right\}$$

respectively. Let (X_n) be a sequence of measurable multifunctions taking values in E'_s. The sequential weak* upper limit $w^*\text{-}ls\ X_n$ of (X_n) is defined by

$$w^*\text{-}ls\ X_n = \left\{x' \in E' : x' = \sigma(E', E)\text{-} \lim_{j\to\infty} x'_{n_j};\ x'_{n_j} \in X_{n_j}\right\}.$$

By $cwk(E'_s)$ we denote the set of all nonempty $\sigma(E', E)$-compact convex subsets of E'_s. A multifunction $X : \Omega \rightrightarrows E'_s$ is scalarly measurable if, for every $x \in E$, the function $\omega \to \delta^*(x, X(\omega))$ is measurable. Let us recall that any scalarly measurable $cwk(E'_s)$-valued multifunction, X, is measurable. Indeed, let $(e_k)_{k\in\mathbb{N}}$ be a sequence in E which separates the points of E', then we have $x \in X(\omega)$ iff, $\langle e_k, x\rangle \le \delta^*(e_k, X(\omega))$ for all $k \in \mathbb{N}$. Further, we denote by $\mathcal{G}^1_{cwk(E'_s)}(\Omega, \mathcal{F}, \mu)$ (shortly $\mathcal{G}^1_{cwk(E'_s)}(\mu)$) the space of all *scalarly integrable* $cwk(E'_s)$-valued multifunctions $X : \Omega \to cwk(E'_s)$, that is, for every $x \in E$, the function $\omega \to \delta^*(x, X(\omega))$ is integrable. By $\mathcal{L}^1_{cwk(E'_s)}(\Omega, \mathcal{F}, \mu)$ (shortly $\mathcal{L}^1_{cwk(E'_s)}(\mu)$) we denote the subspace of $\mathcal{G}^1_{cwk(E'_s)}(\mu)$ of all *integrably bounded* multifunctions X that is the function $|X| : \omega \to |X(\omega)|$ is integrable, here $|X(\omega)| := \sup_{y\in X(\omega)} ||y||_{E'_b}$, by the above consideration, it is easy to see that $|X|$ is measurable. A sequence (X_n) in $\mathcal{L}^1_{cwk(E'_s)}(\mu)$ is *bounded* (resp. *uniformly integrable*) if $(|X_n|)$ is bounded (resp. uniformly integrable) in $\mathcal{L}^1_{\mathbb{R}}(\Omega, \mathcal{F}, \mu)$. In the sequel, we apply the usual convention $|\emptyset| = 0$ and $1_\emptyset = 0$. Our main purpose is to introduce some new types of *tightness condition* so-called *Mazur tightness condition* for sequences in the spaces $\mathcal{L}^1_{cwk(E'_s)}(\mu)$ and $\mathcal{G}^1_{cwk(E'_s)}(\mu)$. These considerations led to several new results of convergence in this space with application to Fatou lemma. In §3 we show the relationships between these tightness conditions. In §4 we present our main result of convergence for a Mazur-tight sequence in the space $L^1_{E'}[E](\mu)$ of scalarly integrable and mean norm bounded E'-valued mappings. In §5, some new convergence results are developed for the space $G^1_{E'}[E](\mu)$ of scalarly integrable E'-valued mappings. These results allow to obtain new types of convergence for the spaces $\mathcal{L}^1_{cwk(E'_s)}(\mu)$ and $\mathcal{G}^1_{cwk(E'_s)}(\mu)$ that we present in §6. We also provide here several variants of Fatou Lemma. The existence of Conditional Expectations of $\sigma(E', E)$ closed random sets in the dual is also stated in §7. Here the L^1-bounded condition is no longer required by contrast of most results given in the literature.

3. Mazur tightness condition

In this section new tightness properties of Mazur type are introduced and examined for sequences in the space $\mathcal{L}^0_{cwk(E'_s)}(\mu)$ of all measurable $cwk(E'_s)$-valued multifunctions. Actually, they find their origin in [12, 15, 16]. First, let us recall the following tightness definition [15]:

Definition 3.1. *A sequence (X_n) in $\mathcal{L}^0_{cwk(E'_s)}(\mu)$ is $cwk(E'_s)$-tight (resp. compactly $cwk(E'_s)$-tight) if there is a scalarly measurable (resp. scalarly measurable and integrably bounded) $cwk(E'_s)$-valued multifunction $\Gamma_\varepsilon : \Omega \rightrightarrows E'$ such that*

$$\inf_n \mu(\{\omega \in \Omega : X_n(\omega) \subset \Gamma_\varepsilon(\omega)\}) \geq 1 - \varepsilon.$$

The measurability of $\{\omega \in \Omega : X_n(\omega) \subset \Gamma_\varepsilon(\omega)\}$ is immediate using the considerations developed in the beginning of this section.

Definition 3.2. *A sequence (X_n) in $\mathcal{L}^0_{cwk(E'_s)}(\mu)$ is said to be L^0-* lim sup*-Mazur tight, (resp. L^1-* lim sup*-Mazur tight) if, for every subsequence (Y_i) of (X_n), there exists a sequence (r_n) in $L^1_{\mathbb{R}}(\Omega, \mathcal{F}, \mu)$ with $r_n \in co\{|Y_i|(.) : i \geq n\}$ such that* $\limsup_n r_n < \infty$ *(resp.* $\limsup_n r_n \in L^1_{\mathbb{R}}(\Omega, \mathcal{F}, \mu)$*).*

Similarly, we introduce a weaker notion of the above Mazur tightness, namely, L^0- lim inf-*Mazur tightness* and L^1- lim inf-*Mazur tightness*:

Definition 3.3. *A sequence (X_n) in $\mathcal{L}^0_{cwk(E'_s)}(\mu)$ is said to be L^0-* lim inf*-Mazur tight, (resp. L^1-* lim inf*-Mazur tight) if, for every subsequence (Y_n) of (X_n), there exists a sequence (r_n) in $L^1_{\mathbb{R}}(\Omega, \mathcal{F}, \mu)$ with $r_n \in co\{|Y_i|(.) : i \geq n\}$ such that for every sequence (s_n) in $L^1_{\mathbb{R}}(\mu)$ such that $s_n \in co\{r_i : i \geq n\}$, one has* $\liminf s_n < \infty$ *(resp.* $\liminf_n s_n \in L^1_{\mathbb{R}}(\Omega, \mathcal{F}, \mu)$*).*

These new notions are denoted respectively: L^ℓ- lim sup-MT and L^ℓ- lim inf-MT, $\ell = 0, 1$. A sequence (X_n) in $\mathcal{L}^0_{cwk(E'_s)}(\mu)$ is said to be scalarly L^ℓ- lim sup-MT (resp. L^ℓ- lim inf-MT), $\ell = 0, 1$ if, for each $x \in E$, the sequence $(\delta^*(x, X_n))$ is L^ℓ- lim sup-MT (resp. L^ℓ- lim inf-MT). From Proposition 2.1 in [15] we derive directly a useful characterization of L^ℓ- lim sup-Mazur tightness condition which may be regarded as an extension of the Biting lemma (see, e.g., [13, 24]), since every $\mathcal{L}^1_{cwk(E'_s)}(\mu)$-bounded sequence is obviously L^1- lim sup-MT. This result will be used extensively in all this work.

Proposition 3.4. *Let (X_n) be a sequence in $\mathcal{L}^0_{cwk(E'_s)}(\mu)$ and let $\ell = 0, 1$. Then the following are equivalent:*

(1) (X_n) is L^ℓ- lim sup-*MT.*
(2) Given any subsequence (Y_n) of (X_n), there exist a subsequence (Z_n) of (Y_n), φ_∞ in $L^\ell_{\mathbb{R}}(\Omega, \mathcal{F}, \mu)$ and an increasing sequence (C_k) in $\mathcal{F}$ with $\lim_{k\to\infty} \mu(C_k) = 1$ *such that for every $k \in \mathbb{N}$, $1_{C_k}\varphi_\infty \in L^1_{\mathbb{R}}(\Omega, \mathcal{F}, \mu)$ and*

$$\forall A \in \mathcal{F}, \quad \lim_{n\to\infty} \int_{A\cap C_k} |Z_n|\, d\mu = \int_{A\cap C_k} \varphi_\infty\, d\mu.$$

As a consequence of this proposition we deduce the following useful property.

Proposition 3.5. *Let (X^1_n) and (X^2_n) be two sequences in $\mathcal{L}^0_{cwk(E'_s)}(\mu)$. If (X^1_n) and (X^2_n) are L^ℓ-* lim sup-*MT, ($\ell = 0, 1$), then the sequence $(|X^1_n| + |X^2_n|)$ is L^ℓ-* lim sup-*MT. Consequently, $(X^1_n + X^2_n)$ is L^ℓ-* lim sup-*MT.*

Proof. Let (φ_n) be any subsequence of $(|X^1_n| + |X^2_n|)$. Each φ_n is of the form $\varphi_n := |Y^1_n| + |Y^2_n|$, where (Y^1_n) and (Y^2_n) are two subsequences of (X^1_n) and (X^2_n) respectively. Applying Proposition 3.4 successively to the sequences (X^1_n) and (X^2_n) we can find a subsequence (ψ_n) of (φ_n) with $\psi_n := |Z^1_n| + |Z^2_n|$, where (Z^1_n) and (Z^2_n) are two subsequences of (Y^1_n) and (Y^2_n) respectively, two functions φ^1_∞, φ^2_∞ in $L^\ell_{\mathbb{R}}(\Omega, \mathcal{F}, \mu)$ and two increasing sequences (C^1_k) and (C^2_k) in $\mathcal{F}$ with $\lim_{k\to\infty} \mu(C^1_k) = 1$ and $\lim_{k\to\infty} \mu(C^2_k) = 1$ such that for every $k \in \mathbb{N}$, the functions $1_{C^1_k}\varphi^1_\infty$ and $1_{C^2_k}\varphi^2_\infty$ are integrable and

$$\lim_{n\to\infty} \int_{A\cap C^1_k} |Z^1_n|\, d\mu = \int_{A\cap C^1_k} \varphi^1_\infty\, d\mu,$$
$$\lim_{n\to\infty} \int_{A\cap C^2_k} |Z^2_n|\, d\mu = \int_{A\cap C^2_k} \varphi^2_\infty\, d\mu,$$

for all $A \in \mathcal{F}$. Then taking $C_k := C^1_k \cap C^2_k$ and $\varphi_\infty := \varphi^1_\infty + \varphi^2_\infty$ we get

$$\lim_{n\to\infty} \int_{A\cap C_k} \psi_n\, d\mu = \int_{A\cap C_k} \varphi^1_\infty\, d\mu + \int_{A\cap C_k} \varphi^1_\infty\, d\mu = \int_{A\cap C_k} \varphi_\infty\, d\mu,$$

for all $A \in \mathcal{F}$. Since $1_{C_k}\varphi_\infty \in L^1_{\mathbb{R}}(\Omega, \mathcal{F}, \mu)$, applying again Proposition 3.4 we deduce that $(|X^1_n| + |X^2_n|)$ is L^ℓ- lim sup-MT. □

In the following proposition, the L^1- lim inf-Mazur tightness and the L^0- lim sup-Mazur tightness conditions together are connected to the L^1- lim sup-Mazur tightness:

Proposition 3.6. *Let (X_n) be a sequence in $\mathcal{L}^0_{cwk(E'_s)}(\mu)$. Then the following two statement (a) and (b) are equivalent:*

(a) (X_n) is L^1- lim sup-MT.
(b) (X_n) is L^1- lim inf-MT and L^0- lim sup-MT.

Proof. The implication $(a) \Rightarrow (b)$ is trivial. To prove $(b) \Rightarrow (a)$ let (Y_n) be any subsequence of (X_n) satisfying (b). Using the L^0- lim sup-Mazur tightness and Proposition 3.4, we find a measurable function $\varphi_\infty : \Omega \mapsto \mathbb{R}^+$, a subsequence of (Y_n) still denoted (Y_n) and a sequence (C_k) in $\mathcal{F}$ with $\lim_k \mu(C_k) = 1$ such that, for every $k \in \mathbb{N}$, $1_{C_k}\varphi_\infty \in L^1_{\mathbb{R}}(\mu)$, and the following holds:

$$\forall A \in \mathcal{F}, \quad \lim_{n\to\infty} \int_{A\cap C_k} |Y_n|\, d\mu = \int_{A\cap C_k} \varphi_\infty\, d\mu.$$

Let (r_n) be a sequence of measurable functions as in the definition of the L^1 – lim inf-Mazur tightness. From the preceding equality it follows that

$$\forall A \in \mathcal{F}, \quad \lim_{n\to\infty} \int_{A\cap C_k} r_n\, d\mu = \int_{A\cap C_k} \varphi_\infty\, d\mu.$$

Invoking Mazur's Theorem and appealing to a diagonal procedure (see, e.g., Lemma 3.1 in [14]), one can construct a sequence (s_n) with $s_n \in co\{r_i : i \geq n\}$ such that, for every k, $(1_{C_k}s_n)$ converges a.e. to $1_{C_k}\varphi_\infty$. Since $\mu(C_k)\mapsto 1$, (s_n) converges a.e. to φ_∞, which, in view of condition (b), shows that $\varphi_\infty \in L^1_{\mathbb{R}}(\mu)$. Returning to Proposition 3.4, we deduce that (X_n) satisfies (a). □

According to the two following results,the notion of L^0- lim inf-Mazur tightness (resp. L^1- lim inf-Mazur tightness) is in some sense stronger than $cwk(E'_s)$-tightness (resp. compactly $cwk(E'_s)$-tightness). The first one is a variant of Proposition 3.2 in [16] dealing with primal space E.

Proposition 3.7. *Suppose that E is a separable Banach space and (X_n) is a sequence in $\mathcal{L}^0_{cwk(E'_s)}(\mu)$ satisfying the condition L^0- lim sup-MT. Then (X_n) admits a $cwk(E'_s)$-tight subsequence.*

Proof. By Proposition 3.4, there exist a subsequence (Y_n) of (X_n) and a $\mathcal{F}$-measurable partition (C_k) of Ω such that for every $k \in \mathbb{N}$ the sequence $(|Y_n|_{|C_k})$ is bounded in the space $L^1_{\mathbb{R}}(C_k, C_k \cap \mathcal{F}, \mu_{|C_k})$. Hence $(|Y_n|_{|C_k})$ is $cwk(E'_s)$-tight with respect to the measure space $(C_k, C_k \cap \mathcal{F}, \mu_{|C_k})$, making use of the Markov inequality. Therefore, for every $\epsilon > 0$, there is a scalarly measurable $cwk(E'_s)$-valued multifunction $\Gamma_{k,\epsilon}$ such that

$$\sup_n \mu(C_k \setminus \{\omega \in C_k : Y_{n|C_k})(\omega) \subset \Gamma_{k,\epsilon}(\omega)\}) \le \epsilon\mu(C_k). \qquad (*)$$

Now define the multifunction Γ_ϵ on Ω by

$$\Gamma_\epsilon = 1_{C_1}\,\Gamma_{1,\epsilon} + \sum_{k\ge 2} 1_{C_k}\,\Gamma_{k,\epsilon}$$

Then, since

$$\{\omega \in \Omega : Y_n(\omega) \subset \Gamma_\epsilon(\omega)\} = \bigcup_k \{\omega \in C_k : Y_{n|C_k}(\omega) \subset \Gamma_{k,\epsilon}(\omega)\},$$

(*) entails

$$\begin{aligned}
\mu(\{\omega \in \Omega : Y_n(\omega)) \subset \Gamma_\epsilon(\omega)\} &= \mu(\bigcup_k \{\omega \in C_k : Y_{n|C_k}(\omega) \subset \Gamma_{k,\epsilon}(\omega)\}) \\
&= \sum_k \mu(\{\omega \in C_k : Y_{n|C_k}(\omega) \subset \Gamma_{k,\epsilon}(\omega)\}) \\
&\ge \sum_k \mu(C_k)(1-\epsilon) = 1-\epsilon.
\end{aligned}$$

Thus the sequence (Y_n) is $cwk(E'_s)$-tight. □

It is worthy to mention that the L^1- lim sup-Mazur tightness condition does not imply that $(|X_n|)$ is bounded in $\mathcal{L}^1_{\mathbb{R}}(\Omega, \mathcal{F}, \mu)$. Indeed, it suffices to consider the space $\mathcal{L}^1_{\mathbb{R}}(\Omega, \mathcal{F}, \mu)$ where $\Omega = [0, 1]$ endowed with the Lebesgue measure and f_n is given by $f_n(\omega) := n^2 1_{[0,1/n]}(\omega),\ \omega \in \Omega$. Then, (f_n) is not bounded in $\mathcal{L}^1_{\mathbb{R}}(\Omega, \mathcal{F}, \mu)$ but satisfies (*), because it converges a.e. to 0. However, we have the following result

Proposition 3.8. *Suppose that E is a separable Banach space and (X_n) is a sequence in $\mathcal{L}^0_{cwk(E'_s)}(\mu)$ satisfying the condition L^1- lim sup-MT. Then (X_n) admits a $cwk(E'_s)$-compactly tight subsequence.*

Proof. Applying Proposition 3.4, to the sequence $(|X_n(.)|)$ provides a subsequence (Y_n) of (X_n) a function $\varphi \in L^1_{\mathbb{R}^+}(\mu)$ and an increasing sequence (C_k) in $\mathcal{F}$ with $\lim_k \mu(C_k) = 1$ such that for every $k \in \mathbb{N}$,

$$\lim_{n\to\infty} \int_{C_k} |Y_n| d\mu = \int_{C_k} \varphi d\mu,$$

for all $A \in \mathcal{F}$. Let $\epsilon > 0$ and choose $p_\epsilon \ge 1$ such that $\frac{1}{p_\epsilon}\int_\Omega \varphi d\mu \le \epsilon$. Applying the Lemma 3.9 below we get

$$\limsup_n \mu(\{\omega \in \Omega : |Y_n|(\omega) > p_\epsilon\}) \leq \frac{1}{p_\epsilon} \int_\Omega \varphi d\mu \leq \epsilon.$$

Hence, there exists $N_\epsilon \in \mathbb{N}$, such that

$$\sup_{n > N_\epsilon} \mu(\{\omega \in \Omega : |Y_n|(\omega) > p_\epsilon\}) \leq \epsilon.$$

Since the functions $|Y_1|, \ldots, |Y_{N_\epsilon}|$ are integrable, one can find $\rho_\epsilon > p_\epsilon$ such that

$$\sup_{n \leq N_\epsilon} \mu(\{\omega \in \Omega : |Y_n|(\omega) > \rho_\epsilon\}) \leq \epsilon.$$

Whence we get

$$\sup_{n \in \mathbb{N}} \mu(\{\omega \in \Omega : |Y_n|(\omega) > \rho_\epsilon\}) \leq \epsilon.$$

This shows that (Y_n) is compactly $cwk(E'_s)$-tight, indeed, it suffices to take $\Gamma_\epsilon := \overline{B}_{E'_b}(0, \rho_\epsilon)$. □

Lemma 3.9. *Let (φ_n) be sequence in $L^1_{\mathbb{R}^+}$ which biting converges to an integrable function φ. Then*

$$\forall p \geq 1, \quad \limsup_n \mu(\{\omega \in \Omega : \varphi_n(\omega) > p\}) \leq \frac{1}{p} \int_\Omega \varphi d\mu.$$

Proof. There exists an increasing sequence (C_k) in $\mathcal{F}$ with $\lim_k \mu(C_k) = 1$ such that for every $k \in \mathbb{N}$,

$$\lim_{n \to \infty} \int_{C_k \cap A} \varphi_n d\mu = \int_{C_k \cap A} \varphi d\mu,$$

for all $A \in \mathcal{F}$. Using the Markov inequality we get

$$\limsup_n \mu(\{\omega \in C_k : \varphi_n(\omega) > p\}) \leq \frac{1}{p} \lim_n \int_{C_k} \varphi_n d\mu = \frac{1}{p} \int_{C_k} \varphi d\mu$$

whence

$$\begin{aligned} \limsup_n \mu(\{\omega \in \Omega : \varphi_n(\omega) > p\}) &\leq \frac{1}{p} \int_{C_k} \varphi d\mu \\ &\quad + \limsup_n \mu(\{\omega \in \Omega \setminus C_k : \varphi_n(\omega) > p\}) \\ &\leq \frac{1}{p} \int_{C_k} \varphi d\mu + \mu(\Omega \setminus C_k). \end{aligned}$$

Letting $k \to \infty$ we get

$$\limsup_n \mu(\{\omega \in \Omega : \varphi_n(\omega) > p\}) \leq \frac{1}{p} \int_\Omega \varphi d\mu.$$

□

We are ready to present general convergence results in $\mathcal{L}^1_{cwk(E'_s)}(\mu)$ with localization of the limit which can be applied to various places in the study of Fatou lemma in Mathematical Economics. A key ingredient in our proofs relies to integrability of the weak* sequential limit of a sequence of measurable multifunctions taking values in E' [12] and the Mazur-tightness conditions introduced above. Further these results constitute a sharp continuation of a similar study initiated in [14] dealing convergences and Fatou lemma in the space $\mathcal{L}^1_{cwk(E)}(\mu)$ of scalarly integrable and integrably bounded multifunctions with convex weakly compact values in the primal space E. For this purpose, we introduce the following convergences in $\mathcal{G}^1_{cwk(E'_s)}(\mu)$. A sequence (X_n) in $\mathcal{G}^1_{cwk(E'_s)}(\mu)$ *weakly Komlós converges* to X_∞, if

$$\forall x \in E, \quad \frac{1}{n}\sum_{i=1}^{n} \delta^*(x, Y_i(\omega)) \to \delta^*(x, X_\infty(\omega)), \quad \text{a.e.} \quad \omega \in \Omega,$$

(X_n) $d_{E'_{m^*}}$-*Wijsman Komlós converges* to X_∞, if

$$\forall x' \in E', \quad \lim_n d_{E'_{m^*}}(x', \frac{1}{n}\sum_{i=1}^{n} Y_i) = d_{E'_{m^*}}(x', X_\infty) \quad a.e.$$

for every subsequence (Y_n) of (X_n), here the negligible set depends only on the subsequence under consideration. (X_n) *weakly biting converges* to X_∞, if there exist a sequence (C_k) in $\mathcal{F}$ with $\lim_k \mu(C_k) = 1$ such that

$$\forall k \geq 1, \quad \forall v \in L^\infty_E(\Omega, \mathcal{F}, \mu), \quad \lim_{n\to\infty} \int_{C_k} \delta^*(v, X_n)d\mu = \int_{C_k} \delta^*(v, X_\infty)d\mu.$$

This study will be achieved from its single-valued specialization, namely we will deal first with the spaces $L^1_{E'}[E](\mu)$ and $G^1_{E'}[E](\mu)$.

4. Convergences in $L^1_{E'}[E](\mu)$

The main result in this section is concerned with the following with application to Fatou lemma.

Theorem 4.1. *Let E is a separable Banach space. Let (f_n) be a sequence in $L^1_{E'}[E](\mu)$ satisfying the L^1-$\limsup$-MT condition. Then there exist a function $f_\infty \in L^1_{E'}[E](\mu)$, a subsequence (g_n) of (f_n) and an increasing sequence (C_k) in $\mathcal{F}$ with $\lim_k \mu(C_k) = 1$ such that the following holds:*

(1) $(1_{C_k} \|g_n\|_{E'_b})$ is uniformly integrable in $L^1_{\mathbb{R}}(\mu)$ for each k.

(2) (g_n) *weakly biting converges to* f_∞.
(3) (g_n) *weakly Komlós converges to* f_∞.
(4) $f_\infty(\omega) \in w^*\text{-cl}\, co\,[w^*\text{-}ls\, g_n(\omega)]$ *a.e.*
(5) If μ *is nonatomic then*

$$\forall A \in \mathcal{F}, \qquad \int_A f_\infty\, d\mu \in w^*\text{-cl}\left(\int_A w^*\text{-}ls\, g_n\, d\mu\right).$$

The proof of Theorem 4.1 involves the three following lemmas. The first one, Lemma 4.2, is an adaptation of Lemma 4.1 in [16] in the framework of a dual space. Its proof follows the same lines but needs a careful look and involves a sequential $\sigma\left(L^1_{E'}[E], L^\infty_E\right)$-compactness result. The second one, Lemma 4.3, is derived from Proposition 3.5 in [15]. The third one, Lemma 4.4 transforms Theorem 5.6 (jjj) [16] into a general result on integration of multifunctions, in particular, it yields an extension of Ljapunov's theorem for the sequential weak* upper limit of a sequence of measurable multifunctions with values in E'.

Lemma 4.2. *Let* $\Delta : \Omega \rightrightarrows E'$ *be a nonempty valued measurable and integrably bounded multifunction. Then*

$$\mathcal{S}^1{}_{w^*-cl(\Delta)} \subset \text{sequ.}\, \sigma(L^1_{E'}[E], L^\infty_E)\text{-cl}(\mathcal{S}^1_\Delta). \qquad (\dagger)$$

Consequently,

$$\int_A w^*\text{-cl}(\Delta) d\mu \subset \text{seq}\, w^*\text{-cl}\left(\int_A \Delta d\mu\right) = w^*\text{-cl}\left(\int_A \Delta d\mu\right). \qquad (\dagger\dagger)$$

Proof. Since the multifunction Δ has a $\mathcal{F} \otimes \mathcal{B}(E'_s)$-measurable graph and E'_s is a Suslin space, invoking Theorem III.22, [17], one can find a sequence $(\sigma_n)_{n\geq 1}$ of scalarly measurable selectors of Δ such that for every $\omega \in \Omega$, $w^* - cl(\Delta(\omega)) = w^* - cl(\{\sigma_n(\omega)\}_{n\geq 1})$. Since Δ is integrably bounded, the functions σ_n are necessary $L^1_{E'}[E]$-integrable and one has

$$d_{E'_{m^*}} - cl(\Delta(\omega)) = d_{E'_{m^*}} - cl(\{\sigma_n(\omega)\}_{n\geq 1}), \qquad (4.2.1)$$

because the restriction of the w^*-topology to the closed ball $|\Delta(\omega)|\overline{B}_{E'}$ of E' is metrizable by the metric $d_{E'_{m^*}}$. Now take σ in $\mathcal{S}^1{}_{w^*-cl(\Delta)}$. For each $q \geq 1$, let us define the sets

$$A^q_n := \left\{\omega \in \Omega : d_{E'_{m^*}}(\sigma(\omega), \sigma_n(\omega)) < \frac{1}{q}\right\} \qquad (n \geq 1),$$

$$\Omega^q_1 := A^q_1, \quad \Omega^q_n := A^q_n \setminus \cup_{i<n} A^q_i \text{ for } n > 1$$

and the function

$$\varsigma_q := \sum_{n=1}^{+\infty} 1_{\Omega_n^q} \sigma_n.$$

Since the functions $\omega \to d_{E'_{m^*}}(\sigma(\omega), \sigma_n(\omega))$ are $\mathcal{F}$-measurable, $A_n^q \in \mathcal{F}$ for all n. Further, from (4.2.1) it follows that $\cup_n A_n^q = \Omega$ a.e. Then $(\Omega_n^q)_n$ constitutes a sequence of pairwise disjoint members of $\mathcal{F}$ which satisfies $\cup_n \Omega_n^q = \Omega$ a.e. So ς_q is a scalarly measurable selector of Δ. As Δ is integrably bounded, we conclude that $\varsigma_q \in \mathcal{S}_\Delta^1$. Furthermore, we have

$$d_{E'_{m^*}}(\sigma(\omega), \varsigma_q(\omega)) < \frac{1}{q}, \qquad \forall \omega \in \Omega.$$

By integrating we get

$$\int_\Omega d_{E'_{m^*}}(\sigma, \varsigma_q)\, d\mu \le \frac{1}{q}.$$

Letting $q \to +\infty$, this inequality entails

$$\forall p \in \mathbb{N}^*, \quad \forall A \in \mathcal{F}, \quad \langle x_p, \int_A \sigma\, d\mu \rangle = \lim_{q \to \infty} \langle x_p, \int_A \varsigma_q\, d\mu \rangle. \tag{4.2.2}$$

On the other hand, since the sequence (ς_q) is mean norm bounded in the space $L^1_{E'}[E](\mu)$, there exists, by Theorem 6.5.9 [13], a subsequence of (ς_q) still denoted in the same way and a function $\sigma' \in L^1_{E'}[E](\mu)$ such that

$$\forall v \in L^\infty_E(\Omega, \mathcal{F}, \mu), \quad \lim_{q \to \infty} \int_\Omega \langle v, \varsigma_q \rangle d\mu = \int_\Omega \langle v, \sigma' \rangle d\mu. \tag{4.2.3}$$

From (4.2.2) and (4.2.3) it follows that $\sigma' = \sigma$ a.e. Hence

$$\sigma \in \text{sequ.}\,\sigma(L^1_{E'}[E], L^\infty_E)\text{-cl}(\mathcal{S}^1_\Delta),$$

which proves (†). To prove (††) let a be an arbitrary element of $\int_A w^*\text{-cl}(\Delta) d\mu$. Then there exists $f \in L^1_{E'}[E](\mu)$ such that $a = \int_\Omega f\, d\mu$. Since, by (†), $f \in \text{seq}\,\sigma(L^1_{E'}[E], L^\infty E)\text{-cl}(\mathcal{S}^1_\Delta)$, there is a sequence (f_n) in $\mathcal{S}^1_\Delta$ which $\sigma(L^1_{E'}[E], L^\infty_E)$ converges to f so that, for every $A \in \mathcal{F}$, $w^*\text{-}\lim_n \int_A f_n d\mu = \int_A f d\mu$, whence $\int_A f d\mu \in \text{seq w}^*\text{-cl}\left(\int_A \Delta d\mu\right)$. □

Lemma 4.3. *Assume that μ is nonatomic, and $\Gamma : \Omega \rightrightarrows E'$ is a $\sigma(E', E)$ compact valued measurable multifunction satisfying $\Gamma(\omega) \subset \Phi(\omega), \forall \omega \in \Omega$ where $\Phi : \Omega \rightrightarrows E'$ is a scalarly integrable $cwk(E'_s)$-valued multifunction. Then*

$$\forall A \in \mathcal{F}, \; G\text{-}\int_A w^*\text{-cl}\, co\Gamma d\mu = w^*\text{-cl}\left(G\text{-}\int_A \Gamma d\mu\right).$$

Proof. It is obvious that $G\text{-}\mathcal{S}^1_\Gamma \subset G\text{-}\mathcal{S}^1_{w^*\text{-}cl\, co\Gamma} \subset G\text{-}\mathcal{S}^1_\Phi$. By [17, Theorem V-13], $G\text{-}\mathcal{S}^1_{w^*\text{-}cl\, co\Gamma}$ is convex and $\sigma(G^1_{E'}[E], L^\infty \otimes E)$ compact. Arguing as in the $L^1_E(\mu)$ case [26, Lemma 2 and Theorem 3], it is not difficult to see that $G\text{-}\mathcal{S}^1_\Gamma$ is dense in $\mathcal{S}^1_{w^*\text{-}cl\, co\Gamma}$ with respect to the $\sigma(G^1_{E'}[E], L^\infty \otimes E)$ topology. Since $f \mapsto \int_\Omega f d\mu$ from $G^1_{E'}[E](\mu)$ into E' is continuous with respect to the $\sigma(L^1_{E'}[E], L^\infty \otimes E)$, the conclusion follows. □

Lemma 4.4. *Assume in addition that μ is nonatomic and let $(\Delta_q)_{q\geq 1}$ be a sequence of measurable multifunctions from Ω to $\sigma(E', E)$- compact subsets of E'. Suppose that Δ_q is integrably bounded, for all q, and $\mathcal{S}^1_{\cup_{q\geq 1}\Delta_q} \neq \emptyset$. Then for all $A \in \mathcal{F}$, the following equalities hold:*
(a) $w^*\text{-}cl \int_A \cup_q w^*\text{-}cl co \Delta_q\, d\mu = w^*\text{-}cl \int_A \cup_q \Delta_q\, d\mu$.
(b) $w^*\text{-}cl(\int_A co \cup_q \Delta_q\, d\mu) = w^*\text{-}cl(\int_A \cup_q \Delta_q\, d\mu)$.

Proof. Let σ be a fixed element of $\mathcal{S}^1_{\cup_{q\geq 1}\Delta_q}$ and set

$$\Lambda_q := \cup_{i=1}^{i=q}(1_{dom\Delta_i}\Delta_i + 1_{\Omega\setminus dom\Delta_i}\sigma).$$

Then (Λ_q) is increasing, $dom\Lambda_q = \Omega$, for all q, and $\cup_q \Lambda_q = \cup_q \Delta_q$. Next, for each $q \in \mathbb{N}$ and each $F \in \mathcal{F}$, define the following multifunction:

$$\Lambda_{F,q} := 1_F w^*\text{-}cl\, co\Lambda_q + 1_{\Omega\setminus F}\sigma.$$

We claim that

$$\mathrm{seq}\,\sigma(L^1_{E'}[E], L^\infty_E)\text{-cl}\,[\mathcal{S}^1{}_{\cup_{q\in\mathbb{N}} w^*\text{-}cl\, co\,\Lambda_q}] = \mathrm{seq}\,\sigma(L^1_{E'}[E], L^\infty_E)\text{-cl}\,[\bigcup_{q\in\mathbb{N}}\bigcup_{F\in\mathcal{F}} \mathcal{S}^1_{\Lambda_{F,q}}].$$

Here $\mathrm{seq}\,\sigma(L^1_{E'}[E], L^\infty_E)\text{-cl}(A)$ denotes the sequential $\sigma(L^1_{E'}[E], L^\infty_E)$-closure of a set $A \subset L^1_{E'}[E](\mu)$. Since, for each $q \in \mathbb{N}$ and each $F \in \mathcal{F}$, $\Lambda_{F,q} \subset \cup_{q\in\mathbb{N}} w^*\text{-}cl\, co\Lambda_q$, it suffices to prove the inclusion

$$\mathcal{S}^1_{\cup_{q\geq 1} w^*\text{-}cl\, co\,\Lambda_q} \subset \mathrm{seq}\,\sigma(L^1_{E'}[E], L^\infty_E)\text{-cl}\left(\bigcup_{q\in\mathbb{N}}\bigcup_{F\in\mathcal{F}} \mathcal{S}^1_{\Lambda_{F,q}}\right). \tag{4.4.1}$$

To show this, take $s \in \mathcal{S}^1_{\cup_{q\geq 1} w^*\text{-}cl\, co\Lambda_q}$ and for each $q \in \mathbb{N}$, define a set $F_q \in \mathcal{F}$ and an $L^1_{E'}[E](\mu)$ selector, s_q, of $\Lambda_{F_q,q}$ as follows:

$$F_q := \{\omega \in \Omega : s(\omega) \in w^*\text{-}cl\, co\Lambda_q(\omega)\} \quad \text{and} \quad s_q := 1_{F_q}s + 1_{\Omega\setminus F_q}\sigma.$$

Then we have

$$\int_\Omega |s - s_q|\, d\mu \leq \int_{\Omega\setminus F_q} |s| d\mu + \int_{\Omega\setminus F_q} |\sigma| d\mu.$$

Since $\lim_{q\to\infty}\mu(\Omega\setminus F_q)=0$, the preceding estimation implies that

$$s\in \text{seq}\,\sigma(L^1_{E'}[E],L^\infty_E)\text{-cl}\left(\bigcup_{q\in\mathbb{N}}\bigcup_{F\in\mathcal{F}}\mathcal{S}^1_{\Lambda_{F,q}}\right).$$

Thus the desired inclusion follows.

Using (4.4.1) it is immediate that

$$\forall A\in\mathcal{F},\ \int_A \cup_{q\geq 1} w^*\text{-}cl\; co\Lambda_q d\mu := \left\{\int_A f d\mu : f\in \mathcal{S}^1_{\cup_{q\geq 1}w^*\text{-}cl\; co\Lambda_q}\right\}$$

$$\subset\left\{\int_A f d\mu : f\in \text{sequ.}\,\sigma\left(L^1_{E'}[E],L^\infty_E\right)\text{-cl}\left(\bigcup_{q\in\mathbb{N}}\bigcup_{F\in\mathcal{F}}\mathcal{S}^1_{\Lambda_{F,q}}\right)\right\} \quad (4.4.2)$$

$$\subset w^*\text{-}cl\left(\left\{\int_A f d\mu : f\in \bigcup_{q\in\mathbb{N}}\bigcup_{F\in\mathcal{F}}\mathcal{S}^1_{\Lambda_{F,q}}\right\}\right)=w^*\text{-}cl\left(\bigcup_{q\in\mathbb{N}}\bigcup_{F\in\mathcal{F}}\int_A \Lambda_{F,q}\,d\mu\right).$$

On the other hand, since Λ_q is measurable, w^* compact valued and integrably bounded for every $q\in\mathbb{N}$ and every $F\in\mathcal{F}$, it follows from Lemma 4.3 that

$$\forall q\in\mathbb{N},\ \ \forall A\in\mathcal{F},\quad \int_A w^*\text{-}cl\; co\Lambda_q d\mu = w^*\text{-}cl\left(\int_A \Lambda_q d\mu\right).$$

Consequently $\forall q\in\mathbb{N}, \forall F\in\mathcal{F}, \forall A\in\mathcal{F}$,

$$\begin{aligned}\int_A \Lambda_{F,q} d\mu &= \int_A 1_F w^*\text{-}cl\; co\Lambda_q d\mu + \int_A 1_{\Omega\setminus F}\sigma d\mu\\ &= w^*\text{-}cl\left(\int_A 1_F\Lambda_q d\mu\right)+\int_A 1_{\Omega\setminus F}\sigma d\mu\\ &= w^*\text{-}cl\left(\int_A 1_F\Lambda_q + 1_{\Omega\setminus F}\sigma d\mu\right).\end{aligned}$$

This yields $\forall A\in\mathcal{F}$,

$$w^*\text{-}cl\left(\bigcup_{q\in\mathbb{N}}\bigcup_{F\in\mathcal{F}}\int_A \Lambda_{F,q}\,d\mu\right)=w^*\text{-}cl\left(\bigcup_{q\in\mathbb{N}}\bigcup_{F\in\mathcal{F}}\int_A 1_F\Lambda_q + 1_{\Omega\setminus F}\sigma d\mu\right). \quad (4.4.3)$$

Since $1_F\Lambda_q + 1_{\Omega\setminus F}\sigma\subset\cup_{q\in\mathbb{N}}\Delta_q$, for all $q\in\mathbb{N}$ and all $F\in\mathcal{F}$, from (4.4.2) and (4.4.3) we deduce

$$\forall A\in\mathcal{F},\quad w^*\text{-}cl\left(\int_A \cup_{q\geq 1} w^*\text{-}cl\; co\Delta_q\, d\mu\right)\subset w^*\text{-}cl\left(\int_A \cup_{q\in\mathbb{N}}\Delta_q d\mu\right)$$

and the equality (a) follows. Whereas (b) is a consequence of the preceding inclusion and the fact that

$$co \cup_{q\in\mathbb{N}} \Delta_q \subset \cup_{q\geq 1} w^*\text{-}cl\, co\Delta_q.$$

□

Before going further let us give a useful application of the preceding lemma to the sequential weak* upper limit of a sequence of measurable multifunctions.

Proposition 4.5. *Assume that μ is nonatomic and (X_n) is a sequence of measurable multifunctions with values in E'. If $\mathcal{S}^1_{w^*\text{-}ls\, X_n} \neq \emptyset$, then the following equalities hold*

$$w^*\text{-}cl \int_\Omega \cup_q w^*\text{-}clcow^*\text{-}ls\,(X_n \cap \overline{B}_{E'}(0,q))\, d\mu = w^*\text{-}cl \int_\Omega w^*\text{-}ls\, X_n\, d\mu.$$

$$\forall A \in \mathcal{F}, \quad w^*\text{-}cl\left(\int_A cow^*\text{-}ls\, X_n\, d\mu\right) = w^*\text{-}cl\left(\int_A w^*\text{-}ls\, X_n\, d\mu\right)$$

Moreover, the set w^*-cl$(\int_A w^*\text{-}ls\, X_n\, d\mu)$ is w^*-closed and convex.

In particular, if $X_n = \Gamma$, for all n, where $\Gamma : \Omega \rightrightarrows E'$ is a measurable multifunction such that $\mathcal{S}^1_\Gamma \neq \emptyset$, then

$$\forall A \in \mathcal{F}, \quad w^*\text{-}cl\left(\int_A co\Gamma\right) = w^*\text{-}cl\left(\int_A \Gamma\, d\mu\right).$$

Consequently the set w^*-cl $\left(\int_A \Gamma\, d\mu\right)$ is w^*-closed and convex

Proof. Take $\Delta_q := w^*\text{-}ls(X_n \cap q\overline{B}_{E'})$. Then Δ_q is integrably bounded and, since $q\overline{B}_{E'}$ is compact metrizable with respect to the weak* topology, it is not difficult to see that Δ_q is w^*-compact valued and measurable (see, e.g., Theorem 5.4 in [12]). Furthermore, since a w^*-convergent sequence is bounded in E', we have for all $\omega \in \Omega$

$$w^*\text{-}ls\, X_n = \bigcup_{q\in\mathbb{N}} \Delta_q.$$

Then, in view of the condition $\mathcal{S}^1_{w^*\text{-}ls\, X_n} \neq \emptyset$, the multifunction $\bigcup_{q\in\mathbb{N}} \Delta_q$ admits at least one $L^1_{E'}[E](\mu)$-selection. Consequently, it is possible to apply Lemma 4.4 to the sequence (Δ_q), which entails the desired equalities. □

The next corollary shows that for a measurable multifunction having at least one $L^1_{E'}[E](\mu)$-integrable selector the integral is dense in the G-integral with respect to the w^*-topology.

Corollary 4.6. *Assume that μ is nonatomic, and $\Gamma : \Omega \rightrightarrows E'$ is a measurable multifunction. If $\mathcal{S}^1_\Gamma \neq \emptyset$, then the following equality holds*

$$\forall A \in \mathcal{F},\ w^*\text{cl}\left(\int_A \Gamma d\mu\right) = w^*\text{-cl}\left(G\text{-}\int_A \Gamma d\mu\right).$$

Proof. It suffices to prove the inclusion

$$G\text{-}\int_A \Gamma d\mu \subset w^*\text{cl}\left(\int_A \Gamma d\mu\right).$$

Let a be an arbitrary element of $G\text{-}\int_A \Gamma\, d\mu$. Then there exists a function $f \in G\text{-}\mathcal{S}^1_\Gamma$ such that $a = \int_A f\, d\mu$. For each $p \in \mathbb{N}$, define the measurable set

$$M_p := \{\omega \in \Omega : \|f(\omega) - \sigma(\omega)\|_{E'_b} \leq p\},$$

where σ is a fixed $L^1_{E'}[E](\mu)$-integrable selector of Γ. Then, since $0 \in \Gamma - \sigma$ a.e., one has

$$\forall x \in E,\quad \int_A 1_{M_p}(\Gamma - \sigma)\, d\mu \subset \int_A \Gamma - \sigma\, d\mu.$$

Therefore

$$\begin{aligned}\langle x, \int_A f - \sigma\, d\mu\rangle &= \int_A \langle x, f - \sigma\rangle\, d\mu = \lim_{p\to\infty} \int_A \langle x, 1_{M_p}(f - \sigma)\rangle\, d\mu \\ &= \lim_{p\to\infty} \langle x, \int_A 1_{M_p}(f - \sigma)\, d\mu\rangle \\ &\leq \lim_{p\to\infty} \delta^*(x, \int_A 1_{M_p}(\Gamma - \sigma\, d\mu)) \\ &\leq \delta^*(x, w^*\text{-cl}\,(\int_A \Gamma - \sigma\, d\mu)),\end{aligned}$$

for every $x \in E$ and for every $A \in \mathcal{F}$. Moreover, by Proposition 4.5, the set $w^*\text{-cl}\,(\int_A \Gamma\, d\mu)$ is convex w^*-closed and so is $w^*\text{-cl}\,\left(\int_A \Gamma - \sigma\, d\mu\right)$. Consequently,

$$\int_A f - \sigma\, d\mu \in w^*\text{-cl}\left(\int_A \Gamma - \sigma\, d\mu\right),$$

which is equivalent to

$$a \in w^*\text{-cl}\left(\int_A \Gamma\, d\mu\right).$$

This finishes the proof. □

Proof of Theorem 4.1. By Theorem 2.3 in [15] and its proof, there exist an increasing sequence (C_k) in $\mathcal{F}$ with $\lim_k \mu(C_k) = 1$, a subsequence (g_n) of (f_n) and $f_\infty \in L^1_{E'}[E](\Omega, \mathcal{F}, \mu)$ satisfying (1), (2) and (3). Now let us prove the localization properties (4) and (5). We shall proceed in two steps.
Step 1. In view of Proposition 3.7, we may suppose, for simplicity, that (g_n) is compactly $cwk(E'_s)$-tight. Consequently, we can construct a non decreasing sequence, $(\Gamma_q)_q$, of $cwk(E'_s)$-valued scalarly measurable integrably bounded multifunctions (in the special case we consider here, we may take for Γ_q the closed ball $\overline{B}_{E'}(0, \rho_q)$ of center 0 and with radius ρ_q) such that

$$\forall n, \quad \mu(\Omega \setminus A_{n,q}) \leq \frac{1}{q}, \tag{4.1.1}$$

where

$$A_{n,q} := \{\omega \in \Omega : g_n(\omega) \in \Gamma_q(\omega)\}.$$

Now, from the condition L^1- lim sup-MT and Theorem 5.7 in [16] it follows that the multifunction w^*-$ls\, g_n$ admits a $L^1_{E'}[E](\mu)$ selector σ. Let (e'_m) be a fixed dense sequence in $\bar{B}_{E'}$ for the Mackey topology and define

$$g^m_{n,q} = 1_{A_{n,q}}(g_n - \ell\sigma - e'_m), \quad (q, m \in \mathbb{N}), \quad (\ell = 0, 1).$$

It is obvious that the sequence $(g^m_{n,q})_n$ satisfies the condition L^1- lim sup-MT so that we may apply again Theorem 2.3 in [15]. Thus, using a standard diagonal procedure, it is possible to find a subsequence (not relabeled) of $(g^m_{n,q})$ and $f^m_{\infty,q} \in L^1_{E'}[E](\Omega, \mathcal{F}, \mu)$ such that

$$\forall e \in E, \quad \lim_{n\to\infty} \frac{1}{n} \sum_{i=1}^{n} \langle e, h_i(\omega)\rangle \to \langle e, f^m_{\infty,q}(\omega)\rangle, \quad \text{a.e.} \quad \omega \in \Omega, \tag{4.1.2}$$

for every subsequence (h_n) of $(g^m_{n,q})$ with

$$f^m_{\infty,q}(\omega) \in w^*\text{-}cl\ co\left(\bigcap_{p=1} w^*\text{-}cl\{g^m_{i,q}(\omega) : i \geq p\}\right), \quad \text{a.e.} \quad \omega \in \Omega.$$

As

$$\sup_n \|g^m_{n,q}(\omega)\|_{E'_b} \leq |\Gamma_q|(\omega) + \ell\|\sigma(\omega)\|_{E'_b} + 1 < \infty$$

and the restriction of the w^*-topology to the closed ball $(|\Gamma_q|(\omega) + \ell\|\sigma(\omega)\|_{E'_b} + 1)\overline{B}_{E'}$ is metrisable, it follows that

$$w^*\text{-}ls\ g^m_{n,q}(\omega) = \bigcap_{p=1} w^*\text{-}cl(\{g^m_{i,q}(\omega) : i \geq p\}),$$

for all $q \in \mathbb{N}$, for all $m \in \mathbb{N}$ and for all $\omega \in \Omega$. Hence

$$f^m_{\infty,q}(\omega) \in w^* - cl\, co\,[w^*\text{-}ls\; g^m_{n,q}(\omega)], \quad \text{a.e.} \quad \omega \in \Omega \tag{4.1.3}$$

for all $q \in \mathbb{N}$ and for all $m \in \mathbb{N}$. Next, putting

$$L_q := \bigcup_{i=1}^{i=q} 1_{D_i} w^*\text{-}ls\,(g_n \cap \Gamma_i) + 1_{\Omega \setminus D_i}\sigma, \quad \text{where} \quad D_i := \text{dom}\, w^*\text{-}ls\,(g_n \cap \Gamma_i),$$

$$\phi(\omega) := \liminf_{n\to\infty} \frac{1}{n}\sum_{i=1}^{n} \|g_i(\omega)\|_{E'_b},$$

and

$$F^\ell_{m,\sigma}(\omega) := \overline{B}_{E'}(f_\infty(\omega) - \ell\sigma(\omega),\, \phi(\omega) + \ell\|\sigma(\omega)\|_{E'_b} + \|e'_m\|_{E'_b}), \quad (\ell = 0, 1),$$

we claim that

$$f_\infty(\omega) - \ell\sigma(\omega) \in w^* - cl(\cup_{q\ge 1} w^* - cl co[(L_q(\omega) - \ell\sigma(\omega)) \cup \{e'_m\}] \cap F^\ell_{m,\sigma}(\omega)) \tag{4.1.4}$$

a.e., for all $m \in \mathbb{N}$. Indeed, it follows from (3) and (4.1.2) that

$$\begin{aligned}
&\|(f_\infty(\omega) - \ell\sigma(\omega) - e'_m) - f^m_{\infty,q}(\omega)\|_{E'_b} \\
&= \sup_{e\in\overline{B}_E} |\langle e, f_\infty(\omega) - \ell\sigma(\omega) - e'_m\rangle - \langle e, f^m_{\infty,q}(\omega)\rangle| \\
&= \sup_{e\in\overline{B}_E} \lim_{n\to\infty} \frac{1}{n} |\sum_{i=1}^{n} \langle e, g_i(\omega) - \ell\sigma(\omega) - e'_m\rangle - \langle e, g^m_{i,q}(\omega)\rangle| \\
&= \sup_{e\in\overline{B}_E} \lim_{n\to\infty} \frac{1}{n} |\sum_{i=1}^{n} \langle e, 1_{A^c_{i,q}}(g_i(\omega) - \ell\sigma(\omega) - e'_m)\rangle| \\
&\le \liminf_{n\to\infty} \frac{1}{n} \sum_{i=1}^{n} 1_{\Omega\setminus A_{i,q}} \|g_i(\omega) - \ell\sigma(\omega) - e'_m\|_{E'_b} := \phi^m_q(\omega)
\end{aligned} \tag{4.1.5}$$

a.e. Using Fatou lemma and (4.1.1) we get

$$\begin{aligned}
\lim_{q\to\infty} \int_{C_k} \phi^m_q(\omega)d\mu &\le \lim_{q\to\infty} \liminf_{n\to\infty} \frac{1}{n} \sum_{i=1}^{n} \int_{C_k\cap(\Omega\setminus A_{i,q})} \|g_i(\omega) - \ell\sigma(\omega) - e'_m\|_{E'_b}\, d\mu \\
&\le \lim_{q\to\infty} \sup_n \int_{C_k\cap(\Omega\setminus A_{n,q})} \|g_n(\omega) - \ell\sigma(\omega) - e'_m\|_{E'_b}\, d\mu = 0,
\end{aligned}$$

for every $k \in \mathbb{N}$. Hence the sequence $(\phi^m_q(\omega))_q$ converges to 0 in the Banach space $L^1_{\mathbb{R}}(C_k)$ when $q \to \infty$. By extracting subsequences, we may assume that $(\phi^m_q)_q$ converges to 0 a.e. on each C_k. From (4.1.3) and (4.1.5) we have

$$f^m_{\infty,q}(\omega) \in \overline{co}[w^*\text{-}ls g^m_{n,q}(\omega)] \cap \overline{B}_{E'}(f_\infty(\omega) - \ell\sigma(\omega) - e'_m, \phi^m_q(\omega)))$$

$$\subset \overline{co}[(L_q(\omega) - \ell\sigma(\omega) - e'_m) \cup \{0\}] \cap (F^\ell_{m,\sigma}(\omega) - e'_m) \ a.e,$$

because

$$\overline{co}[w^*\text{-}ls g^m_{n,q}(\omega)] \subset \overline{co}[w^*\text{-}ls((g_n(\omega) - \ell\sigma(\omega) - e'_m) \cap (\Gamma_q(\omega) - \ell\sigma(\omega) - e'_m)) \cup \{0\}]$$

$$\subset \overline{co}[(L_q(\omega) - \ell\sigma(\omega) - e'_m) \cup \{0\}],$$

and

$$\phi^m_q(\omega) \le \phi(\omega) + \ell\|\sigma(\omega)\|_{E'_b} + \|e'_m\|_{E'_b}.$$

We deduce that

$$d_{E'_b}(f_\infty(\omega) - \ell\sigma(\omega) - e'_m, w^* - clco[(L_q(\omega) - \ell\sigma(\omega) - e'_m) \cup \{0\}] \cap (F^\ell_{m,\sigma}(\omega) - e'_m)$$

$$\le \|f_\infty(\omega) - \ell\sigma(\omega) - e'_m - f^m_{\infty,q}(\omega)\|_{E'_b} \le \phi^m_q(\omega).$$

As $(\phi^m_q)_q$ converges to 0 a.e. on each C_k and $\mu(C_k) \to 1$, it follows that

$$f_\infty(\omega) - \ell\sigma(\omega) - e'_m$$
$$\in w^* - cl\big(\cup_{q\ge 1} w^* - clco[(L_q(\omega) - \ell\sigma(\omega) - e'_m) \cup \{0\}] \cap (F^\ell_{m,\sigma}(\omega) - e'_m)\big)$$

a.e., which is equivalent to (4.1.4). Now, to prove (4) we repeat an argument in the proof of Theorem 8 in [2]. We assert that, for every subset C in E',

$$w^*cl\,co\,C = \bigcap_m w^*cl\,co[C \cup \{e'_m\}]. \qquad (\ddagger)$$

Indeed, assume that C is nonempty. If $x' \notin w^*cl\,co\,C$, there is $e \in E$ and $r \in \mathbb{R}$ such that

$$\delta^*(e, C) < r < \langle e, x'\rangle.$$

Taking e'_m in $\{y \in E' : \delta^*(e, C) < \langle e, y\rangle < r\}$ we get

$$w^*\text{-}cl\,co[C \cup \{e'_m\}] \subset \{y \in E' : \langle e, y\rangle \le r\}.$$

Hence $x \notin w^*\text{-}cl\,co[C \cup \{e'_m\}]$.

Applying $(\ddagger)$ in our case we get

$$w^* - cl(\cup_{q\ge 1} w^* - cl\,co\,L_q(\omega))$$
$$= \bigcap_{m\ge 1} w^*cl\,co[(\cup_{q\ge 1} w^*cl\,co\,L_q(\omega)) \cup \{e'_m\}]$$
$$= \bigcap_m w^* - cl(\cup_{q\ge 1} w^* - clco[L_q(\omega) \cup \{e'_m\}]), \qquad (4.1.6)$$

for all $\omega \in \Omega$, where the last equality follows from the fact that the sequence (L_q) is increasing. Consequently, (4) follows from (4.1.4) for $\ell = 0$, and (4.1.6). It remains to prove (5).
Step 2. Writing

$$F^1_{m,\sigma}(\omega) = f_\infty(\omega) - \sigma(\omega) + (\phi(\omega) + \|\sigma(\omega)\|_{E'_b} + \|e'_m\|_{E'_b})\overline{B}_{E'}(0,1),$$

we deduce easily that $F^1_{m,\sigma} \in \mathcal{L}^1_{cwk(E'_s)}(\mu)$. On the other hand, it is not difficult to see that L_q is measurable (see, e.g., Theorem 5.4 in [12]) and so is the multifunction $w^*\text{-cl}\, co[L_q - \sigma \cup \{e'_m\}]$. From these facts and (4.1.4) for $\ell = 1$, it follows that the multifunction $\cup_{q\geq 1} w^*\text{-cl}\, co[L_q - \sigma \cup \{e'_m\}] \cap F^1_{m,\sigma}$ satisfies the conditions of Lemma 4.2. Then

$$\begin{aligned}
&\int_A w^* - cl[\cup_{q\geq 1} w^*\text{-cl}\, co[L_q - \sigma \cup \{e'_m\}] \cap F^1_{m,\sigma}]\, d\mu \\
&\subset w^*\text{-cl}\left(\int_A \cup_{q\geq 1} w^*\text{-cl}\, co[L_q - \sigma \cup \{e'_m\}] \cap F^1_{m,\sigma}\, d\mu\right) \\
&\subset w^*\text{-cl}\left(\int_A \cup_{q\geq 1} w^*\text{-cl}\, co[L_q - \sigma \cup \{e'_m\}]\, d\mu\right), \qquad (4.1.7)
\end{aligned}$$

for every m. Now an appeal to Lemma 4.4 shows that

$$\begin{aligned}
&w^*\text{-cl}\left(\int_A \cup_{q\geq 1} w^*\text{-cl}\, co[L_q - \sigma \cup \{e'_m\}]\right) d\mu \\
&= w^*\text{-cl}\left(\int_A \cup_{q\geq 1} L_q - \sigma \cup \{e'_m\}\, d\mu\right). \qquad (4.1.8)
\end{aligned}$$

Thus using (4.1.4) for $\ell = 1$, (4.1.7) and (4.1.8) we get

$$\begin{aligned}
\int_A f_\infty - \sigma\, d\mu &\in \int_A \bigcap_m w^* - cl[\cup_{q\geq 1}(w^*\text{-cl}\, co[L_q - \sigma \cup \{e'_m\}] \cap F^1_{m,\sigma})]\, d\mu \\
&\subset \bigcap_m \int_A w^* - cl[\cup_{q\geq 1}\left(w^*\text{-cl}\, co[L_q - \sigma \cup \{e'_m\}] \cap F^1_{m,\sigma}\right)]\, d\mu \\
&\subset \bigcap_m w^*\text{-cl}\left(\int_A \cup_{q\geq 1} L_q - \sigma \cup \{e'_m\}\, d\mu\right) \\
&\subset \bigcap_m w^*\text{-cl}\left(\int_A w^*\text{-}ls\, g_n - \sigma \cup \{e'_m\}\, d\mu\right),
\end{aligned}$$

where the last inclusion follows from the fact that, $\cup_{q\geq 1} L_q \subset w^*\text{-}ls\, g_n$. On the other hand, noting that the multifunction $w^*\text{-}ls\, g_n$ is measurable, (by Theorem 5.5 in [12]) and $0 \in w^*\text{-}ls\, g_n - \sigma$, we can prove easily that

$$\int_A w^*\text{-}ls\, g_n - \sigma \cup \{e'_m\}\, d\mu \subset \int_A w^*\text{-}ls\, g_n - \sigma\, d\mu + \int_A \{e'_m\} \cup \{0\}\, d\mu,$$

which implies

$$w^*\text{-cl}\left(\int_A w^*\text{-}ls\, g_n - \sigma \cup \{e'_m\}\, d\mu\right)$$
$$\subset w^*\text{-cl}\left(\int_A w^*\text{-}ls\, g_n - \sigma\, d\mu\right) + \int_A \{e'_m\} \cup \{0\}\, d\mu,$$

since the set $\int_A \{e'_m\} \cup \{0\}\, d\mu$ is compact. Hence, there exists

$$a \in w^*\text{-cl}\left(\int_A w^*\text{-}ls\, g_n - \sigma\, d\mu\right) \quad \text{and} \quad b_m \in \int_A \{e'_m\} \cup \{0\}\, d\mu$$

such that

$$\int_A f_\infty - \sigma\, d\mu = a + b_m,$$

for every m. But, taking a subsequence (e'_{m_k}) of (e'_m) which w^*-converges to 0 one has $\lim_{k\to\infty}\langle x, b_{m_k}\rangle = 0$. Indeed, choose s_m in $\mathcal{S}^1_{\{e'_m\}\cup\{0\}}$ such that $\int_A s_m\, d\mu = b_m$. Then we have

$$|\langle x, b_m\rangle| = |\langle x, \int_A s_m\, d\mu\rangle| = |\int_A \langle x, s_m\rangle\, d\mu|$$
$$\leq \int_A |\langle x, s_m\rangle|\, d\mu \leq \int_A |\langle x, e'_m\rangle|\, d\mu = \mu(A)|\langle x, e'_m\rangle|.$$

Hence

$$\int_A f_\infty - \sigma\, d\mu \in w^*\text{-cl} \int_A w^*\text{-}ls\, g_n - \sigma\, d\mu.$$

Equivalently

$$\int_A f_\infty\, d\mu \in w^*\text{-cl}\left(\int_A w^*\text{-}ls\, g_n\, d\mu\right).$$

□

From Theorem 4.1, we get easily the following version of Fatou lemma.

Corollary 4.7. *Let E be a separable Banach space. Let (f_n) be sequence in the space $L^1_{E'}[E](\mu)$ such that:*

(i) (f_n) satisfies the condition L^1- lim sup-MT.
(ii) For every $x \in E$, the sequence $(\langle x, f_n\rangle)$ is uniformly integrable.
(iii) There exists $b \in E'$ such that $b = w^*\text{-}\lim_{n\to\infty} \int_\Omega f_n d\mu$.

Then there exists $f_\infty \in L^1_{E'}[E](\mu)$ *such that:*

(j) $b = \int_\Omega f_\infty d\mu$.
(jj) For almost all $\omega \in \Omega$ *one has* $f_\infty(\omega) \in w^*\text{-}cl\, co\,[w^*\text{-}ls f_n(\omega)]$.
(jjj) In particular, if μ *is nonatomic, then*

$$\int_\Omega f_\infty d\mu \in w^*\text{-}cl\left(\int_\Omega w^*\text{-}ls\; f_n\, d\mu\right).$$

We end this section by the following version of Fatou which is an analog of Corollary 4.4 [16] in the framework of $L^1_{E'}[E](\mu)$ space.

Corollary 4.8. *Let* E *is a separable Banach space. Let* (f_n) *be a sequence in* $L^1_{E'}[E](\Omega, \mathcal{F}, \mu)$ *satisfying the condition* L^1- lim sup-*MT. If* μ *is nonatomic, then the following inclusion holds*

$$w^*\text{-}ls \int_\Omega f_n\, d\mu \subset w^*\text{-cl} \int_\Omega w^*\text{-}ls\; f_n\, d\mu - C^*,$$

where C *is the cone of all* $x \in E$ *for which* $(max[0, \langle -x, f_n\rangle])$ *is uniformly integrable and* C^* *is the polar cone of* C.

Proof. Let b be an arbitrary element of $w^*\text{-}ls \int_\Omega f_n\, d\mu$. Then there exist a subsequence of (f_n) (not relabeled) such that $b = w^* - \lim_n \int_\Omega f_n\, d\mu$. An appeal to Theorem 4.1 produces a function $f_\infty \in L^1_{E'}[E](\mu)$, a subsequence (g_n) of (f_n) and an increasing sequence (C_k) in $\mathcal{F}$ with $\lim_k \mu(C_k) = 1$ for which (1)–(5) hold.

Let $\varepsilon > 0$ and $x \in C$ be given. Pick $k_0 \geq 1$ such that

$$\int_{C_{k_0}} \langle x', f_\infty\rangle\, d\mu \geq \int_\Omega \langle x', f_\infty\rangle\, d\mu - \epsilon$$

and that

$$\limsup_n \int_{\Omega\setminus C_{k_0}} \langle x, g_n\rangle^-\, d\mu \leq \varepsilon.$$

These two inequalities combined with (1) and a routine computation give

$$\begin{aligned}
\langle x, b\rangle &\geq \lim_n \int_{C_{k_0}} \langle x, g_n\rangle\, d\mu - \limsup_n \int_{\Omega\setminus C_{k_0}} \langle x, g_n\rangle^-\, d\mu \\
&\geq \lim_n \int_{C_{k_0}} \langle x, g_n\rangle\, d\mu - \epsilon \\
&= \int_{C_{k_0}} \langle x, f_\infty\rangle\, d\mu - \epsilon \\
&\geq \int_\Omega \langle x, f_\infty\rangle\, d\mu - 2\epsilon.
\end{aligned}$$

Thus $\langle x, b\rangle \geq \int_\Omega \langle x, f_\infty\rangle \, d\mu$. As μ is nonatomic, by (5), we conclude that

$$b \in \int_\Omega f_\infty \, d\mu - C^* \in w^*\text{-}cl\left(\int_\Omega w^*\text{-}ls\ f_n d\mu\right) - C^*.$$

□

5. Convergences in $G^1_{E'}[E](\mu)$

In this section we proceed to a new convergence result in the space $G^1_{E'}[E](\mu)$ of scalarly integrable mappings $f : \Omega \to E'$ and its applications to Fatou lemma. Since $|f| \notin L^1_{\mathbb{R}}(\mu)$, this study involves both the L^0- lim sup-Mazur and the scalar L^1- lim inf-Mazur tightness conditions by contrast with the L^1- lim sup-Mazur tightness condition occurring in the space $L^1_{E'}[E](\mu)$. Before going further, we need the following $G^1_{E'}[E]$-extension of Lemma 4.4.

Lemma 5.1. *Assume that μ is nonatomic and let $(\Delta_q)_{q\geq 1}$ be a sequence of measurable multifunctions from Ω to $\sigma(E', E)$- compact subsets of E'. Suppose that $1_{dom\Delta_q}\Delta_q$ is scalarly integrable, for all q,and $G\text{-}\mathcal{S}^1_{\cup_{q\geq 1}\Delta_q} \neq \emptyset$. Then:*
(a) $w^*\text{-}cl\,(G - \int_\Omega \cup_q w^*\text{-}clco\Delta_q\, d\mu) = w^*\text{-}cl\,(G - \int_\Omega \cup_q \Delta_q\, d\mu)$.
(b) $\forall A \in \mathcal{F}, \quad w^*\text{-}cl\,(G - \int_A co \cup_q \Delta_q\, d\mu) = w^*\text{-}cl\,(G - \int_A \cup_q \Delta_q\, d\mu)$.

Proof. Let σ be a fixed element of $G\text{-}\mathcal{S}^1_{\cup_{q\geq 1}\Delta_q}$ and set

$$\Lambda_q := \cup_{i=1}^{i=q}(1_{dom\Delta_i}\Delta_i + 1_{\Omega\setminus dom\Delta_i}\sigma).$$

Then (Λ_q) is increasing, $dom\Lambda_q = \Omega$, for all q, and $\cup_q\Lambda_q = \cup_q\Delta_q$. Next, for each $q \in \mathbb{N}$ and each $F \in \mathcal{F}$, define the following multifunction:

$$\Lambda_{F,q} := 1_F w^*\text{-}cl\ co\Lambda_q + 1_{\Omega\setminus F}\sigma.$$

We claim that

$$\text{seq}\, w^*\text{-cl}\left(G\text{-}\int_A \cup_{q\in\mathbb{N}} w^*\text{-}cl\ co\ \Lambda_q\, d\mu\right) = \text{seq}\, w^*\text{-cl}\left(G\text{-}\int_A \cup_{q\in\mathbb{N}} \cup_{F\in\mathcal{F}} \Lambda_{F,q}\, d\mu\right).$$

Here seq w^*-cl(Y) denotes the sequential w^*-closure of a set $Y \subset E'$. Since, for each $q \in \mathbb{N}$ and each $F \in \mathcal{F}$, $\Lambda_{F,q} \subset \cup_{q\in\mathbb{N}} w^*\text{-}cl\ co\Lambda_q$, it suffices to prove the inclusion

$$G\text{-}\int_A \cup_{q\in\mathbb{N}} w^*\text{-}cl\ co\ \Lambda_q\, d\mu \subset \text{seq}\, w^*\text{-cl}\left(\bigcup_{q\in\mathbb{N}}\bigcup_{F\in\mathcal{F}} G\text{-}\int_A \Lambda_{F,q}\, d\mu\right). \tag{5.1.1}$$

To show this, take $s \in G\text{-}\mathcal{S}^1_{\cup_{q\geq 1} w^*\text{-}cl\, co\Delta_q}$ and for each $q \in \mathbb{N}$, define a set $F_q \in \mathcal{F}$ and an $G^1_{E'}[E](\mu)$ selector, s_q, of $\Lambda_{F_q,q}$ as follows:

$$F_q := \{\omega \in \Omega : s(\omega) \in w^*\text{-}cl\, co\Lambda_q(\omega)\} \quad \text{and} \quad s_q := 1_{F_q} s + 1_{\Omega\setminus F_q}\sigma.$$

Then we have

$$\forall x \in E, \quad \int_\Omega |\langle x, s - s_q\rangle| d\mu \leq \int_{\Omega\setminus F_q} |\langle x, s\rangle| d\mu + \int_{\Omega\setminus F_q} |\langle x, \sigma\rangle| d\mu.$$

Since $\lim_{q\to\infty} \mu(\Omega \setminus F_q) = 0$, the preceding estimation implies that

$$s \in \text{seq}\, w^*\text{-cl}\,(G\text{-}\int_A \cup_{q\in\mathbb{N}} \cup_{F\in\mathcal{F}} \Lambda_{F,q}\, d\mu).$$

Thus the desired inclusion follows.

On the other hand, since, for each $q \in \mathbb{N}$, the multifunction Λ_q satisfies all the conditions of Lemma 4.3. we have

$$\forall q \in \mathbb{N}, \ \ \forall A \in \mathcal{F}, \quad G\text{-}\int_A w^*\text{-}cl\, co\Lambda_q d\mu = w^*\text{-}cl\,(G\text{-}\int_A \Lambda_q d\mu).$$

Consequently $\forall q \in \mathbb{N}, \forall F \in \mathcal{F}, \forall A \in \mathcal{F}$,

$$\begin{aligned} G\text{-}\int_A \Lambda_{F,q} d\mu &= G\text{-}\int_A 1_F w^*\text{-}cl\, co\Lambda_q d\mu + \int_A 1_{\Omega\setminus F}\sigma d\mu \\ &= w^*\text{-}cl\,(G\text{-}\int_A 1_F \Lambda_q d\mu) + \int_A 1_{\Omega\setminus F}\sigma d\mu \\ &= w^*\text{-}cl\,(G\text{-}\int_A (1_F\Lambda_q + 1_{\Omega\setminus F}\sigma) d\mu). \end{aligned}$$

This yields $\forall A \in \mathcal{F}$,

$$w^*\text{-}cl\,(\bigcup_{q\in\mathbb{N}} \bigcup_{F\in\mathcal{F}} G\text{-}\int_A \Lambda_{F,q}\, d\mu) = w^*\text{-}cl\,(\bigcup_{q\in\mathbb{N}} \bigcup_{F\in\mathcal{F}} G\text{-}\int_A 1_F\Lambda_q + 1_{\Omega\setminus F}\sigma\, d\mu). \tag{5.1.2}$$

Since $1_F\Lambda_q + 1_{\Omega\setminus F}\sigma \subset \cup_{q\in\mathbb{N}}\Delta_q$, for all $q \in \mathbb{N}$ and all $F \in \mathcal{F}$, from (5.1.1) and (5.1.2) we deduce

$$\forall A \in \mathcal{F}, \ w^*\text{-}cl\,(G\text{-}\int_A \cup_{q\geq 1} w^*\text{-}cl\, co\Delta_q\, d\mu) \subset w^*\text{-}cl\,(G\text{-}\int_A \cup_{q\in\mathbb{N}}\Delta_q d\mu).$$

Hence the equality (a) follows. Finally, the equality (b) is a consequence of the preceding inclusion and the fact that

$$co \cup_{q\in\mathbb{N}} \Delta_q \subset \cup_{q\geq 1} w^*\text{-}cl\, co\Delta_q.$$

□

The following result is a reformulation of Proposition 4.5 for the multi-valued Gelfand integral. Its proof is similar using Lemma 5.1.

Proposition 5.2. *Let (X_n) be a sequence of measurable multifunctions with values in E'. If μ is nonatomic and if the set $G\text{-}\mathcal{S}^1_{w^*\text{-}ls\, X_n}$ is nonempty, then for all $A \in \mathcal{F}$, the equalities*

$$w^*\text{-}cl\left(G\text{-}\int_A \cup_q w^*\text{-}clco w^*\text{-}ls\,(X_n \cap \overline{B}_{E'}(0,q))\,d\mu\right) = w^*\text{-}cl\left(G\text{-}\int_A w^*\text{-}ls\, X_n\,d\mu\right),$$

$$w^*\text{-}cl\left(G\text{-}\int_A co w^*\text{-}ls\, X_n\,d\mu\right) = w^*\text{-}cl\left(G\text{-}\int_A w^*\text{-}ls\, X_n\,d\mu\right),$$

hold. Moreover, the set $w^*\text{-}\mathrm{cl}\left(G\text{-}\int_A w^*\text{-}ls\, X_n\,d\mu\right)$ is w^*-closed and convex.

In particular, if $X_n = \Gamma$, for all n, where $\Gamma : \Omega \rightrightarrows E'$ is a measurable multifunction such that $G\text{-}\mathcal{S}^1_\Gamma \neq \emptyset$, then

$$\forall A \in \mathcal{F}, \quad w^*\text{-}cl\left(G\text{-}\int_A co\Gamma\right) = w^*\text{-}cl\left(G\text{-}\int_A \Gamma\,d\mu\right).$$

Consequently the set $w^*\text{-}\mathrm{cl}\left(G\text{-}\int_A \Gamma\,d\mu\right)$ is w^*-closed and convex

Theorem 5.3. *Let E is a separable Banach space. Let (f_n) be a in $G^1_{E'}[E](\mu)$ satisfying the following conditions:*

(i) (f_n) is L^0- lim sup*-MT.*
(ii) (f_n) is scalarly L^1- lim inf*-MT.*

Then there exist a function $f_\infty \in G^1_{E'}[E](\mu)$, a subsequence (g_n) of (f_n) and a sequence (C_k) in $\mathcal{F}$ with $\lim_k \mu(C_k) = 1$ such that the following hold:

(1) $\forall k \in \mathbb{N}$, $\forall n \geq k$, $1_{C_k} g_n \in L^1_{E'}[E](\mu)$, $1_{C_k} f_\infty \in L^1_{E'}[E](\mu)$.
(2) $(1_{C_k} \|g_n\|_{E'_b})_{n \geq k}$ is uniformly integrable in $L^1_{\mathbb{R}}(\mu)$ for each k.
(3)

$$\forall v \in L^\infty_E(\Omega, \mathcal{F}, \mu), \quad \lim_{n\to\infty, n\geq k} \int_{C_k} \langle v, g_n\rangle d\mu = \int_{C_k} \langle v, f_\infty\rangle d\mu.$$

(4) (g_n) weakly Komlós converges to f_∞.
(5) $f_\infty(\omega) \in w^*\text{-}\mathrm{cl}\,co\,[w^*\text{-}\,ls\, g_n(\omega)]$ a.e.
(6) If μ is nonatomic, then $\forall A \in \mathcal{F}$,

$$(\in_1) \qquad \int_A 1_{C_k} f_\infty\,d\mu \in w^*\text{-}\mathrm{cl}\left(\int_A 1_{C_k} w^*\text{-}ls\, g_n\,d\mu\right).$$

$(\in_2)$

$$\int_A f_\infty\,d\mu \in w^*\text{-}\mathrm{cl}\left(G\text{-}\int_A w^*\text{-}ls\, f_n\,d\mu\right) \quad \text{provided that} \quad G\text{-}\mathcal{S}^1_{w^*\text{-}ls\, f_n} \neq \emptyset.$$

Proof. On account of the L^0- lim sup-MT tightness condition (i) and Proposition 3.4, we provide a subsequence (g_n) of (f_n), a measurable function $\varphi_\infty : \Omega \mapsto \mathbb{R}^+$, and a sequence (C_k) in $\mathcal{F}$ with $\lim_k \mu(C_k) = 1$ such that

$$\lim_{n\to\infty} \int_{A\cap C_k} |g_n|\, d\mu = \int_{A\cap C_k} \varphi_\infty\, d\mu < \infty,$$

for all $k \in \mathbb{N}$ and for all $A \in \mathcal{F}$. In view of this equality, we observe that, for each $k \in \mathbb{N}$, every subsequence (h_n) of (g_n) admits a subsequence (h_n^k) with $\int_{C_k} |h_n^k|\, d\mu < \infty$, for all $n \in \mathbb{N}$, such that $(1_{C_k} h_n^k)$ is uniformly integrable. Using this fact and applying Theorem 4.1 to $(1_{C_k} g_n)$ via a standard diagonal procedure, it is possible to find a subsequence of (g_n) (not relabeled) and a function $f_\infty^k \in L^1_{E'}[E](\mu)$ such that

$$(1_{C_k} g_n)_{n\ge k} \quad \text{is uniformly integrable in} \quad L^1_{E'}[E](\mu),$$

$$(1_{C_k} g_n) \quad \text{weakly Komlós converges to} \quad f_\infty^k,$$

$$\forall k \in \mathbb{N},\ \ \forall v \in L^\infty_E(\Omega, \mathcal{F}, \mu), \qquad \lim_{n\to\infty, n\ge k} \int_\Omega \langle v, 1_{C_k} g_n\rangle d\mu = \int_\Omega \langle v, f_\infty^k\rangle d\mu,$$

$$f_\infty^k(\omega) \in w^*\text{-cl}\, co\, [w^*\text{-}ls\, g_n(\omega)] \quad \text{a.e} \quad \omega \in C_k.$$

Furthermore, if μ is nonatomic, then

$$\forall A \in \mathcal{F}, \qquad \int_A f_\infty^k\, d\mu \in w^*\text{-cl}\left(\int_A w^*\text{-}ls\, 1_{C_k} g_n\, d\mu\right).$$

Put

$$C'_1 := C_1 \quad \text{and} \quad C'_k := C_k \setminus C_{k-1} \quad \text{for} \quad k > 1,$$

and

$$f_\infty := \sum_{k=1}^{k=\infty} 1_{C'_k} f_\infty^k.$$

Since $\frac{1}{n}\sum_{i=1}^n g_i$ w^*-converges to f_∞^k a.e. on each C_k and $(C_k) \uparrow$, it follows that

$$\forall k, \forall j \le k, \quad f_\infty^j = f_\infty^k \quad \text{a.e on} \quad C_j,$$

and then

$$\forall k, \quad f_\infty = f_\infty^k \quad \text{a.e on} \quad C_k.$$

Consequently we get

$$(g_n) \quad \text{weakly Komlós converges to} \quad f_\infty,$$

$$\forall k \in \mathbb{N},\ \ \forall v \in L^\infty_E(\Omega, \mathcal{F}, \mu), \qquad \lim_{n\to\infty, n\ge k} \int_{C_k} \langle v, g_n\rangle d\mu = \int_{C_k} \langle v, f_\infty\rangle d\mu,$$

$$f_\infty(\omega) \in w^*\text{-cl}\, co\, [w^*\text{-}ls\, g_n(\omega)] \quad \text{a.e.}$$

and, if μ is nonatomic, we have

$$\forall A \in \mathcal{F}, \quad \int_{A\cap C_k} f_\infty\, d\mu = \int_{A\cap C_k} f_\infty^k\, d\mu \in w^*\text{-cl}\left(\int_{A\cap C_k} w^*\text{-}ls\, 1_{C_k} g_n\, d\mu\right)$$

$$= w^*\text{-cl}\left(\int_A w^*\text{-}ls\, 1_{C_k} g_n\, d\mu\right).$$

thus proving (1), (2), (3), (4), (5) and (6)-($\in_1$). Next, let us show that f_∞ is scalarly integrable. Fix x in E. By conditions (i), (ii) and Proposition 3.6, the sequence $(\langle x, g_n\rangle)$ is L^1- lim sup-MT. So, applying Proposition 3.4 to the sequence $(\langle x, g_n\rangle)$, provides a function $\varphi_\infty^x \in L^1_{\mathbb{R}^+}(\mu)$, a subsequence of (g_n) still denoted (g_n) and an increasing sequence (C_k^x) in $\mathcal{F}$ with $\lim_k \mu(C_k^x) = 1$ such that, for every $k \in \mathbb{N}$, the following holds:

$$\forall A \in \mathcal{F}, \quad \lim_{n\to\infty} \int_{A\cap C_k^x} |\langle x, g_n\rangle|\, d\mu = \int_{A\cap C_k^x} \varphi_\infty^x\, d\mu.$$

Using successively this equality, conclusion (4) and the classical Fatou lemma we get

$$\int_{C_k^x} |\langle x, f_\infty\rangle|\, d\mu = \int_{C_k^x} \lim_{n\to\infty} |\frac{1}{n}\sum_{i=1}^n \langle x, g_i\rangle|\, d\mu \le \int_{C_k^x} \liminf_{n\to\infty} \frac{1}{n}\sum_{i=1}^n |\langle x, g_i\rangle| d\mu$$

$$\le \liminf_{n\to\infty} \frac{1}{n}\sum_{i=1}^n \int_{C_k^x} |\langle x, g_i\rangle| d\mu$$

$$= \lim_{n\to\infty} \int_{C_k^x} |\langle x, g_n\rangle|\, d\mu = \int_{C_k^x} \varphi_\infty^x\, d\mu$$

for all $k \in \mathbb{N}$. Whence

$$\int_\Omega |\langle x, f_\infty\rangle|\, d\mu = \lim_{k\to\infty} \int_{C_k^x} |\langle x, f_\infty\rangle|\, d\mu \le \lim_{k\to\infty} \int_{C_k^x} \varphi_\infty^x\, d\mu = \int_\Omega \varphi_\infty^x\, d\mu < \infty,$$

proving the required integrability property. Finally, let us prove the second inclusion of (6). Let $\sigma \in G\text{-}\mathcal{S}^1_{w^*\text{-}ls\, f_n}$. Then from ($\in_1$) and the inclusion $0 \in w^*\text{-}ls\, f_n - \sigma$, it follows that

$$\int_{A\cap C_k} (f_\infty - \sigma)\, d\mu \in w^*\text{-cl}\left(G - \int_A 1_{C_k}\left(w^*\text{-}ls\, f_n - \sigma\right) d\mu\right)$$

$$\subset w^*\text{-}cl\left(G - \int_A w^*\text{-}ls\, f_n - \sigma\, d\mu\right),$$

for every $k \in \mathbb{N}$ and every $A \in \mathcal{F}$. Consequently, since f_∞ and σ are scalarly integrable, one has $\forall x \in E, \forall A \in \mathcal{F}$,

$$\begin{aligned}\left\langle x, \int_A f_\infty - \sigma \, d\mu \right\rangle &= \int_A \langle x, f_\infty - \sigma \rangle \, d\mu = \lim_{k\to\infty} \int_A \langle x, 1_{C_k}(f_\infty - \sigma)\rangle \, d\mu \\ &= \lim_{k\to\infty} \left\langle x, \int_A 1_{C_k}(f_\infty - \sigma) \, d\mu \right\rangle \\ &\le \delta^*\left(x, w^*\text{-cl}\left(G - \int_A w^*\text{-}ls \, f_n - \sigma \, d\mu\right)\right).\end{aligned}$$

Moreover, by Proposition 5.2, the set $w^*\text{-cl}(G - \int_A w^*\text{-}ls\, f_n \, d\mu)$ is w^*-closed convex and so is $w^*\text{-cl}(G - \int_A w^*\text{-}ls\, f_n - \sigma \, d\mu)$. Hence we get

$$\forall A \in \mathcal{F}, \quad \int_A f_\infty - \sigma \, d\mu \in w^*\text{-cl}\left(G - \int_A w^*\text{-}ls\, f_n - \sigma \, d\mu\right).$$

Thus

$$\int_A f_\infty \, d\mu \in w^*\text{-cl}\left(G - \int_A w^*\text{-}ls\, f_n \, d\mu\right).$$

This completes the proof. □

The following result is a direct consequence of Theorem 5.3, Corollary 4.6 and Theorem 5.8 in [12].

Corollary 5.4. *Let E is a separable Banach space. Let (f_n) be a sequence in $G^1_{E'}[E](\mu)$ satisfying the following two conditions*

(i) (f_n) *is* L^0- lim sup-*MT.*
(ii) (f_n) *is scalarly* L^1- lim inf-*MT.*
(iii) $\liminf |f_n| \in L^1_{\mathbb{R}}(\mu)$.

Then there exist a function $f_\infty \in G^1_{E'}[E](\mu)$, a subsequence (g_n) of (f_n) and a sequence (C_k) in $\mathcal{F}$ with $\lim_k \mu(C_k) = 1$ satisfying (1)–(5) of Theorem 5.3 and, if μ is nonatomic, then

$$(6') \qquad \forall A \in \mathcal{F}, \quad \int_A f_\infty \, d\mu \in w^*\text{-cl}\left(\int_A w^*\text{-}ls\, f_n \, d\mu\right).$$

Theorem 5.3 extends Theorem 4.1 to the space $G^1_{E'}[E](\mu)$, by the way, we get the following $G^1_{E'}[E](\mu)$-extension of Corollary 4.8.

Corollary 5.5. *Suppose that μ is nonatomic, E is a separable Banach space and (f_n) is a sequence in $G^1_{E'}[E](\mu)$ satisfying the following two conditions*

(i) (f_n) *is* L^0- lim sup-*MT.*
(ii) (f_n) *is scalarly* L^1- lim inf-*MT.*
(iii) $\liminf |f_n| \in L^1_{\mathbb{R}}(\mu)$.

Then the following inclusion holds

$$w^*\text{-}ls \int_\Omega f_n\,d\mu \subset w^*\text{-cl}\left(\int_\Omega w^*\text{-}ls\, f_n\,d\mu\right) - C^*,$$

where C is the cone of all $x \in E$ for which $(max[0, \langle -x, f_n\rangle])$ is uniformly integrable and C^* is the polar cone of C.

The proof is the same as that of Corollary 4.8 using Corollary 5.4 and is omitted. □

6. Convergences in $\mathcal{L}^1_{cwk(E'_s)}(\mu)$ and $\mathcal{G}^1_{cwk(E'_s)}(\mu)$

Our main result in this section is concerned with new convergence results in the space $\mathcal{L}^1_{cwk(E'_s)}(\mu)$ and $\mathcal{G}^1_{cwk(E'_s)}(\mu)$.

Theorem 6.1. *Let (X_n) be a sequence in $\mathcal{L}^1_{cwk(E'_s)}(\mu)$ satisfying the condition L^1-$\limsup$-MT. Then there exist a subsequence (X'_n) of (X_n), $X_\infty \in \mathcal{L}^1_{cwk(E'_s)}(\mu)$ and a sequence (D_k) in $\mathcal{F}$ with $\lim_k \mu(D_k) = 1$ such that the following hold:*

(1) $(|X'_n|)$ is uniformly integrable in $L^1_{\mathbb{R}}(D_k)(\mu)$ on each D_k.
(2) (X'_n) weakly Komlós converges to X_∞.
(3) (X'_n) d_{m^*}-Wijsman Komlós converges a.e. to X_∞.
(4) (X'_n) weakly biting converges to X_∞.

$$\forall k \geq 1, \forall v \in L^\infty_E(\Omega, \mathcal{F}, \mu), \quad \lim_{n\to\infty} \int_{D_k} \delta^*(v, X'_n)d\mu = \int_{D_k} \delta^*(v, X_\infty)d\mu,$$

(5) $X_\infty(\omega) \subset w^*\text{-cl}\,co\,[w^*\text{-}ls\, X_n(\omega)]$ a.e.
(6) If μ is nonatomic then

$$\forall A \in \mathcal{F}, \quad \int_A X_\infty\,d\mu \subset w^*\text{-cl}\left(\int_A w^*\text{-}ls\, X'_n\,d\mu\right).$$

Proof. We will use several arguments of the proof of Theorem 4.1 with appropriate modifications.
Step 1. On account of the condition L^1-$\limsup$-M, Theorem 2.1 in [15] and Proposition 3.4, there exist a subsequence (X'_n) of (X_n) a function $\varphi \in L^1_{\mathbb{R}}(\mu)$ and an increasing sequence (D_k) in $\mathcal{F}$ with $\lim_k \mu(D_k) = 1$ such that

$$(|X'_n|) \quad \text{is uniformly integrable in} \quad L^1_{\mathbb{R}}(D_k)(\mu) \quad \text{on each} D_k, \qquad (6.1.1)$$

$$\lim_{n\to\infty} \frac{1}{n} \sum_{i=1}^{n} |Y_i|(\omega) = \varphi(\omega) \quad \text{exists a.e., and} \tag{6.1.2}$$

$$\lim_{n\to\infty} \delta^* \left(x_p, \frac{1}{n} \sum_{i=1}^{n} Y_i \right) \quad \text{exists a.e.} \tag{6.1.3}$$

for every subsequence (Y_n) of (X'_n). On the other hand, in view of Proposition 3.8, we may suppose, for simplicity, that (X'_n) is compactly $cwk(E'_s)$-tight. Consequently, we can construct a non decreasing sequence, (K_q), in $\mathcal{L}^1_{cwk(E'_s)}(\mu)$ such that

$$\forall n, \quad \mu(\Omega \setminus \{\omega \in \Omega : X'_n(\omega) \subset K_q(\omega)\}) \leq \frac{1}{q}. \tag{6.1.4}$$

Next, for every $p \in \mathbb{N}$, pick a maximal $L^1_{E'}[E](\mu)$-selection $v_{n,p}$ of X'_n, that is

$$\delta^*(x_p, X'_n) = \langle x_p, v_{n,p} \rangle.$$

It is clear that $(v_{n,p})$ is also L^1- lim sup-MT and we have

$$\forall n, \; \mu(\Omega \setminus \{\omega \in \Omega : v_{n,p}(\omega) \subset K_q(\omega)\}) \leq \mu(\Omega \setminus \{\omega \in \Omega : X'_n(\omega) \subset K_q(\omega)\}) \leq \frac{1}{q}.$$

As in the proof of Theorem 4.1, let us set

$$Q_q := \bigcup_{i=1}^{i=q} 1_{B_i} w^*\text{-}ls\,(X'_n \cap K_i) + 1_{\Omega \setminus B_i} \tau,$$

where $B_i := \operatorname{dom} w^*\text{-}ls\,(X'_n \cap Q_i)$ and τ a fixed $L^1_{E'_s}(\mu)$-integrable selector of $w^*\text{-}ls X'_n$ (such a function is ensured by Theorem 5.7 in [16]). Repeating mutandis the arguments of the proof of Theorem 4.1 for the sequence $(v_{n,p})_n$ instead of (f_n) but replacing (C_k), Γ_q, L_q, ϕ and σ respectively by (D_k), K_q, Q_q, φ and τ, we can always find a subsequence of $(v_{n,p})$ (not relabeled) and $v_{\infty,p} \in L^1_{E'}[E](\mu)$ for each $p \in \mathbb{N}$, such that

$$(v_{n,p}) \;\; \text{weakly Komlós converges to} \;\; v_{\infty,p} \in L^1_{E'}[E](\mu) \;\; \text{for each} \;\; p \in \mathbb{N} \tag{6.1.5}$$

$$v_{\infty,p}(\omega) - \ell\tau(\omega) \in w^* - cl[\cup_{q\geq 1}(w^*\text{-cl}\, co[Q_q(\omega) - \ell\tau(\omega) \cup \{e'_m\}] \cap G^{\ell}_{m,\tau}(\omega))], \tag{6.1.6}$$

where

$$G^{\ell}_{m,\tau}(\omega) := \overline{B}_{E'}(v_{\infty,p}(\omega) - \ell\tau(\omega), \varphi(\omega) + \ell\|\tau(\omega)\|_{E'_b} + \|e'_m\|_{E'_b}), \quad (\ell = 0, 1).$$

Step 2. Let us prove (2) and (3). To do this consider the multifunctions

$$S_n = \frac{1}{n}\sum_{i=1}^{n} X'_i \quad \text{and} \quad X_\infty = w^*\text{-}li\ \frac{1}{n}\sum_{i=1}^{n} X'_i,$$

where w^*-$li\ C_n$ is the sequential weak* lower limit of a sequence (C_n) in $2^{E'}$ defined by

$$w^*\text{-}li\ C_n = \{x' \in E' : x' = \sigma(E', E)\text{-}\lim_{n\to\infty} x'_n;\ x'_n \in C_n\}.$$

Then, by (6.1.2), (S_n) is pointwise bounded a.e., and X_∞ is $cwk(E'_s)$-valued, the w^*-closedness of X_∞ follows easily from the fact that the restriction of the weak* topology to bounded sets is metrizable. Moreover, $v_{\infty,p} \in \mathcal{S}^1_{X_\infty}$ and we have

$$\lim_{n\to+\infty} \delta^*(x_p, S_n(\omega)) = \lim_n \left\langle x_p, \frac{1}{n}\sum_{i=1}^{n} v_{i,p} \right\rangle = \langle x_p, v_{\infty,p}\rangle \le \delta^*(x_p, X_\infty(\omega)) \quad \text{a.e.}$$

On the other hand it easy to see that

$$\delta^*(x_p, X_\infty(\omega)) \le \lim_{n\to\infty} \delta^*(x_p, S_n(\omega)) \quad \text{a.e.}$$

Whence we get

$$\lim_{n\to\infty} \delta^*(x_p, S_n(\omega)) = \delta^*(x_p, X_\infty(\omega)) \quad \text{a.e.} \tag{6.1.7}$$

We will use an argument in [10, Lemma 3.2]. We have

$$\begin{aligned} |\delta^*(x, S_n) - \delta^*(x, X_\infty)| \le\ & \max\{\delta^*(x - x_p, S_n), \delta^*(x_p - x, S_n)\} \\ & + |\delta^*(x_p, S_n) - \delta^*(x_p, X_\infty)| \\ & + \max\{\delta^*(x - x_p, X_\infty), \delta^*(x_p - x, X_\infty) \end{aligned}$$

for all $x' \in E'$ and for all j. Now let $x \in \overline{B}_E$ and $\varepsilon > 0$. There is $x_p \in D$ such that $||x - x_p|| \le \varepsilon$. Then we have

$$|\delta^*(x, S_n) - \delta^*(x, X_\infty)| \le \varepsilon \sup_n |S_n| + |\delta^*(x_p, S_n) - \delta^*(x_p, X_\infty)| + \varepsilon\, |X_\infty|.$$

Thus, by (6.1.7) and the pointwise boundedness of (S_n), it follows

$$\forall x \in E, \quad \lim_{n\to\infty} \delta^*(x, S_n(\omega)) = \delta^*(x, X_\infty(\omega)) \quad \text{a.e.} \tag{6.1.8}$$

By this equality, X_∞ is scalarly measurable, and hence measurable, (see, e.g., Corollary 5.3, [12]). Furthermore, returning again to (6.1.2), we get

$$|X_\infty| \le \liminf_{n\to\infty} |S_n| \le \lim_{n\to\infty} \frac{1}{n}\sum_{i=1}^{n} |X'_i|\, d\mu = \varphi,$$

hence $\int_\Omega |X_\infty|\, d\mu < \infty$.
Next, we claim that

$$\lim_n d_{E'_{m^*}}(x', S_n) = d_{E'_{m^*}}(x', X_\infty),$$

for all $x' \in E'$ and almost all $\omega \in \Omega$. Indeed, since the multifunctions S_n and X_∞ are $cwk(E'_s)$-valued and $p(x') := d_{E'_{m^*}}(0, x')$ is a m^*-continuous semi-norm, we can invoke Theorem II.18 in [17], which, together with (6.1.8), entail

$$\begin{aligned}
\liminf_n d_{E'_{m^*}}(x', S_n) &= \liminf_n \sup_{x\in U^0} [\langle x, x'\rangle - \delta^*(x, S_n)] \\
&\ge \sup_{x\in U^0} \lim_n [\langle x, x'\rangle - \delta^*(x, S_n)] \\
&= \sup_{x\in U^0} [\langle x, x'\rangle - \delta^*(x, X_\infty)] \\
&= d_{E'_{m^*}}(x', X_\infty)
\end{aligned}$$

for every $x' \in E'$ and for almost all $\omega \in \Omega$, where $U := \{x' \in E' : p(x') < 1\}$ and U^0 its polar. By definition of X_∞ we have

$$\limsup_n d_{E'_{m^*}}(x', S_n)) \le d_{E'_{m^*}}(x', X_\infty),$$

for every $x' \in E'$ and for almost all $\omega \in \Omega$. Hence

$$\lim_n d_{E'_{m^*}}(x', S_n)) = d_{E'_{m^*}}(x', X_\infty),$$

for every $x' \in E'$ and for almost all $\omega \in \Omega$.

Applying the results obtained above for the sequence (X'_n) to any other subsequence (Y_n) of (X'_n) gives $X'_\infty \in \mathcal{L}^1_{cwk(E^*_s)}(\mu)$ such that

$$\forall x \in E, \quad \lim_{n\to\infty} \delta^*\left(x, \frac{1}{n}\sum_{i=1}^{n} Y_i(\omega)\right) = \delta^*\left(x, X'_\infty(\omega)\right) \quad \text{a.e.}$$

$$\forall x' \in E', \quad \limsup_n d_{E'_{m^*}}\left(x', \frac{1}{n}\sum_{i=1}^{n} Y_i(\omega)\right) = d_{E'_{m^*}}\left(x', X'_\infty\right), \quad \text{a.e.}$$

Then returning to (6.1.3) and (6.1.8) we deduce that $X_\infty = X'_\infty$, thus completing the proof of (2) and (3).
Step 3. Using (6.1.1), conclusion (2) and Lebegue–Vitali theorem, we get

$$\forall k \geq 1,\ \ \forall v \in L^\infty_E(\Omega, \mathcal{F}, \mu),\ \ \lim_{n\to\infty} \int_{D_k} \delta^*(v, \frac{1}{n}\sum_{i=1}^{n} Y_i) d\mu = \int_{D_k} \delta^*(v, X_\infty) d\mu,$$

for every subsequence (Y_n) of (X'_n). This is equivalent to

$$\forall k \geq 1,\ \ \forall v \in L^\infty_E(\Omega, \mathcal{F}, \mu),\ \ \lim_{n\to\infty} \int_{D_k} \delta^*(v, X'_i) d\mu = \int_{D_k} \delta^*(v, X_\infty) d\mu,$$

thus proving (4).
Step 4. To prove (5) and (6) let us set

$$r_1(\omega) := |X_\infty|(\omega) + \varphi(\omega) + \|e'_m\|_{E'_b} \quad \text{and}$$

$$r_2(\omega) := |X_\infty|(\omega) + 2\|\tau(\omega)\|_{E'_b} + \varphi(\omega) + \|e'_m\|_{E'_b}.$$

Since $v_{\infty,k} \in \mathcal{S}^1_{X_\infty}$, it follows from (6.1.6) for $\ell = 0$ that

$$\begin{aligned}
&\delta^*(x_p, X_\infty(\omega)) = \langle x_p, v_{\infty,j}(\omega)\rangle \\
&\quad \leq \delta^*(x_p, w^* - cl\big[\cup_{q\geq 1} w^*\text{-cl}\, co[Q_q(\omega) \cup \{e'_m\}] \\
&\qquad\qquad \cap w^*\text{-cl}\, co \bigcup_{s \in \mathcal{S}^1_{X_\infty}} \overline{B}_{E'}(s(\omega), \varphi(\omega) + \|e'_m\|_{E'_b})\big]) \\
&\quad \leq \delta^*\left(x_p, w^* - cl\big[\cup_{q\geq 1} w^*\text{-cl}\, co[Q_q(\omega) \cup \{e'_m\}] \cap \overline{B}_{E'}(0, r_1(\omega))\big]\right),
\end{aligned}$$

for every p and for every m. Since the multifunction

$$\omega \Rightarrow w^* - cl[\cup_{q\geq 1}(w^*\text{-cl}\, co[Q_q(\omega) \cup \{e'_m\}] \cap \overline{B}_{E'}(0, r_1(\omega)))]]$$

is $cwk(E'_s)$-valued, E'_s is Suslin and its dual is equal to E, by virtue of Proposition III-35 in [17], the preceding inequality entails

$$\begin{aligned}
X_\infty(\omega) &\subset w^* - cl\big[\cup_{q\geq 1} w^*\text{-cl}\, co[Q_q(\omega) \cup \{e'_m\}] \cap \overline{B}_{E'}(0, r_1(\omega))\big] \\
&\subset w^* - cl\,(\cup_{q\geq 1} w^*\text{-cl}\, co[Q_q(\omega) \cup \{e'_m\}]). \qquad (6.1.9)
\end{aligned}$$

Similarly, using again (6.1.6) but this time for $\ell = 1$, we obtain

$$X_\infty(\omega) - \tau(\omega) \subset w^* - cl\big[\cup_{q\geq 1}(w^*\text{-cl}\, co[Q_q(\omega) - \tau(\omega) \cup \{e'_m\}] \cap \overline{B}_{E'}(0, r_2(\omega))\big]. \qquad (6.1.10)$$

Inclusion (5) is a consequence of (6.1.9). Indeed, it suffices to proceed as in the Step 1 of the proof of Theorem 4.1, by using an argument in the proof of Theorem 8 in [2]. Finally, to prove (6) take $u \in \mathcal{S}^1_{X_\infty}$ and note that (6.1.10) entails

$$u(\omega)-\tau(\omega) \in w^*-cl\left[\cup_{q\geq 1} w^*\text{-cl}\, co[Q_q(\omega)-\tau(\omega)\cup\{e'_m\}]\cap \overline{B}_{E'}(0, r_2(\omega))\right].$$

Since the sequence $\big(w^*\text{-cl}\, co[Q_q(\omega) - \tau \cup \{e'_m\}] \cap \overline{B}_{E'}(0, r_2(\omega))\big)$ satisfies all the conditions of Lemma 4.4, repeating exactly the same arguments as in the Step 2 of the proof of Theorem 4.1, we deduce that

$$\int_A u\, d\mu \in w^*\text{-cl}\left(\int_A \cup_{q\geq 1} Q'_q\, d\mu\right) = w^*\text{-cl}\left(\int_A w^*\text{-}ls\, X'_n\, d\mu\right),$$

which yields the desired inclusion (6). □

From Theorem 6.1 we derive the following Biting lemma in $\mathcal{L}^1_{cwk(E'_s)}(\mu)$. We refer to [8, 9, 14] dealing with Biting lemma in $\mathcal{L}^1_{cwk(E)}(\mu)$.

Corollary 6.2. *Suppose that E is a separable Banach space, (X_n) is a bounded sequence in $\mathcal{L}^1_{cwk(E'_s)}(\mu)$. Then there exist a subsequence (X'_n) of (X_n) and $X_\infty \in \mathcal{L}^1_{cwk(E'_s)}(\mu)$ such that the following hold:*

(i) (X'_n) weakly biting converges to X_∞
(ii) $X_\infty(\omega) \subset w^* cl co\,[w^*\text{-}ls\, X'_n(\omega)]$ a.e.

Our second main result presents a version of Theorem 5.3 for multifunctions in the space $\mathcal{G}^1_{cwk(E'_s)}(\mu)$. The L^1- lim sup-MT condition is replaced by the L^0 – lim sup and the scalar L^1 – lim inf Mazur tightness conditions

Theorem 6.3. *Let (X_n) be a sequence in $\mathcal{G}^1_{cwk(E'_s)}(\mu)$ satisfying the following conditions:*

(i) (X_n) is L^0- lim sup-MT.
(ii) (X_n) is scalarly L^1- lim inf-MT.

Then there exist a subsequence (X'_n) of (X_n), $X_\infty \in \mathcal{G}^1_{cwk(E'_s)}(\mu)$ and a sequence (D_k) in $\mathcal{F}$ with $\lim_k \mu(D_k) = 1$ such that the following hold:

(1) $\forall k \in \mathbb{N}$, $\forall n \geq k$, $1_{C_k} X'_n \in \mathcal{L}^1_{cwk(E'_s)}(\mu)$, $1_{C_k} X_\infty \in \mathcal{L}^1_{cwk(E'_s)}(\mu)$.
(2) $(1_{C_k}|X'_n|)_{n\geq k}$ is uniformly integrable in $L^1_{\mathbb{R}}(\mu)$ for each k.
(3) (X'_n) weakly Komlós converges to X_∞.
(4) (X'_n) d_{m^*}-Wijsman Komlós converges a.e. to X_∞.

(5)

$$\forall k \geq 1,\ \ \forall v \in L_E^\infty(\Omega, \mathcal{F}, \mu), \qquad \lim_{n\to\infty, n\geq k} \int_{D_k} \delta^*(v, X_n')d\mu = \int_{D_k} \delta^*(v, X_\infty)d\mu.$$

In particular,

$$\forall x \in E, \quad \lim_{n\to\infty} \int_{C_k} \delta^*(x, X_n')d\mu = \int_{C_k} \delta^*(x, X_\infty)d\mu.$$

(6) $X_\infty(\omega) \subset w^*\text{-cl}\, co\,[w^*\text{-}ls\ X_n'(\omega)]$ *a.e.*
(7) If μ *is nonatomic then* $\forall A \in \mathcal{F}$,

$$(\subset_1) \qquad \textstyle\int_A 1_{D_k} X_\infty\, d\mu \subset w^*\text{-cl}\left(\int_A 1_{D_k} w^*\text{-}ls\ X_n'\, d\mu\right).$$

$$(\subset_2) \quad G\text{-}\int_A X_\infty\, d\mu \subset w^*\text{-cl}\,(G\text{-}\int_A w^*\text{-}ls\, X_n\, d\mu), \quad \textit{provided that} \quad G\text{-}\mathcal{S}^1_{w^*\text{-}ls\, X_n} \neq \emptyset.$$

Proof. Reasoning as in the beginning of the proof of Theorem 5.3 by using Proposition 3.6 and Theorem 6.1, we find a subsequence (X_n') of (X_n), $X_\infty^k \in \mathcal{L}^1_{cwk(E_s')}(\mu)$ and an increasing sequence (D_k) in $\mathcal{F}$ with $\lim_k \mu(D_k) = 1$ such that $\forall k \in \mathbb{N}$,

$$(1_{D_k}|X_n'|)_{n\geq k} \quad \text{is uniformly integrable in} \quad L^1_{E'}[E](\mu).$$

$$(1_{D_k}X_n') \quad \text{weakly Komlós converges to} \quad X_\infty^k.$$

$$\forall v \in L_E^\infty(\Omega, \mathcal{F}, \mu), \qquad \lim_{n\to\infty, n\geq k} \int_\Omega \delta^*(v, 1_{D_k}X_n'(\omega))d\mu = \int_\Omega \delta^*(v, X_\infty^k)d\mu.$$

$$X_\infty^k(\omega) \subset w^*\text{-cl}\, co\, w^*\text{-}ls\ X_n'(\omega) \quad \text{a.e. on each} \quad D_k.$$

Furthermore, if μ is nonatomic, then

$$\forall A \in \mathcal{F}, \quad \int_A X_\infty^k\, d\mu \subset w^*\text{-cl}\left(\int_A w^*\text{-}ls\ 1_{D_k}X_n'\, d\mu\right).$$

Put

$$D_1' := D_1 \quad \text{and} \quad D_k' := D_k \setminus D_{k-1} \quad \text{for} \quad k > 1,$$

and

$$X_\infty := \sum_{k=1}^{k=\infty} 1_{D_k'} X_\infty^k.$$

Since $\frac{1}{n}\sum_{i=1}^n \delta^*(x, X_i'(\omega))$ converges to $\delta^*(x, X_\infty^k(\omega))$ for all $x \in E$ and for almost everywhere $\omega \in D_k$ and $(D_k) \uparrow$, it follows that

$$\forall k, \forall j \leq k, \quad \delta^*(x, X_\infty^j(\omega)) = \delta^*(x, X_\infty^k(\omega)),$$

for all $x \in E$ and for almost everywhere $\omega \in D_j$. Hence

$$\forall k, \forall j \leq k, \quad X^j_\infty = X^k_\infty \quad \text{a.e. on} \quad D_j,$$

which yields

$$\forall k, \quad X_\infty = X^k_\infty \quad \text{a.e. on} \quad D_k.$$

Consequently we get

$$(X'_n) \quad \text{weakly Komlós converges to} \quad X_\infty,$$

$$\forall k \in \mathbb{N}, \forall v \in L^\infty_E(\Omega, \mathcal{F}, \mu), \quad \lim_{n\to\infty, n\geq k} \int_{D_k} \delta^*(v, X'_n) d\mu = \int_{D_k} \delta^*(v, X_\infty) d\mu,$$

$$X_\infty(\omega) \subset w^*\text{-cl}\, co\, [w^*\text{-}ls\, X'_n(\omega)] \quad \text{a.e.}$$

and, if μ is nonatomic, we have

$$\forall A \in \mathcal{F}, \quad \int_A 1_{D_k} X_\infty \, d\mu = \int_A 1_{D_k} X^k_\infty \, d\mu = \int_{A\cap D_k} X^k_\infty \, d\mu$$

$$\subset w^*\text{-cl}\,\Big(\int_{A\cap D_k} w^*\text{-}ls\, 1_{D_k} X'_n \, d\mu\Big) = w^*\text{-cl}\,\Big(\int_A w^*\text{-}ls\, 1_{D_k} X'_n \, d\mu\Big)$$

whence follow (1), (2), (3), (4), (5), (6) and (7)-($\subset_1$). Next, let us show that X_∞ is scalarly integrable. Fix x in E. By conditions (i), (ii) and Proposition 3.5, the sequence $(\delta^*(x, X'_n))$ is L^1-lim sup-MT. Applying Proposition 3.4, provides a function $\theta^x_\infty \in L^1_{\mathbb{R}^+}(\mu)$, a subsequence of (X'_n) still denoted (X'_n) and a sequence (B^x_k) in $\mathcal{F}$ with $\lim_k \mu(B^x_k) = 1$ such that, for every $k \in \mathbb{N}$, the following holds:

$$\forall A \in \mathcal{F}, \quad \lim_{n\to\infty} \int_{A\cap B^x_k} |\delta^*(x, X'_n)| \, d\mu = \int_{A\cap B^x_k} \theta^x_\infty \, d\mu.$$

This equality, conclusion (3) and the classical Fatou lemma entail

$$\begin{aligned}
\int_{B^x_k} |\delta^*(x, X_\infty)| \, d\mu &= \int_{B^x_k} \lim_{n\to\infty} \Big|\frac{1}{n}\sum_{i=1}^n \delta^*(x, X'_i)\Big| \, d\mu \\
&\leq \int_{B^x_k} \liminf_{n\to\infty} \frac{1}{n}\sum_{i=1}^n |\delta^*(x, X'_i)| d\mu \\
&\leq \liminf_{n\to\infty} \frac{1}{n}\sum_{i=1}^n \int_{B^x_k} |\delta^*(x, X'_i)| d\mu \\
&= \lim_{n\to\infty} \int_{B^x_k} |\delta^*(x, X'_n)| \, d\mu = \int_{B^x_k} \theta^x_\infty \, d\mu
\end{aligned}$$

for all $k \in \mathbb{N}$. Whence

$$\int_{\Omega} |\delta^*(x, X_\infty)| \, d\mu = \lim_{k\to\infty} \int_{B_k^x} |\delta^*(x, X_\infty)| \, d\mu$$
$$\leq \lim_{k\to\infty} \int_{B_k^x} \theta_\infty^x, d\mu = \int_{\Omega} \theta_\infty^x, d\mu < \infty,$$

which shows the desired integrability property.

Finally, let us show the second inclusion of (7). Let $\sigma \in G\text{-}\mathcal{S}^1_{w^*\text{-}ls\, X_n}$, then from inclusion $(\subset_1)$ we deduce

$$\forall x \in E,\ G\text{-}\int_A 1_{D_k}(X_\infty - \sigma)\, d\mu \subset w^*\text{-cl}\left(G\text{-}\int_A 1_{D_k}(w^*\text{-}ls\, X_n - \sigma)\, d\mu\right)$$
$$\subset w^*\text{-cl}\left(G\text{-}\int_A w^*\text{-}ls\, X_n - \sigma\, d\mu\right), \quad (6.3.1)$$

where the last inclusion follows the fact $0 \in w^*\text{-}ls\, X_n - \sigma$ a.e. Since $1_{D_k} X_\infty \in \mathcal{L}^1_{cwk(E_s')}(\mu)$, for all $k \in \mathbb{N}$, by Strassen formula (see again Theorem V-14, [17]), it follows

$$\forall k \in \mathbb{N},\quad \int_A \delta^*(x, 1_{D_k}(X_\infty - \sigma))\, d\mu$$
$$= \int_A \delta^*(x, 1_{D_k} X_\infty)\, d\mu - \int_A \langle x, 1_{D_k}\sigma\rangle\, d\mu$$
$$= \delta^*(x, \int_A 1_{D_k} X_\infty\, d\mu) - \left\langle x, \int_A 1_{D_k}\sigma\, d\mu\right\rangle$$
$$= \delta^*(x, G\text{-}\int_A 1_{D_k}(X_\infty - \sigma)\, d\mu). \quad (6.3.2)$$

From (6.3.1), (6.3.2) and the fact that $\mu(D_k) \uparrow 1$ it follows

$$\forall x \in E,\ \forall A \in \mathcal{F},\quad \delta^*\left(x, G - \int_A X_\infty - \sigma\, d\mu\right)$$
$$\leq \int_A \delta^*(x, X_\infty - \sigma)\, d\mu$$
$$= \lim_{k\to\infty} \int_A \delta^*(x, 1_{D_k}(X_\infty - \sigma))\, d\mu$$
$$= \lim_{k\to\infty} \delta^*(x, G\text{-}\int_A 1_{D_k}(X_\infty - \sigma) d\mu)$$
$$\leq \delta^*(x, w^*\text{-cl}\,(G\text{-}\int_A w^*\text{-}ls\, X_n - \sigma\, d\mu)). \quad (6.3.3)$$

Moreover, by Proposition 5.2, the set $w^*\text{-cl}\,(G\text{-}\int_A w^*\text{-}ls\, X_n\, d\mu)$ is convex w^*-closed and so is $w^*\text{-cl}\,(G\text{-}\int_A w^*\text{-}ls\, X_n - \sigma\, d\mu)$. Therefore (6.3.3) entails

$$G\text{-}\int_A X_\infty - \sigma\, d\mu \subset w^*\text{-cl}\left(G\text{-}\int_A w^*\text{-}ls\, X_n - \sigma\, d\mu\right).$$

Equivalently

$$G\text{-}\int_A X_\infty\, d\mu \subset w^*\text{-cl}\left(G\text{-}\int_A w^*\text{-}ls\, X_n\, d\mu\right),$$

which is the desired inclusion ($\subset_2$). □

As a direct consequence of Theorem 6.3, Corollary 4.6 and Theorem 5.8 in [12] we have the following

Corollary 6.4. *Let* (X_n) *be a sequence in* $\mathcal{G}^1_{cwk(E'_s)}(\mu)$ *satisfying the following conditions:*

(i) (X_n) *is* L^0- lim sup-*MT.*
(ii) (X_n) *is scalarly* L^1- lim inf -*MT.*
(iii) $\liminf d_{E'_b}(0, X_n) \in L^1_{\mathbb{R}}(\mu)$.

Then there exist a multifunction $X_\infty \in \mathcal{G}^1_{cwk(E'_s)}(\mu)$, *a subsequence* (X'_n) *of* (X_n) *and a sequence* (D_k) *in* $\mathcal{F}$ *with* $\lim_k \mu(D_k) = 1$ *satisfying (1)–(6) of Theorem 6.3, and if* μ *is nonatomic*

$$(7') \qquad \forall A \in \mathcal{F}, \quad G\text{-}\int_A X_\infty\, d\mu \subset w^*\text{-cl}\left(\left(\int_A w^*\text{-}ls\, X_n\, d\mu\right)\right).$$

The following is an application of the preceding result to weak compactness in the space $\mathcal{G}^1_{cwk(E'_s)}(\mu)$

Corollary 6.5. *Let* (X_n) *be a sequence in* $\mathcal{G}^1_{cwk(E'_s)}(\mu)$ *satisfying the following conditions:*

(i) (X_n) *is* L^0- lim sup-*MT.*
(ii) $(\delta^*(x, X_n))$ *is uniformly integrable.*

Then there exist a subsequence (X'_n) *of* (X_n) *and* $X_\infty \in \mathcal{G}^1_{cwk(E^*_s)}(\mu)$ *such that*
$\forall A \in \mathcal{F}, \forall x \in E,$

$$\lim_{n\to\infty} \int_A \delta^*(x, X'_n)\, d\mu = \int_A \delta^*(x, X_\infty)\, d\mu$$

with $X_\infty(\omega) \subset w^*clco\,[w^*\text{-}\,ls\, X'_n(\omega)]$ *a.e.*

We finish this section by providing the following Fatou lemma which is a multivalued version of Corollary 5.5. Its proof is essentially based on Theorem 5.3 and Proposition 3.5.

Proposition 6.6. *Suppose that μ is nonatomic, E is a separable Banach space and (X_n) in $\mathcal{G}^1_{cwk(E'_s)}(\mu)$ satisfying the following conditions:*

(i) (X_n) *is* L^0- lim sup-*MT.*
(ii) (X_n) *is scalarly* L^1- lim inf -*MT.*
(iii) $\liminf d_{E'_b}(0, X_n) \in L^1_{\mathbb{R}}(\mu)$.

Then the following inclusion holds

$$w^*\text{-}ls\, G\text{-}\int_\Omega X_n\, d\mu \subset w^*\text{-cl}\left(\int_\Omega w^*\text{-}ls\, X_n\, d\mu\right) - C^*,$$

where C is the cone of all $x \in E$ for which $(max[0, \delta^*(-x, X_n)])$ is uniformly integrable and C^* is the polar cone of C.

Proof. Let b be an arbitrary element of $w^*\text{-}ls\, G\text{-}\int_\Omega X_n\, d\mu$. Then there exist a subsequence of (X_n) (not relabeled) and an associated sequence (f_n) of $G^1_{E'}[E](\mu)$-selectors such that $b = w^*\text{-}\lim_{n\to\infty} \int_\Omega f_n\, d\mu$. By (i) the sequence (f_n) is L^0- lim sup-MT. Furthermore, by (i), (ii) and Proposition 3.6, (X_n) is scalarly L^1- lim sup-MT. Using the inequality

$$\forall x \in E, \quad |\langle x, f_n(\omega)\rangle| \le |\delta^*(x, X_n(\omega)| + |\delta^*(-x, X_n(\omega)| \quad \text{a.e.},$$

and Proposition 3.5, we conclude that (f_n) is scalarly L^1- lim sup-MT. Consequently, according to Theorem 5.3, we find $f_\infty \in G^1_{E'}[E](\mu)$, a subsequence (g_n) of (f_n) and a sequence (C_k) in $\mathcal{F}$ with $\lim_k \mu(C_k) = 1$ such that

$$\forall k \in \mathbb{N},\ \ \forall x \in E,\ \ \forall A \in \mathcal{F} \quad \lim_{n\to\infty} \int_{A\cap C_k} \langle x, g_n\rangle d\mu = \int_{A\cap C_k} \langle x, f_\infty\rangle d\mu, \tag{6.6.1}$$

$$\forall A \in \mathcal{F}, \quad \int_A 1_{C_k} f_\infty\, d\mu \in w^*\text{-cl}\left(\int_A 1_{C_k} w^*\text{-}ls\, g_n\, d\mu\right). \tag{6.6.2}$$

We claim that

$$\int_A f_\infty\, d\mu \in w^*\text{-cl}\left(\int_A w^*\text{-}ls\, X_n\, d\mu\right). \tag{6.6.3}$$

Indeed, since condition (iii) ensures that $\mathcal{S}^1_{w^*\text{-}ls\, X_n}$ is non empty, thanks to Theorem 5.8 in [12], we can choose σ in $\in \mathcal{S}^1_{w^*\text{-}ls\, X_n}$. Then from (6.6.2) and the inclusion $0 \in w^*\text{-}ls\, X_n - \sigma$ a.e., it follows that

$$\forall x \in E, \quad \int_A 1_{C_k}(f_\infty - \sigma)\, d\mu \in w^*\text{-cl}\left(\int_A 1_{C_k}(w^*\text{-}ls\, g_n - \sigma)\, d\mu\right)$$
$$\subset w^*\text{-cl}\left(\int_A w^*\text{-}ls\, X_n - \sigma\, d\mu\right).$$

This inclusion and the same arguments used in the proof of Theorem 5.3 - ($\in_2$) prove our claim. On the other hand, let C' be the cone of all $x \in E$ for which $(max[0, -\langle x, f_n\rangle])$ is uniformly integrable and C' its polar cone. Since, for each $n \in \mathbb{N}$, g_n is a selector of X_n, necessary $C \subset C'$. Using (6.6.1) and reasoning as in the proof of Corollary 4.8 we deduce

$$b \in \int_\Omega f_\infty\, d\mu - C' \subset \int_\Omega f_\infty\, d\mu - C^*. \tag{6.6.4}$$

Combining (6.6.3)) and (6.6.4) gives

$$b \in w^*\text{-cl}\left(\int_A w^*\text{-}ls\, X_n\, d\mu\right) - C^*.$$

□

7. Conditional expectation of weakly* closed convex random sets in the dual

We finish our paper by providing the existence of conditional expectation of w^*-closed random sets which led to Fatou lemma for conditional expectation in the space $L^1_{E'}[E](\mu)$ and $\mathcal{L}^1_{cwk(E'_s)}(\mu)$.

In the following, $\mathcal{B}$ is a complete sub σ-algebra of $\mathcal{F}$. For any subset $\mathcal{H}$ in $L^1_{E'}[E](\mathcal{B}, \mu)$, and for any $v \in L^\infty_E(\mathcal{B}, \mu)$ we set

$$\delta^*(v, \mathcal{H}) = \sup_{u \in \mathcal{H}} \langle v, u\rangle.$$

Definition 7.1. *We shall say that Γ is a $\mathcal{F}$-random (resp. $\mathcal{B}$-random) closed convex set in E'_s, if the multifunction $\Gamma : \Omega \rightrightarrows E'_s$ is $\mathcal{F}$ (resp. $\mathcal{B}$) measurable, that is, the graph of Γ belongs to $\mathcal{F} \times \mathcal{B}(E'_s)$ (resp. $\mathcal{B} \times \mathcal{B}(E'_s)$).*

We begin to state the existence and uniqueness of conditional expectation of an integrably bounded $\mathcal{F}$-random closed convex set Γ in E'_s (that is, $|\Gamma| \in L^1_{\mathbb{R}}(\mathcal{F})$) .

Definition 7.2. *A $\mathcal{B}$-random closed convex set Σ in E'_s is called conditional expectation of Γ if:*
(i) There is $\beta \in L^1_{\mathbb{R}^+}(\mathcal{B})$ such that $\Sigma(\omega) \subset \beta(\omega)\overline{B}_{E'}$ a.e.
(ii) $\forall x \in E, \forall B \in \mathcal{B}, \quad \int_B \delta^*(x, \Sigma(\omega))d\mu(\omega) = \int_B \delta^*(x, \Gamma(\omega))d\mu(\omega)$.

Since E'_s is Suslin and its dual is equal to E, by virtue of Theorem V.14 (ii) is equivalent to

$$\forall B \in \mathcal{B}, \quad \int_B \Sigma(\omega) d\mu(\omega) = \int_B \Gamma(\omega) d\mu(\omega),$$

which is equivalent to

$$\forall x \in E, \quad \delta^*(x, \Sigma(\omega)) = E^{\mathcal{B}} \delta^*(x, \Gamma(\omega)) \quad \text{a.e.}$$

here $E^{\mathcal{B}} f$ denotes the usual conditional expectation of an integrable function f. We provide an existence and uniqueness result of conditional expectation of an integrably bounded $\mathcal{F}$-random closed convex set in E'_s extending Theorem VIII.34 in [17] because here the strong dual E'_b of E is no longer separable. This need a careful look involving a sequentially compactness result in [13, Corollary 6.5.10], and some other techniques.

Theorem 7.3. *Under the foregoing hypotheses there exists a unique (for equality a.e.) conditional expectation of* Γ, Σ. *Moreover* Σ *has the properties:*

(a) $\Sigma(\omega) \subset E^{\mathcal{B}}(|\Gamma])(\omega)\overline{B}_{E'}$ *a.e.*
(b) The integral functionals

$$I_\Sigma : v \mapsto \int_\Omega \delta^*(v(\omega), \Sigma(\omega)) d\mu(\omega) \quad \text{and} \quad I_\Gamma : v \mapsto \int_\Omega \delta^*(v(\omega), \Gamma(\omega)) d\mu(\omega)$$

are continuous on the closed unit ball $\overline{B}_{L^\infty_E(\mathcal{B})}$ *of* $L^\infty_E(\Omega, \mathcal{B}, \mu)$ *endowed with the topology of convergence in measure and coincide on the subset of all simple functions* $v = \sum_{i=1}^n 1_{B_i} x_i$, *with the disjoint* $B_i \in \mathcal{B}$, $x_i \in E$.
(c) $\mathcal{S}^1_\Sigma(\mathcal{B})$ *is sequentially* $\sigma(L^1_{E'}[E](\mathcal{B}), L^\infty_E(\mathcal{B}))$ *compact (here* $\mathcal{S}^1_\Sigma(\mathcal{B})$ *denotes the set of all* $L^1_{E'}[E](\Omega, \mathcal{B}, \mu)$ *selections of* Σ*) and satisfies the inclusion*

$$E^{\mathcal{B}} \mathcal{S}^1_\Gamma(\mathcal{F}) \subset \mathcal{S}^1_\Sigma(\mathcal{B}).$$

(d) Furthermore one has

$$\delta^*(v, E^{\mathcal{B}} \mathcal{S}^1_\Gamma(\mathcal{F}) = \delta^*(v, \mathcal{S}^1_\Sigma(\mathcal{B}))$$

for all $v \in L^\infty_E(\mathcal{B})$.

Proof. Step 1 To prove the existence of Σ we apply Theorem V.17 in [17] by recalling that E'_s is a e.l.c Suslin space and E is its dual. Then we take in this theorem $\Lambda = L^1_{\mathbb{R}}(\Omega, \mathcal{B}, \mu)$ and $\Lambda^* = L^\infty_{\mathbb{R}}(\Omega, \mathcal{B}, \mu)$. We put $M(f) = \int f \Gamma d\mu$ for $f \in \Lambda^*$. Since $E' = \cup_n n\overline{B}_{E'}$, the mapping M mets conditions (i)–(iv) of Theorem V.17 in [17]. So there exist a $\mathcal{B}$-measurable convex $\sigma(E', E)$ compact valued, scalarly integrable multifunction Σ such that, $\forall f \in \Lambda^*, M(f) = \int f\Sigma d\mu$. Taking $f = 1_B(B \in \mathcal{B})$, we obtain $\int_B \Sigma d\mu = \int_B \Gamma d\mu$. The uniqueness follows easily as in the proof of Theorem VIII.34 in [17]. Indeed, let Σ_1 and Σ_2 be two convex $\mathcal{B}$-measurable convex $\sigma(E', E)$ compact valued, scalarly integrable multifunction such that

$$\forall f \in \Lambda^*, \quad M(f) = \int f\Sigma_1 d\mu = \int f\Sigma_2 d\mu.$$

By Strassen Theorem V.14 in [17], we have, for every $x \in E, \delta^*(x, \Sigma_1(\omega)) = \delta^*(x, \Sigma_2(\omega))$ a.e. By Proposition III.35, we deduce that $\Sigma_1(\omega) = \Sigma_2(\omega)$ a.e.

We will denote $E^{\mathcal{B}}\Gamma = \Sigma$ the unique $\mathcal{B}$-measurable convex $\sigma(E', E)$ compact valued, scalarly integrable multifunction Σ which verifies

$$\forall f \in \Lambda^*, \quad M(f) = \int f\Sigma d\mu.$$

Taking $f = 1_B(B \in \mathcal{B})$, we obtain

$$\int_B E^{\mathcal{B}}\Gamma d\mu = \int_B \Gamma d\mu.$$

Now we provide the properties of the conditional expectation $E^{\mathcal{B}}\Gamma$. It is worthy to mention that, when $\Gamma = u \in L^1_{E'}[E](\mathcal{F})$, then the EB of u, $E^{\mathcal{B}}u$, belongs to $L^1_{E'}[E](\mathcal{B})$ and satisfies

$$\forall f \in L^\infty_{\mathbb{R}}(\Omega, \mathcal{B}, \mu), \quad \int fu\, d\mu = \int fE^{\mathcal{B}}u\, d\mu.$$

Step 2 (a) For $x \in E$, one has

$$\begin{aligned}\delta^*(x, \Sigma(\omega)) &= E^{\mathcal{B}}(\delta^*(x, \Gamma(.))(\omega) \le E^{\mathcal{B}}(||x||.|\Gamma|)(\omega)\\ &= ||x||E^{\mathcal{B}}(|\Gamma|)(\omega) = E^{\mathcal{B}}(|\Gamma|)(\omega)\delta^*(x, \overline{B}_{E'}).\end{aligned}$$

for a.e. $\omega \in \Omega$. Again by [17, Proposition III.35], we have $\Sigma(\omega) \subset E^{\mathcal{B}}(|\Gamma|)(\omega)\overline{B}_{E'}$.

(b) It is clear that the formula

$$\int \delta^*(v(\omega), \Sigma(\omega))d\mu(\omega) = \int \delta^*(v(\omega), \Gamma(\omega))d\mu(\omega)$$

holds if $v = \sum_{i=1}^n 1_{B_i}x_i$, with the disjoint $B_i \in \mathcal{B}, x_i \in E$. Now we claim that the integral functionals

$$I_\Sigma : v \mapsto \int_\Omega \delta^*(v(\omega), \Sigma(\omega))d\mu(\omega) \quad \text{and} \quad I_\Gamma : v \mapsto \int_\Omega \delta^*(v(\omega), \Gamma(\omega))d\mu(\omega)$$

are continuous on the closed unit ball $\overline{B}_{L^\infty_E(\mathcal{B})}$ of $L^\infty_E(\Omega, \mathcal{B}, \mu)$ endowed with the topology of convergence in measure. Indeed we have for $v, w \in \overline{B}_{L^\infty_E(\mathcal{B})}$ the estimate

$$\begin{aligned}
&\left| \int_\Omega \delta^*(v(\omega), \Sigma(\omega)) d\mu(\omega) - \int_\Omega \delta^*(w(\omega), \Sigma(\omega)) d\mu(\omega) \right| \\
&\leq \int_\Omega |\delta^*(v(\omega), \Sigma(\omega)) - \delta^*(w(\omega), \Sigma(\omega))| d\mu(\omega) \\
&\leq \int_\Omega \max(\delta^*(v(\omega) - w(\omega), \Sigma(\omega)), \delta^*(w(\omega) - v(\omega), \Sigma(\omega))) d\mu(\omega) \\
&\leq 2 \int ||v(\omega) - w(\omega)|| E^{\mathcal{B}}(|\Gamma|)(\omega) d\mu(\omega)
\end{aligned}$$

and similarly

$$\begin{aligned}
&\left| \int \delta^*(v(\omega), \Gamma(\omega)) d\mu(\omega) - \int \delta^*(w(\omega), \Gamma(\omega)) d\mu(\omega) \right| \\
&\leq \int |\delta^*(v(\omega), \Gamma(\omega)) - \delta^*(w(\omega), \Gamma(\omega))| d\mu(\omega) \\
&\leq \int_\Omega \max(\delta^*(v(\omega) - w(\omega), \Gamma(\omega)), \delta^*(w(\omega) - v(\omega), \Gamma(\omega))) d\mu(\omega) \\
&\leq 2 \int ||v(\omega) - w(\omega)|| |\Gamma|(\omega) d\mu(\omega).
\end{aligned}$$

So (b) follows. If E is reflexive, one can see that I_Σ and I_Γ are Mackey continuous since the topology of convergence in measure on $\overline{B}_{L^\infty_E(\mathcal{B})}$ coincides with the Mackey convergence $\tau(L^\infty_E, L^1_{E'})$.

(c) The sequential $\sigma(L^1_{E'}[E](\mathcal{B}), L^\infty_E(\mathcal{B}))$ compactness of $\mathcal{S}^1_\Sigma(\mathcal{B})$ follows from Step 1 and Corollary 6.5.10 in [13]. Let $u \in \mathcal{S}^1_\Gamma(\mathcal{F})$ and $x \in E$. Then

$$\langle x, E^{\mathcal{B}} u \rangle \leq E^{\mathcal{B}}[(\delta^*(x, \Gamma(.))] = \delta^*(x, \Sigma(.)) \quad \text{a.e.}$$

So again by [17, Proposition III.35], $E^{\mathcal{B}} u \in \mathcal{S}^1_\Sigma(\mathcal{B})$ and hence

$$E^{\mathcal{B}} \mathcal{S}^1_\Gamma(\mathcal{F}) \subset \mathcal{S}^1_\Sigma(\mathcal{B}). \tag{*}$$

(d) By (*), it is immediate that

$$\delta^*(v, E^{\mathcal{B}} \mathcal{S}^1_\Gamma(\mathcal{F})) \leq \delta^*(v, \mathcal{S}^1_\Sigma(\mathcal{B}))$$

for all $v \in L^\infty_E(\mathcal{B})$. Let us prove the converse inequality

$$\delta^*(v, E^{\mathcal{B}}\mathcal{S}^1_\Gamma(\mathcal{F})) \geq \delta^*(v, \mathcal{S}^1_\Sigma(\mathcal{B})). \qquad (**)$$

Let $v \in L^\infty_E(\mathcal{B})$. Let u be a maximal $\mathcal{F}$ measurable selection of Γ associated with v, that is

$$\langle v(\omega), u(\omega)\rangle = \delta^*(v(\omega), \Gamma(\omega)), \quad \forall \omega \in \Omega.$$

See [17, Theorem III.22]. Then it is obvious that $u \in L^1_{E'}[E](\Omega, \mathcal{F}, \mu)$. Furthermore, by applying the equality of conditional expectation given in Step 2(b)

$$\int \langle v, u\rangle\, d\mu = \int \langle v, E^{\mathcal{B}}u\rangle\, d\mu.$$

One has

$$\begin{aligned}
\delta^*(v, E^{\mathcal{B}}\mathcal{S}^1_\Gamma(\mathcal{F})) &\geq \langle v, E^{\mathcal{B}}u\rangle = \int \langle v, E^{\mathcal{B}}u\rangle\, d\mu \\
&= \int \langle v, u\rangle\, d\mu = \langle v, u\rangle = \int_\Omega \delta^*(v(\omega), \Gamma(\omega))\, d\mu(\omega) \\
&= \int_\Omega \delta^*(v(\omega), \Sigma(\omega))\, d\mu(\omega) \quad \text{(by (b) and approximation)} \\
&\geq \langle v, u_1\rangle \quad \text{for any} \quad u_1 \in \mathcal{S}^1_\Sigma(\mathcal{B}).
\end{aligned}$$

Finally

$$\delta^*(v, E^{\mathcal{B}}\mathcal{S}^1_\Gamma(\mathcal{F})) = \delta^*(v, \mathcal{S}^1_\Sigma(\mathcal{B})) \qquad (***)$$

for all $v \in L^\infty_E(\mathcal{B})$. □

Remarks. When E is a reflexive separable Banach space and $\Gamma \in \mathcal{L}^1_{cwk(E')}(\Omega, \mathcal{F}, \mu)$, then conditional expectation $E^{\mathcal{B}}\Gamma$ of Γ belongs to $\mathcal{L}^1_{cwk(E')}(\Omega, \mathcal{B}, \mu)$ and satisfies

$$\delta^*(v, E^{\mathcal{B}}\mathcal{S}^1_\Gamma(\mathcal{F})) = \delta^*(v, \mathcal{S}^1_\Sigma(\mathcal{B}))$$

for all $v \in L^\infty_E(\mathcal{B})$ so that

$$E^{\mathcal{B}}\mathcal{S}^1_\Gamma(\mathcal{F}) = \mathcal{S}^1_\Sigma(\mathcal{B})$$

because $E^{\mathcal{B}}\mathcal{S}^1_\Gamma(\mathcal{F})$ and $\mathcal{S}^1_\Sigma(\mathcal{B})$ are convex $\sigma(L^1_{E'}(\mathcal{B}), L^\infty_E(\mathcal{B}))$ compact, meanwhile the existence and uniqueness of EB met in Theorem 7.3 are unusual because the dual space is not strongly separable. See also [27] dealing with CE of Random Sets in the dual of a separable Fréchet space via the regular conditional probability.

To end the paper we provide the existence and uniqueness of conditional expectation of a closed convex $\mathcal{F}$ random set in E'_s in the line of [17, Theorem VIII.35].

Theorem 7.4. *Let Γ be a closed convex $\mathcal{F}$-random set in E'_s which admits an selection $u_0 \in L^1_{E'}[E](\mathcal{F})$. For every n and very ω, let*

$$\Gamma_n(\omega) := \Gamma(\omega) \bigcap_n (u_0(\omega) + n\overline{B}_{E'}),$$

$$\Sigma(\omega) = w^* cl \left[\bigcup_n E^{\mathcal{B}}(\Gamma_n)(\omega) \right].$$

Then: (a) Σ which is a.e. convex, is a unique (for the equality a.e.) $\mathcal{B}$ closed convex random set in E'_s with

$$\forall v \in L^\infty_E(\mathcal{B}), \quad \int_\Omega \delta^*(v(\omega), \Sigma(\omega)) d\mu(\omega) = \int_\Omega \delta^*(v(\omega), \Gamma(\omega)) d\mu(\omega).$$

(b) Σ is the smallest (for inclusion a.e.) of the $\mathcal{B}$ closed convex random set Θ such that

$$E^{\mathcal{B}} \mathcal{S}^1_\Gamma(\mathcal{F}) \subset \mathcal{S}^1_\Theta(\mathcal{B}).$$

We shall denote $E^{\mathcal{B}}\Gamma = \Sigma$ and says that Σ is the conditional expectation of Γ.

Proof. The proof is the same as in [17, Theorem VIII.35], using Theorem 7.3, the monotone convergence theorem and measurable projection theorem which ensures the uniqueness. Here the measurability of Σ is ensured thanks to Corollary 5.3 in [12]; at this point, let us mention that Γ admits a $L^1_{E'}[E](\mathcal{F})$ selection iff $d(0, \Gamma)$ is μ-integrable (see Lemma 5.6 in [12]). □

The results obtained in this section led to Fatou lemma for conditional expectation of weak-star random sets in a dual space.

References

1. Artstein, Z.: A note on Fatou lemma's in several dimensions. J. Math. Econ. **6**, 277–282 (1979)
2. Amrani, A., Castaing, C., Valadier, M.: Méthodes de troncatures appliquées à des problèmes de convergences faible ou forte dans L^1. Arch. Rational Mech. Anal **117**, 167–191 (1992)
3. Balder, E.J.: A Fatou lemma for Gelfand integrals by means of Young measure theory. Positivity **6**, 317–329 (2002)
4. Balder, E.J., Hess, Ch.: Two generalizations of Komlós theorem with lower closure-type aplications. J. Convex Anal. **3**, 25–44 (1996)

5. Balder, E.J., Sambucini, A.R.: Fatou's lemma for multifunctions with unbounded values in a dual space. J. Convex Anal. **12**, 383–395 (2005)
6. Benabdellah, H., Castaing, C.: Weak compactness and convergences in $L^1_{E'}[E]$. Adv. Math. Econ. **3**, 1–44 (2001)
7. Castaing, C.: Quelques résultats de convergences des suites adaptées. Sém. Anal. Conv. Exp **2**, 2.1–2.24 (1987); Acta Mathematica Vietnamica **14**(1), 51–66 (1989)
8. Castaing, C.: Méthodes de compacité et de decomposition, applications: minimisation, convergences des martingales, lemme de Fatou multivoque. Ann. Math. Pura Apli. **164**, 51–75 (1993)
9. Castaing, C., Clauzure, P.: Lemme de Fatou multivoque, Ann. Math. Pura Appl. **XXXIX**, 303–320 (1991)
10. Castaing, C., Ezzaki, F.: Some convergence results for multivalued martingales in the limit. Séminaire d Analyse Convexe Montpellier 1990, Exposé No 1
11. Castaing, C., Ezzaki, F., Hess, Ch.: Convergence of conditional expectations for unbounded closed convex random sets. Stud. Math. **124**(2), 133–148 (1997)
12. Castaing, C., Hess, Ch., Saadoune, M.: Tightness conditions and integrability of the sequential upper limit of a sequence of multifunctions. Adv. Math. Econ. **11**, 1–34 (2008)
13. Castaing, C., Raynaud de Fitte, P., Valadier, M.: Young measures on topological spaces. With applications in control theory and probability theory. Dordrecht: Kluwer 2004
14. Castaing, C., Saadoune, M.: Dunford–Pettis-types theorem and convergences in set-valued integration. J. Nonlinear Convex Anal. **1**, 37–71 (1999)
15. Castaing, C., Saadoune, M.: Komlós type convergence with applications. Adv. Math. Econ. **10**, 1–26 (2007)
16. Castaing, C., Saadoune, M.: On various versions of Fatou lemma. Submitted (2008)
17. Castaing, C., Valadier, M.: Convex analysis and measurable multifunctions. Lectures Notes in Mathematics, vol. 580. Berlin: Springer 1977
18. Cornet, B., Martins da Rocha, V.F.: Fatou's lemma for unbounded Gelfand integrable mapping. Preprint 109, CERNSEM, Université Paris 1 (2002)
19. Cornet, B., Médecin, J.P.: Fatou's lemma for Gelfand integrable mappings. Positivity **6**, 297–315 (2002)
20. Hiai, F.: Convergence of conditional expectations and strong laws of large numbers for multivalued random variables. TAMS **291**(2), (613–627) 1985
21. Hiai, F., Umegaki, H.: Integrals, Conditional expectations, and martingales of multivalued functions. J. Multivariate Anal. **7**, 149–182 (1977)
22. Hildenbrand, W.: Core and equilibria of a large economy. Princeton: Princeton University Press 1974
23. Khan, M.A., Majumdar, M.: Weak sequential convergence in $L_1(\mu, X)$ and an approximate version of Fatou's lemma. J. Math. Anal. Appl. **114**, 569–573 (1986)
24. Saadoune, M., Valadier, M.: Extraction of a good subsequence from a bounded sequence of integrable functions. J. Convex Anal. **2**(1/2), 345–357 (1995)
25. Schmeidler, D.: Fatou's lemma in several dimensions, Proc. Am. Math. Soc. **24**, 300–306 (1970)

26. Valadier, M.: Semi-continuité de fonctionnnelles integrales, Séminaire d Analyse Convexe, Montpellier 1977, Exposé No 2
27. Valadier, M.: On conditional expectation of random sets. Annali di Mathematica pura ed applicata (IV) **CXXVI**, 81–91 (1980)
28. Yannelis, N.C.: Fatou's lemma in infinite-dimensional space. Proc. Am. Math. Soc. **102** 303–310 (1988)

Adv. Math. Econ. 12, 71–95 (2009)

Advances in
MATHEMATICAL
ECONOMICS

©Springer 2009

Variational analysis and mathematical economics 1: Subdifferential calculus and the second theorem of welfare economics

A.D. Ioffe

Department of Mathematics, Technion, Haifa 32000, Israel
(e-mail: ioffe@math.technion.ac.il)

Received: September 3, 2008
Revised: November 3, 2008

JEL classification: D11, D61

Mathematics Subject Classification (2000): 49K27, 49J52, 90C48, 91B50

Abstract. The paper consists of two parts. The first is devoted to a general subdifferential theory based on an axiomatic approach. Along with the list of "axioms" which summarizes properties shared by all major subdifferentials studied in variational analysis, we also consider four "optional" properties which specific subdifferentials may or may not have, such as trustworthiness, robustness, tightness (validity of a certain fuzzy subdifferential inequality) and geometric compatibility (connection between subdifferentials and normal cones). The concluding result says that the approximate G-subdifferential is the only subdifferential that has the four properties on all Banach space.

The second part is devoted to application of the general subdifferential theory to a model of welfare economics with a Banach commodity space. Here we begin with subdifferential characterization of nonconvex separation property in general and also for a special case of one of the sets being a shifted kernel of a linear epimorphism, and then apply the results to characterize Pareto and weak Pareto optimal allocations in welfare economics. The final result is a strengthening of earlier versions of the second welfare theorem due to Khan-Vohra, Cornet, Joffre and Mordukhovich. In particular, a weaker and more symmetric version of Cornet's qualification condition appears in the characterization of Pareto optimality.

Key words: general subdifferential theory, nonconvex separation, Pareto optimality, qualification conditions, welfare economics

DOI: 10.1007/978-4-431-92935-2_3,

1. Introduction

The paper is an extended transcript of the first part of the Simon Newcomb lecture (under the same title) I gave in the John Hopkins University in October 2007. The lecture was concentrated on mathematical aspects of two well known problems of mathematical economics: price equilibrium for Pareto optimal points in models of welfare economics and regularity (stability of equilibrium prices under variations of the economy parameters) in models of competitive economics, both for nonsmooth and nonconvex economies. The two problems appeal to two, in a sense oppositely extreme, settings of nonsmooth analysis. The first can be considered with extreme generality of data, practically without any a priori restrictions, the second, on the contrary, needs "reasonable" degree of nonsmoothness to make meaningful results available.

We have pursued two goals when writing this paper. First is to try to develop a coherent "abstract" theory of subdifferentials and then to look from that perspective into the second theorem of welfare economics. Earlier publications, especially [5, 21, 28], also used an extremely general frameworks to treat the subjects. But in these works, as well as in many other publications in variational analysis (see, e.g., [1, 2, 11, 17, 19, 26, 29]) the abstract "axiomatic" approach was mainly applied to prove one or another specific result in maximal possible generality. We here apply it as a gate to a general theory of subdifferentials, partly due to the mere curiosity of how far we can move without using any specific constructions. However the second theorem of welfare economics has also somewhat benefited from that as the qualification condition that has been eventually worked out is weaker and in a sense more symmetric.

For the first time the techniques and language of variational analysis for that purpose were probably used by and Khan and Vohra [25]. The equilibrium prices that appear in their version of the theorem were elements of Clarke's normal cones at the Pareto optimum under assumptions (free disposal and nonsatiation) that excluded any necessity in constraint qualifications at the optimal point. Shortly afterwards ([25] actually appeared in 1984 as a working paper) Cornet [10] extended their result to the "market clear" setting and introduced a constraint qualification which served as a model for further studies. In both cases the case of a finite dimensional commodity space was considered.

We refer to [24] for a detailed discussion of these and earlier developments. Further studies along the lines set by the two mentioned works were focused on generalizations of the mentioned results in three directions:

(a) Passage to models with infinitely dimensional commodity space

(b) Using other (smaller than Clarke's) subdifferentials, in particular nonconvex-valued[1] to get equilibrium prices better associated with the problem[2]
(c) Modifying the qualification condition in order to make it less restrictive

Bonnisseau and Cornet [3] and Khan [23] considered models of welfare economy with locally convex commodity spaces. In the first the decentralizing equilibrium prices were taken from Clarke's normal cones to the corresponding sets, in the second – from the approximate normal cones (as the latter were originally defined).[3] Shortly afterwards Joffre [21] and Mordukhovich [28] observed that (in the Banach space setting) the theorem is valid with any subdifferential/normal cone satisfying certain set of properties

---

[1] Scepticism about suitability of Clarke's generalized gradients and normal cones for necessary optimality conditions in nonsmooth optimization can be traced back to the very early stage of development of nonsmooth analysis. We mention in this connection Rockafellar's result [31] showing, roughly speaking, that Clarke's normal cone to the graph of a Lipschitz mapping from $I\!R^n$ into $I\!R^m$ is the orthogonal complement to the graph of the derivative of the restriction of the intersection of the maximal linear manifolds along which the mapping is strictly differentiable at the given point. As far as real-valued functions are concerned, it is an easy matter to construct an example in which the limiting (Mordukhovich) or approximate subdifferential, on the one hand and generalized gradient, on the other, can differ at a certain point. But it took some time to understand the real relationship between the two. First Katriel [22] proved that for a real valued Lipschitz function of one real variable they can differ at countably many points at most and then D. Borwein, J. Borwein and Wang showed that (a) in dimensions two and higher there are Lipschitz functions whose limiting and Clarke's subdifferentials differ almost everywhere [4] and (b) for a generic (in a suitable sense) Lipschitz function the limiting and Clarke subdifferentials are identically equal [8]. The latter suggests that the passage from Clarke to approximate subdifferential generically may bring about little gain. The important point however is that with functions and sets that are usually appear in "real" situations, a substantial gain is not a rare phenomenon. At the same time, Clarke's generalized gradient proves to be much more efficient for studying real equilibria, which cannot be described in terms of minimization (e.g., [13]). These topics will be discussed in more details in the second paper devoted to regularity.

[2] There is no chance of course that the existence of equilibrium prices in a nonsmooth economy at a certain point is a guarantee that this point is a local Pareto optimum – see, e.g., [13]; in fact this cannot be true unless the economy is convex.

[3] The definition of the approximate subdifferential and normal cone in infinite dimensions in its original form given in [14] leads to unnecessarily large objects in certain cases. For that reason the definition was modified and only smaller versions of approximate normal cones was used in later publications: see, e.g., [19,20]. Later in this paper we shall speak about that in greater details. It is worth noting, however, that the result of [23] extends to the modified definition without any change.

and proved "abstract" versions of the second welfare theorem. Another innovation of these two works was connected with modifications[4] of the Cornet qualification condition (also used in [24] in a finite dimensional setting). We shall discuss the last two developments in more details in § 3, 4.

The next and the longest section can be viewed as an introduction to a "general theory of subdifferentials" based on the axiomatic approach. We begin with a list of basic properties (an elaboration over the one in the original publication by the author [17]) which, we believe, any reasonable subdifferential must have (even though not all of them are used in one or another publication, including this one, by the way), and actually all major subdifferentials used in variational analysis do have. Then we introduce three key properties (called tightness, robustness and trustworthiness on a space) which a subdifferential may or may not have. The main part of the section is concerned with the studies of possible consequences of various combinations of these properties (including, of course those needed to prove our version of the second theorem of welfare economics). The final results state that (a) all tight robust subdifferentials trusted on a certain space coincide on the class of locally Lipschitz functions defined on the space and (b) the approximate G-subdifferential (whose definition we give at the end of the section – it is actually trusted on every Banach space) is the only subdifferential which, in addition to the three properties, possesses a certain "geometric consistency" property (saying, roughly speaking, that the subdifferential of an l.s.c. function can be defined through the normal cone to its epigraph).

2. Subdifferentials: a general view

Emile Picard once noticed that the differential calculus would not have been created if Newton had thought that continuous functions do not necessarily have derivatives.

The idea that nondifferentiability should sometimes be taken into account and explicitly dealt with is still very alien to many analysts. A popular approach when there is a need to work with something nonsmooth has been to take a smooth ε-approximation, do whatever necessary and then pass to the limit as $\varepsilon \to 0$. A convincing illustration of the power of such an approach is given by the degree theory and the famous proof of the Brouwer fixed-point theorem. One of the first attempts to treat nondifferentiability in a systematic way undertaken by Warga was based on this approach. There were a number of good results obtained on this way. However nonuniqueness of resulting

[4] Under different names but actually identical.

objects and essentially finite dimensional character of all constructions determined rather limited applicability of that method.

The approach that eventually gained recognition of the optimization community has lead to creation of a "nonsmooth" calculus which in many respects is modeled by the classical differential calculus and convex analysis and contains both as specific cases. The latter is especially important, both formally and "psychologically," as it creates desirable contiguity of theories and applications.

The concepts of nonsmooth subdifferential and subderivative and their geometric counterparts (normal and tangent cone) play the principal role in the calculus. The terminology underscores certain "one-sidedness," which indeed is in the center of the approach to analysis of nonsmooth objects.

There are several "good" subdifferentials at work in variational analysis: proximal, Fréchet, Dini–Hadamard, their viscosity and limiting versions and already mentioned Clarke's generalized gradient, approximate subdifferential. Below is a list of essential properties shared by all of them. Taking this properties as "axioms" we can develop a consistent and far reaching theory which, though not yet presented in a unified way, does exist in a fragmented form in many journal publications (see, e.g., already quoted [1, 2, 5, 11, 17, 26, 28, 29]).

By a *subdifferential* we always mean a mapping which associates with any extended real-valued function f on a Banach space X and any $x \in X$ a set $\partial f(x) \subset X^*$.[5] It turns out that all mentioned and some others (e.g., "viscosity") subdifferentials share the following eight properties:

- *Substantiality*
  (P1) $\partial f(x) = \emptyset$ if $x \notin \text{dom } f = \{x : |f(x)| < \infty\}$.
- *Locality*
  (P2) If f and g coincide in a neighborhood of x, then $\partial f(x) = \partial g(x)$.
- *Contiguity*
  (P3) If f is continuously (or strictly) Fréchet differentiable at x, then $\partial f(x) = \{f'(x)\}$.
  (P4) If f is convex, then $\partial f(x)$ coincides with the subdifferential of f in the sense of convex analysis, that is $\partial f(x) = \{x^* : \langle x^*, h\rangle \le f(x+h) - f(x),\ \forall\, h\}$.
- *Existence*
  (P5) If f attains a local minimum at x, then $0 \in \partial f(x)$.
- *Boundedness*
  (P6) If f is Lipschitz with constant K near x and $x^* \in \partial f(x)$, then $\|x^*\| \le K$.

[5] In principle it is possible to extend the definitions of certain subdifferentials to a broader class of locally convex spaces – see, e.g., [16, 23]. But it does not seem that such an extension may attract substantial interest.

- *Calculability*
  (P7) If $\varphi(x, y) = f(x) + g(y)$, then $\partial\varphi(x, y) \subset \partial f(x) + \partial g(y)$.[6]
  (P8) If $\lambda > 0$, $A : X \to Y$ is a bounded linear operator with Im $A = Y$, $x^* \in X^*$ and $\varphi(x) = \lambda f(Ax + y) + \langle x^*, x\rangle$, then $\partial\varphi(x) = \lambda A^*\partial f(Ax + y) + x^*$.
- *Order compatibility*
  (P9) If $S \subset X$ is a closed set and f a lower semicontinuous function such that $f(x) = 0$ on S and $f(x) \geq d_S(x)$ for all x, then $\partial d_S(x) \subset \partial f(x)$ for $x \in S$.[7]
  The nine properties is a starting point for a long list of nontrivial calculus rules.[8] Below we prove several facts we specifically need in what follows and a few facts of a general interest.
  Let $Q \subset X$. Then $\delta_Q(x)$, the *indicator* of Q, is the function equal to zero on Q and $+\infty$ outside of Q.
  The set

$$N(Q, x) = \partial\delta_Q(x),$$

(which by (P1) can be nonempty only if $x \in Q$) is called the *normal cone* to Q at x associated with ∂.

Proposition 1. *(a) $N(Q, x) \neq \emptyset$ for every $x \in Q$. If $\overline{x}$ is an interior point of Q, then $N(Q, \overline{x}) = \{0\}$.*
(b) For any $x \in Q$ the cone cone $\partial d_S(x) = \cup_{r>0} r\partial d_S(x)$ *is a subset of $N(Q, x)$ and does not depend of the specific equivalent norm in X.*

Proof. We have $0 \in N(Q, x)$ for every $x \in Q$ by (P5). On the other hand, if $\overline{x} \in$ int Q, we take a small $\varepsilon > 0$ such that $B(\overline{x}, \varepsilon) \subset Q$. and let $g(x)$ be the indicator of the ball. This a convex function and $\partial g(\overline{x}) = \{0\}$ by (P4). Now (P2) implies (a). The first part of (b) follows from (P9) applied to $f = \delta_S$, the second also follows from (P9) applied to the distance functions associated with equivalent norms. □

Of course, it does not follow from the proposition that $N(Q, x)$ contains nonzero elements if x is a boundary point of Q. This is not the case even if

[6] Actually for most of the known subdifferentials the equality holds; Clarke's generalized gradient seems to be the only exception.

[7] This property was introduced by Penot [30] who called a subdifferential satisfying the property *quasi-homotone*.

[8] Most, if not all, publications with discussions of "abstract subdifferential" calculus contain part of the listed above properties, usually only those needed for the proofs of the results presented in the papers. Sometimes this is interpreted as an indication of a greater generality of the results. Such interpretations can hardly be accepted as it is difficult to imagine a workable concept of a subdifferential which would not have all of the properties.

Q is convex.[9] A sufficient condition for that is given later in Proposition 5.

It is said that ∂ can be *trusted* on X, or is *trustworthy* on X, or that X is a *trustworthy space* for ∂ if the following property holds:[10]

(P10) If f_1 and f_2 are lower semicontinuous with one of them being Lipschitz near x and $f_1 + f_2$ attains a local minimum at x, then for any $\varepsilon > 0$ there are $x_1,\ x_2,\ x_1^*,\ x_2^*$ such that

$$\|x_i - x\| < \varepsilon,\ x_i^* \in \partial f_i(x_i), \quad \text{and } \|x_1^* + x_2^*\| < \varepsilon.$$

Proposition 2. *Let ∂ be a subdifferential trusted on X. (a) if f is a lower semicontinuous extended-real-valued function on X, then $\partial f(x) \neq \emptyset$ for all x of a dense subset of* dom f*; (b) if $Q \subset X$ is a closed set and $\overline{x} \in Q$ is a boundary point of Q, then for any $\varepsilon > 0$ there is a $x \in Q$ with $\|x - \overline{x}\| < \varepsilon$ such that $N(Q, x)$ contains a nonzero element.*

Proof. (a) Take an $\overline{x} \in \text{dom } f$ and an $\varepsilon > 0$. We may assume ε small enough to guarantee for example that $f(x) \geq f(\overline{x}) - 1$ if $\|x - \overline{x}\| \leq \varepsilon$. By Ekeland's principle there is a w such that $\|w - \overline{x}\| \leq \varepsilon/2$, and $f(x) + (2/\varepsilon)\|x - w\|$ attains a local minimum at w. By trustworthiness there is an x such that $\|x - w\| < \varepsilon/2$, hence $\|x - \overline{x}\| < \varepsilon$, and $\partial f(x) \neq \emptyset$.

(b) As $\overline{x}$ is a boundary point of Q, we can find a $w \notin Q$ such that $\|w - \overline{x}\| < \varepsilon^2/2$. By Ekeland's principle there is a $\overline{w} \in Q$ with $\|\overline{w} - \overline{x}\| < \varepsilon/2$ such that the function

$$g(x) = \|w - x\| + \delta_Q(x) + \varepsilon\|x - \overline{w}\|$$

attains its minimum at $\overline{w}$. By trustworthiness, there are $x \in Q$ and u such that $\|u - \overline{w}\|$ is strictly smaller that the distance from w to Q, $\|x - \overline{w}\| < \varepsilon/2$ and for some x^* in the subdifferential of $\|w - \cdot\| + \varepsilon\|\cdot - \overline{w}\|$ at u we have $x^* \in N(Q, x) + \varepsilon B$. As $u \neq w$, we conclude that $\|x^*\| > 1 - \varepsilon$. □

A subdifferential is called *robust* if

(P11) $$\bigcap_{\varepsilon>0} cl^*\Big(\bigcup_{\|u-x\|<\varepsilon} \partial f(u)\Big) \subset \partial f(x),$$

provided f is Lipschitz near x.

---

[9] Take for instance the Hilbert parallelepiped $\{x = (x_1, x_2, \ldots) : |x_n| \leq n^{-1}\}$ in the Hilbert space l_2. Zero is a boundary point of this set but the normal cone to it at the origin reduces to zero.

[10] The concept of trustworthiness was first introduced in [15] in a somewhat different form. It was further modified in [12] and in the final form was stated in [19,20]. The definition here is equivalent as one can see from [32] (for viscosity subdifferentials) and [18,26] for the general case. In fact it is possible to assume that one of the functions is convex continuous, not just Lipschitz.

Proposition 3. *Let ∂ be an robust subdifferential which is trusted on X. Then:*

(a) if f is Lipschitz near x, then $\partial f(x)$ is a weak compact set.*
(b) $\partial f(x) \neq \emptyset$ whenever f is Lipschitz near x.
(c) if f_1 and f_2 are Lipschitz near x and f_1+f_2 attains a local minimum at x, then $0 \in \partial f_1(x) + \partial f_2(x)$.

Proof. To prove (a) we only need to observe that we actually have the equality in (P11).

We note further that (b) follows from (c) applied to the function $f(\cdot) + K\|\cdot - x\|$, where K is the Lipschitz constant of f. So let us prove (c). As ∂ is trusted on X, there is a sequence of quadruples $(x_{1n}, x_{2n}, x_{1n}^*, x_{2n}^*)$ such that $x_{in} \to x$, $x_{in}^* \in \partial f_i(x_{in})$ and $\|x_{1n}^* + x_{2n}^*\| \to 0$. By (P6) both (x_{1n}^*) and (x_{2n}^*) are bounded sequences and if x^* is a weak* limit point of one of them, then $-x^*$ is a weak* limit point of the other. Now the result follows from robustness of the subdifferential. □

The two properties are not sufficient to make a meaningful theory as they offer no information about the function that may come from the knowledge that $x^* \in \partial f(x)$ (in particular to estimate, e.g., the subdifferential of $f_1 + f_2$). To get a "real" calculus of subdifferential we need one more property. Namely, we shall say that a subdifferential is *tight* if the following holds whenever $x^* \in \partial f(x)$:

(P12) For any $\varepsilon > 0$ and any finite dimensional subspace $E \subset X$ there is a w such that $\|w - x\| < \varepsilon$ and the function $\varphi(h) = f(w+h) + \varepsilon\|h\| - \langle x^*, h\rangle$ attains a local minimum on E at zero.

As the first application of the tightness property we shall give sufficient conditions for the existence of nonzero elements in the normal cone and in the subdifferential of the distance functions to a set at a boundary point. Recall that a set $Q \in X$ is called *compactly epi-Lipschitz*[11] near $x \in \mathrm{cl}\,Q$ if there are

[11] This concept was first introduced in [7]. For other characterizations and interrelations of this concept with other compactness notions used in variational analysis see [6, 19]. In many applications the compact epi-Lipschitz property can be replaced by a somewhat weaker property known as "sequential normal compactness" [28] (actually compact epi-Lipschitzness is equivalent to a topological counterpart of the second property if the approximate subdifferential is considered [20] and both coincide in weakly compactly generated spaces). However the compact epi-Lipschitz property has a definite advantage over normal compactness because it is a geometric property of the set itself while normal compactness of the set should be verified for any specific type of subdifferential or normal cone.

$\varepsilon > 0$ and a norm compact set $C \subset X$ such that

$$Q \bigcap (x + \varepsilon B) + tB \subset Q + tC \quad \text{for } t \in [0, \varepsilon) \tag{1}$$

Proposition 4. *Suppose that ∂ is a tight subdifferential and $Q \subset X$ is compactly epi-Lipschitz near a certain $\overline{x} \in \text{cl}Q$, that is that* (1) *holds for some $\varepsilon > 0$ and compact $C \subset X$. Then*

$$\alpha = \alpha(x^*) := \sup_{h \in C} \langle x^*, h \rangle \geq \|x^*\|$$

for any pair (x, x^*) such that x is sufficiently close to $\overline{x}$ and either $x^* \in \partial d(\cdot, Q)(x)$ or $x \in Q$ and $x^* \in N(Q, x)$.

Proof. [12] So suppose (1) holds. The statement is trivial if $\overline{x}$ is an interior point of Q. So let $\overline{x}$ be a boundary point. Then C must contain nonzero elements. Set $r = \sup\{\|h\| : h \in C\}$.

We first consider the case of the distance function. Take next an (x, x^*) such that $\|x - \overline{x}\| < \varepsilon$ and $x^* \in \partial d(\cdot, Q)(x)$ and a small $\gamma > 0$ to be sure that $\|x - \overline{x}\| + \gamma < \varepsilon$.

Let $e \in X$ be such that $\|e\| = 1$ and $\langle x^*, e \rangle \geq (1 - \gamma)\|x^*\|$. Let further $h_1, \ldots, h_k$ be a γ-net in C and $E = \text{span}\,\{e, h_1, \ldots, h_n\}$.

As ∂ is tight, we can find a u such that $\|u - x\| < \gamma$ (so that $d(x, Q) < \varepsilon$) and

$$d(u + h, Q) - \langle x^*, h \rangle + \gamma \|h\| \geq d(u, Q) \tag{2}$$

for all sufficiently small $h \in E$. Chose further for any small $t > 0$ (at least such that $d(u, Q) + t(1 + r) < \varepsilon$) an $x_t \in Q$ such that $\|u - x_t\| \leq d(u, Q) + o(t)$. We have $\|u - x_t\| < \varepsilon$, so by (1) for any t we can find $u_t \in Q$ and $h_t \in C$ such that

$$x_t + te = u_t + th_t.$$

We have $x_t + t(e - h_t) \in Q$, so

$$d(u + t(e - h_t), Q) = d(u - x_t + (x_t + t(e - h_t), Q)) \leq d(u, Q) + o(t). \tag{3}$$

Take an $h'_t \in E \cap C$ such that $\|h_t - h'_t\| < \gamma$. We have by (2)

$$d(u + t(e - h'_t), Q) - d(u, Q) - t\langle x^*, e - h'_t \rangle + t\|e - h'_t\| \geq 0. \tag{4}$$

[12] The basic idea of the proof is the same as in the proof of Theorem 2 in [19]. In that paper however the idea of the proof was somewhat obscured by techniques connected with the unnecessarily strong assumption that ∂ is the approximate subdifferential.

As $|d(u+t(e-h'_t),Q)-d(u+t(e-h_t),Q)|<t\gamma$, (3) and (4) imply

$$t\gamma + o(t) - t\langle x^*, e-h'_t\rangle + t(1+r) \geq 0,$$

so dividing by t and taking $t \to 0$, we get

$$\alpha(x^*) \geq \langle x^*, e\rangle - (2+r)\gamma \geq \|x^*\| - (3+r)\gamma.$$

The result now follows as γ can be chosen arbitrarily small.

The proof for the normal cone is basically the same, even simpler. (2) reduces in this case to

$$-\langle x^*, h\rangle + \gamma\|h\| \geq 0$$

for all $h \in E \cap Q$ sufficiently close to zero. We further define $u_t \in Q$ and $h_t \in C$ from $x + te = u_t + h_t$ and get $\langle x^*, h_t\rangle \geq (1-\gamma)\|x^*\| - \gamma(1+r)$ from which the desired inequality is easily obtained. □

Proposition 5. *Suppose that ∂ is a tight and robust subdifferential which is trusted on X. Let Q be a closed subset of X. Then:*

(a) If $\overline{x}$ is a boundary point of Q and Q is compactly epi-Lipschitz near $\overline{x}$, then $\partial d(\cdot, Q)(\overline{x})$, and hence $N(Q, \overline{x})$, contains nonzero vectors.
(b) If f_1 and f_2 are Lipschitz near x, then $\partial(f_1 + f_2)(x) \subset \partial f_1(x) + \partial f_2(x)$.

Proof. (a) Assume that $x \notin Q$. Take a small $\varepsilon > 0$, choose $\tilde{u} \in Q$ such that $\|x - \tilde{u}\| \leq d(x, Q) + \varepsilon^2$ and consider the function $\varphi(u) = \|x - u\| + d(u, Q)$. Clearly $\inf\varphi = d(x, Q)$ and therefore $\varphi(\tilde{u}) \leq \inf\varphi + \varepsilon^2$. By Ekeland's principle there is a $\overline{u}$ with $\|\overline{u}-\tilde{u}\| \leq \varepsilon$ such that $\varphi(u)+\varepsilon\|u-\overline{u}\|$ attains an absolute minimum at $\overline{u}$. A reference to trustworthiness and (P4) allows to conclude that there are a u^* belonging to the subdifferential of $\|\cdot\|$ at a point close to $x - \overline{u}$ and a v close to $\overline{u}$ such that

$$0 \in u^* + \partial d(\cdot, Q)(v) + \varepsilon B$$

(with the level of closeness fully in our disposal). We observe that for ε small enough we may be sure that $x \neq \overline{u}$ and therefore $\|u^*\| = 1$.

Let us return to the proof of our statement. If x is a boundary point of Q, then there is a sequence (x_n) of vectors not belonging to Q and converging to x. As we have just seen, we can associate with this sequence two other sequences: (v_n) also converging to x and (u_n^*) such that $u^* \in \partial d(\cdot, Q)(v_n)$ and $\|u_n^*\| = 1$. As Q is compactly epi-Lipschitz near x, it follows from Proposition 4 that $\sup\{\langle u_n^*, h\rangle : h \in C\} \geq 1$, that is there are $h_n \in C$ such that $\langle u_n^*, h_n\rangle \geq 1$ for all n. Now if h is a limit point of h_n and u^* is a weak*-limit point of u_n^*, then $\langle u^*, h\rangle \geq 1$, that is $u^* \neq 0$ and $u^* \in \partial d(\cdot, Q)(x)$ as ∂ is a robust subdifferential.

(b) Let f_1, f_2 be Lipschitz near x with constant K, and let $x^* \in \partial(f_1 + f_2)(x)$. Then for any finite dimensional E and any $\varepsilon > 0$ we find a w such that

$$f_1(u) + f_2(u) - \langle x^*, u - w\rangle + \varepsilon\|u - w\| + 2Kd(u - w, E)$$

attains a local minimum at w (tightness). As ∂ is trusted on X, there are (u_i, u_i^*), $i = 1, 2$ such that

$$\|u_i - w\| < \varepsilon, \quad u_i^* \in \partial f_i(u_i), \quad x^* \in u_1^* + u_2^* + \varepsilon B + E^{\perp}.$$

We have also $\|u_i^*\| \le K$. Repeating the already standard limiting arguments involving robustness of ∂ we conclude that $x^* \in \partial f_1(x) + \partial f_2(x)$. □

Remarks. A problem which remains open is *what can be said about subdifferentials of the distance functions at points not belonging to the set?*

Proposition 6. *Let ∂ be a tight robust subdifferential which is trusted on X. Let $Q \subset X$ be a closed set, let $\overline{x} \in Q$, and let the following regularity property holds for Q near $\overline{x}$:*

> **(R)** *There is an $r > 0$ such that for any finite dimensional subspace $E' \subset X$ there is a bigger finite dimensional subspace E such that for any $w \in Q$ sufficiently close to $\overline{x}$*
>
> $$d(x, Q \bigcap (w + E)) \le r\big(d(x, Q) + d(x, w + E)\big) \qquad (5)$$
>
> *for all x of a neighborhood of w.*

Then

$$N(Q, \overline{x}) \subset \bigcup_{\lambda \ge 0} \lambda \partial d(\cdot, Q)(\overline{x}),$$

that is for any $x^* \in N(Q, \overline{x})$ there is a $\lambda > 0$ such that $x^* \in \lambda\partial d(\cdot, Q)(\overline{x})$. In fact, we can always find $\lambda \le r(\|x^*\| + 1)$.

Proof. Assume **(R)**, and let $x^* \in N(Q, \overline{x})$. By tightness we can find a small $\varepsilon > 0$ and a $w \in Q$ arbitrarily close to $\overline{x}$ such that

$$-\langle x^*, u - w\rangle + \varepsilon\|u - w\| \ge 0$$

for any $u \in Q \cap (w + E)$. The function on the left is Lipschitz with constant not greater that $\|x^*\| + 1$ (if $\varepsilon < 1$ which we always can assume), so setting $\lambda = r(\|x^*\| + 1)$, we can be sure in view of (5) that

$$\lambda(d(u,Q)+d(u,w+E))+\varepsilon\|u-w\|-\langle x^*,u-w\rangle\geq 0$$

for all u of a neighborhood of w. By trustworthiness and (P4) in any neighborhood of w we can find an x such that

$$x^*\in\lambda\partial d(\cdot,Q)(x)+\varepsilon B+E^{\perp}\cap(\lambda B)$$

and we conclude in the standard way using robustness that $x^*\in\lambda\partial d(\cdot,Q)$. □

Proposition 7. *If f is Lipschitz in a neighborhood of $\overline{x}$, then* epi f *satisfies* (**R**) *in a neighborhood of* $(\overline{x}, f(\overline{x}))$.

Proof. Denote, as earlier, by L the Lipschitz constant of f in a neighborhood of $\overline{x}$. First we observe that whichever norm in $X\times I\!R$ has been chosen, there are $K\geq k>0$ such that

$$k(L\|x\|+|\alpha|)\leq\|(x,\alpha)\|\leq K(L\|x\|+|\alpha|). \tag{6}$$

We have, if (x,α) is sufficiently close to $(\overline{x}, f(\overline{x}))$:

$$\begin{aligned}(f(x)-\alpha)^+ &\geq \inf\{L\|x-x'\|+|\alpha-\alpha'|:\ (x',\alpha')\in \text{epi } f\}\\ &=\inf_{x'}(L\|x-x'\|+(f(x')-\alpha)^+)\\ &\geq\inf_{x'}(L\|x-x'\|+(f(x)-\alpha)^+-|f(x')-f(x)|)\\ &\geq (f(x)-\alpha)^+.\end{aligned}$$

Let now $E'\subset X\times I\!R$, $\dim E'<\infty$. If $\{0\}\times I\!R\subset E'$, set $E=E'$. Otherwise set $E=E'\oplus(\{0\}\times I\!R)$. In either case $E=D\oplus I\!R$ for some finite dimensional subspace $D\subset X$. We obviously have from (6)

$$kLd(x,D)\leq d((x,\alpha),E)\leq KLd(x,D).$$

Furthermore if (u,β) are sufficiently close to $(\overline{x}, f(\overline{x}))$, then

$$\begin{aligned}&d((x,\alpha),\text{epi } f\cap((u,\beta)+E))\\ &\quad=\inf\{\|(x,\alpha)-(x',\alpha')\|:\ \alpha'\geq f(x'),\ (x',\alpha')\in(u,\beta)+E\}\\ &\quad\leq K\inf\{L\|x-x'\|+|\alpha-\alpha'|:\ \alpha'\geq f(x'),\ (x',\alpha')\in(u,\beta)+E\}\\ &\quad=K\inf\{L\|x-x'\|+(f(x')-\alpha)^+:\ x'\in u+D\}\\ &\quad\leq K\big[(f(x)-\alpha)^++\inf\{L\|x-x'\|+|f(x)-f(x')|: x'-u\in D\}\big]\\ &\quad\leq K\big[(f(x)-\alpha)^++2Ld(x-u,D)\big]\\ &\quad\leq K\big[k^{-1}d((x,\alpha),\text{epi } f)+2Ld((x,\alpha),(u,\beta)+E)\big]\end{aligned}$$

and the proof is completed. □

If we look back at Proposition 5 and the proof of Proposition 6, then the last result may suggest that for a Lipschitz function on X tight robust subdifferentials trusted on X should coincide. This is indeed the case and the following proposition gives a direct proof of the fact.

Proposition 8. *Let ∂ be a tight robust subdifferential which is trusted on X. Let f be a function on X which is Lipschitz continuous near $\overline{x}$. Then $x^* \in \partial f(\overline{x})$ if and only if for any $\varepsilon > 0$ and any finite dimensional subspace E of X there are w and $\delta > 0$ such that $\|w - \overline{x}\| < \varepsilon$ and*

$$f(w+h) - f(w) - \langle x^*, h\rangle + \varepsilon\|h\| \geq 0, \quad \forall h \in E, \ \|h\| < \delta. \tag{7}$$

Thus if ∂' is another tight robust subdifferential which is trusted on X, then $\partial f(\overline{x}) = \partial' f(\overline{x})$.

Proof. The tightness property provides the proof in one direction. We therefore have to show that whenever for any $\varepsilon > 0$ and finite dimensional $E \subset X$ there are w with $\|w - \overline{x}\| < \varepsilon$ and $\delta > 0$ such that (7) holds, we conclude that $x^* \in \partial f(\overline{x})$. The proof of this implication is basically the same as the proof of part (b) of Proposition 5. Indeed, it follows from (7) (as f is Lipschitz and ∂ is a trustworthy subdifferential) that, given ε and E, there is an x with $\|x - \overline{x}\| < \varepsilon$ such that (for a sufficiently large K depending only on the Lipschitz constant of f)

$$x^* \in \partial f(x) + E^{\perp} \cap (KB) + \varepsilon B.$$

When $\varepsilon \to 0$, we get using robustness that $x^* \in \partial f(x) + E^{\perp} \cap (KB)$. From here, taking into account that $\partial f(x)$ is a weak*-compact set (Proposition 2), we conclude that $x^* \in \partial f(\overline{x})$. □

Another consequence of Proposition 8 is

Proposition 9. *Let ∂ be a tight robust subdifferential which is trusted on $X \times I\!R$, and let f be Lipschitz continuous in a neighborhood of $\overline{x}$:*

(a) If $x^* \in \partial f(\overline{x})$, then there is an $r > 0$ such that $(x^*, -1) \in r\partial d\,(\cdot, \text{epi } f)\,(\overline{x}, f(\overline{x}))$.

(b) Suppose in addition that the norm in $X \times I\!R$ is defined by $\|(x, \alpha)\| = L\|x\| + |\alpha|$, were L is not smaller than the Lipschitz constant of f in a neighborhood of $\overline{x}$. Then the converse is true: if $(x^*, -1) \in r\partial d(\cdot, \text{epi } f)(\overline{x}, f(\overline{x}))$ for some $r > 0$, then $x^* \in \partial f(\overline{x})$.

(c) Thus

$$\partial f(\overline{x}) = \{x^* : \ (x^*, -1) \in N(\text{epi } f, (\overline{x}, f(\overline{x}))\}.$$

Proof. (a) Let $x^* \in \partial f(\overline{x})$. Then, given $\varepsilon > 0$ and a finite dimensional $D \in X$ we can find a $w \in \text{dom } f$ and $\delta > 0$ such that $\|w - x\| < \varepsilon$ and

$$f(w+h) - f(w) - \langle x^*, h\rangle + \varepsilon\|h\| \geq 0, \quad \forall\, h \in D, \ \ \|h\| < \delta.$$

Taking a small ξ, we can rewrite the expression in the left side as

$$f(w+h) - f(w) - \xi - \langle (x^*, -1), (h, \xi) \rangle + \varepsilon \|h\|.$$

As follows from the proof of Proposition 7, there is an $r > 0$ such that $rd((x, \alpha), \text{epi } f) \geq (f(x) - \alpha)^+$ if (x, α) is sufficiently close to $(\overline{x}, f(\overline{x}))$. Thus we have

$$rd((w+h, f(w)+\xi), \text{epi } f) \geq (f(w+h) - f(w) - \xi)^+ \geq f(w+h) - f(w) - \xi.$$

Now let E be a finite dimensional subspace of $X \times I\!R$, and D its projection onto X. Comparing the last two inequalities, we conclude that, given $\varepsilon > 0$, we can find a w in the ε-neighborhood of $\overline{x}$ such that

$$r[d((w, f(w)) + (h, \xi), \text{epi } f) - d((w, f(w)), \text{epi } f)] - \langle (x^*, -1), (h, \xi) \rangle$$
$$+ \varepsilon \|h\| \geq 0$$

whenever $(h, \xi) \in E$ and the norm of (h, ξ) is sufficiently small. Application of Proposition 8 (possible as ∂ is trusted on $X \times I\!R$) gives $(x^*, -1) \in r\partial(\cdot, \text{epi } f)((\overline{x}, f(\overline{x}))$.

(b) Assume now that the last inclusion holds. Then by tightness, given an $\varepsilon > 0$ and a finite dimensional $D \in X$ we find (again using the proof of Proposition 7) a (w, β) in the ε-neighborhood of $(\overline{x}, f(\overline{x}))$ such that

$$(f(w+h) - (\beta + \xi))^+ - (f(w) - \beta)^+ - \langle (x^*, -1), (h, \xi) \rangle + \varepsilon(\|h\| + |\xi|) \geq 0$$

for all $h \in D$ with $\|h\|$ and $|\xi|$ sufficiently small. As $a^+ - b^+ \leq (a - b)^+$ for any real a and b, we get from here

$$(f(w+h) - (f(w) + \xi))^+ - \langle (x^*, -1), (h, \xi) \rangle + \varepsilon(\|h\| + |\xi|) \geq 0$$

for the same h and ξ. Set $\xi = f(w+h) - f(w)$. Then the last inequality gives

$$f(w+h) - f(w) - \langle x^*, h \rangle + \varepsilon(L+1)\|h\| \geq 0.$$

Again, an application of Proposition 8 proves the claim.

(c) The inclusion

$$\partial f(\overline{x}) \subset \{x^* : \ (x^*, -1) \in N(\text{epi } f, (\overline{x}, f(\overline{x}))\}.$$

follows from (a) and Proposition 1(b). The opposite inclusion is a combination of (b) and Propositions 6 and 7. It has to be taken into account that the definition of a subdifferential and normal cone does not involve a reference to any specific norm in the space. □

Thus, for Lipschitz functions we get a nice geometric characterization of a tight robust subdifferential which is trusted on $X \times I\!R$. We shall call a subdifferential *geometrically consistent* on X if for *any* lower semi-continuous function on X, not just Lipschitz, the relations $x^* \in \partial f(x)$ and $(x^*, -1) \in N(\text{epi } f, (x, f(x))$ are equivalent.

To state the final result of this section we have to recall the definition of the approximate G-subdifferential. Given a function f, the *lower Dini–Hadamard directional derivative* of f at x is

$$d^- f(x; h) = \liminf_{(u,t)\to(h,+0)} t^{-1}(f(x+tu) - f(x)),$$

and the *Dini–Hadamard subdifferential* of f at x is

$$\partial^- f(x) = \{x^* : \langle x^*, h\rangle \le d^- f(x; h), \ \forall\, h\}.$$

Let further E be a finite dimensional subspace of X and $f|_Q$ stand for the restriction of f to Q (that is the function equal to f on Q and infinity outside of Q). Now, if f is Lipschitz near x with constant L, we define the G-subdifferential of f at x by

$$\partial f(x) = \bigcap_{E\in\mathcal{F}} \bigcap_{\varepsilon>0} \text{cl}^*\Big(\bigcup_{\|u-x\|<\varepsilon} \partial^- f_{u+E}(u) \cap B(0, L)\Big),$$

where $\mathcal{F}$ is the collection of finite dimensional subspaces of X.

Finally, if f is a lower semi-continuous function, we define the G-subdifferential of f at x by

$$\partial f(x) = \{x^* : (x^*, -1) \in \bigcup_{\lambda\ge 0} \lambda \partial d(\cdot, \text{epi } f)(x, f(x))\}.[13]$$

As well known the result does not depend on the choice of the norm in $X \times I\!R$. The G-subdifferential has all the three properties: it is trusted on every Banach space, tight and robust. It is also more or less clear from the definitions that it is geometrically consistent. Thus Proposition 9 leads to

Theorem 10. *Approximate G-subdifferential is the only tight robust subdifferential which is trusted and geometrically consistent on every Banach space.*[14]

---

[13] As we have already mentioned, this definition differs from the original definition of [14] in which we defined the subdifferential as the weak*-closure of the union on the right. It turned out later that closure operation is not needed in the proofs and moreover, it kills some good properties, e.g., the one analogous to the property (c) in Proposition 9.

[14] A parallel theory can be developed for *sequentially* robust subdifferentials which however does impose some a priori restrictions to the choice of a Banach space. We hope to consider it elsewhere.

3. A scheme relevant to the second theorem of welfare economics

We shall now turn to the question we need to answer in order to approach the second theorem of welfare economics with the general concept of subdifferential. Namely, given two closed sets Q_1 and Q_2 in a Banach space X having at least one common point $\overline{x}$, – when we can guarantee that the normal cones to the sets at $\overline{x}$ contain a common nonzero vector? An alternative formulation is the existence of a common nonzero vector in $\partial d(\cdot, Q_1)(\overline{x})$ and $\partial d(\cdot, Q_1)(\overline{x})$. In the last case the a priori requirement that the sets are closed is not essential. Actually, in the situation typical for models of welfare economics, one of the sets may have a very special structure being the preimage of a point (for a more general set as well) under a linear bounded mapping onto a Banach space.

We shall prove two results which are closely connected although basically independent. The first is a sort of a calculus rule for the distance functions, while the second result, essentially answering the questions, is of the kind that is usually interpreted as a "nonconvex separation property."

Proposition 11. *Let ∂ be a tight and robust subdifferential that can be trusted on X. Let further Q_1 and Q_2 be closed subsets of X. Then for any $x_i \in Q_i$ we have*

$$\partial d(\cdot, Q_1 + Q_2)(x_1 + x_2) \subset \partial d(\cdot, Q_1)(x_1) \bigcap \partial d(\cdot, Q_2)(x_2).$$

Proof. Set for brevity $x = x_1 + x_2$, and let $x^* \in \partial d(\cdot, Q_1 + Q_2)(x)$. Take a finite dimensional subspace $E \subset X$. By tightness, for any $\varepsilon > 0$ there is a w such that $\|w - x\| < \varepsilon$, and

$$d(w + h, Q_1 + Q_2) + \varepsilon\|h\| - \langle x^*, h\rangle \geq d(x, Q_1 + Q_2)$$

for all $h \in E$ of a neighborhood of zero. As the function on the left is Lipschitz, with constant not exceeding $1 + \varepsilon$, this amounts to

$$\|w + h - (u_1 + u_2)\| + \varepsilon\|h\| + (1 + \varepsilon)\big(d(h, E) + d(u_1, Q_1) + d(u_2, Q_2)\big) \\ - \langle x^*, h\rangle \geq d(x, Q_1 + Q_2)$$

for all h of a neighborhood of zero, e.g., satisfying $\|h\| < \delta$ for some $\delta > 0$ and all u_i, $i = 1, 2$. (We may assume that $\delta \leq \varepsilon$.) Denote by $g(h, u_1, u_2)$ the function in the left-hand side of the inequality.

By Ekeland's variational principle, there are $\overline{h}$ and $\overline{u}_i \in Q_i$ such that $\|\overline{h}\| < \sqrt{\varepsilon}$, $\|\overline{u}_i - x\| < \sqrt{\varepsilon}$ and the function

$$g(h, u_1, u_2) + \sqrt{\varepsilon}(\|h - \overline{h}\| + \|u_1 - \overline{u}_1\| + \|u_2 - \overline{u}_2\|)$$

attains local minimum at $(\overline{h}, \overline{u}_1, \overline{u}_2)$. As all terms of the latter function are Lipschitz (and all but $d(\cdot, Q_i)$ convex), we apply Proposition 5(b) and get as a result that there is a $u^* \in x^* + E^{\perp}$, $\|u^*\| \le 1$ such that

$$0 \in -u^* + \sqrt{\varepsilon}B + (1+\varepsilon)\partial d(\cdot, Q_1)(\overline{u}_1);$$
$$0 \in -u^* + \sqrt{\varepsilon}B + (1+\varepsilon)\partial d(\cdot, Q_2)(\overline{u}_2).$$

By robustness, the set $U(E)$ of u^* such that $\|u^*\| \le 1$, $u^* \in x^* + E^{\perp}$ and $u^* \in \partial d(\cdot, Q_1)(x) \cap \partial d(\cdot, Q_2)(x)$ is nonempty for any E, these sets are weak* compact and do not increase with E. Therefore the intersection of all these sets over all finite dimensional subspaces of X is nonempty. It is also obvious that the only element in the intersection obtained this way may be x^*. □

This nicely looking proposition may not, however, be fully satisfactory. Our ultimate goal is to find conditions which guarantee that $\partial d(\cdot, Q_i)(x_i)$ have a common nonzero element. The proposition may guarantee this only if $x = x_1 + x_2$ is a boundary point of the closure of $Q_1 + Q_2$. A more delicate analysis allows to get it without a priori assuming the latter.

We say following [5] that two closed sets Q_1 and Q_2 are *separable* at $(\overline{x}_1, \overline{x}_2) \in Q_1 \times Q_2$ if $\overline{x} = \overline{x}_1 + \overline{x}_2$ is a boundary point of $Q_1 + Q_2$, that is if $Q_1 + Q_2$ contains no neighborhood of $\overline{x}$. The sets are *locally separable* at $(\overline{x}_1, \overline{x}_2)$ if there is a neighborhood of zero $U \subset X$ such that $Q_i \cap (\overline{x}_i + U)$ are separable at $(\overline{x}_1, \overline{x}_2)$.[15]

Theorem 12. *(a) Assume that ∂ is trusted on X and Q_i, $i = 1, 2$, are closed subsets of X. Assume that Q_1 and Q_2 are locally separable at $(\overline{x}_1, \overline{x}_2)$. Then for any $\varepsilon > 0$ there are $x_i \in Q_i$ and an x^* such that $\|x_i - \overline{x}_i\| < \varepsilon$, $\|x^*\| = 1$ and $x^* \in N(Q_i, x_i) + \varepsilon B$.*

(b) If, moreover, ∂ is a robust tight subdifferential and one of the sets Q_i is compactly epi-Lipschitz near $\overline{x}_i$, then $\partial d(\cdot, Q_1)(\overline{x}_1) \cap \partial d(\cdot, Q_2)(\overline{x}_2)$ and therefore $N(Q_1, \overline{x}_1) \cap N(Q_2, \overline{x}_2)$ contain nonzero vectors.

The first statement is sometimes referred to as the "ε-separation theorem" while the second as the "exact separation theorem."

Proof. Set $\overline{x} = \overline{x}_1 + \overline{x}_2$. We can assume without loss of generality that the entire sets Q_i are separable at $(\overline{x}_1, \overline{x}_2)$. Take an $\varepsilon > 0$ and let $x \notin Q_1 + Q_2$ be such that $\|x - \overline{x}\| < \varepsilon^2$. Consider the function $\varphi(x_1, x_2) = \|x - x_1 - x_2\|$ on the set $Q_1 \times Q_2$. This is a complete metric space in the induced metric, so

---

[15] This property introduced probably in [5] is closely connected with $\overline{x}_1$ being an *extremal point* of Q_1 and $\overline{x} - Q_2$ in the sense of [27,29] – see [9]. We use separability because it is a weaker property and in terms of separability the formulation of Pareto optimality properties in welfare economics is a bit more convenient.

by Ekeland's variational principle there are $\overline{u}_i \in Q_i$ such that $\|\overline{u}_i - \overline{x}_i\| < \varepsilon$ and

$$\psi(x_1, x_2) = \varphi(x_1, x_2) + \varepsilon(\|x_1 - \overline{u}_1\| + \|x_2 - \overline{u}_2\|) \geq \varphi(\overline{u}_1, \overline{u}_2), \quad \forall\, x_i \in Q_i.$$

This amounts to saying that the function

$$g(x_1, x_2) = \delta_{Q_1}(x_1) + \delta_{Q_2}(x_2) + \psi(x_1, x_2)$$

attains an unconditional minimum at $(\overline{u}_1, \overline{u}_2)$.

As $\overline{u}_i \in Q_i$, we have $\rho = \psi(\overline{u}_1, \overline{u}_2) = \|x - \overline{u}_1 - \overline{u}_2\| > 0$. By trustworthiness, we can find (x_1, x_2) with $\|x_i - \overline{u}_i\| < \varepsilon$ and (w_1, w_2) with $\|w_i - \overline{u}_i\| < \rho/2$ such that

$$(0, 0) \in N(Q_1)(x_1) \times N(Q_2, x_2) - (x^*, x) + \varepsilon(B \times B),$$

where x^* belongs to the subdifferential of the norm at $x - w_1 - w_2$. As this vector is not equal to zero, we have $\|x^*\| = 1$. This completes the proof of the first statement.

The simplest way to prove (b) is just to refer to [5] with a reference to the property in third part of Proposition 3 (which was used in [5] as one of axioms of subdifferentials).[16]

Remark. It is appropriate to compare here Theorem 12 with the corresponding results of [5,21,28] (also [29]). Using the property of Proposition 3(c) as an axiom as in [5, 21] exclude nonrobust subdifferentials (as say Fréchet or Dini–Hadamard) from consideration. In [28] the part of the exact statement involving distance functions is absent (and it is not clear whether it is obtainable within the axiomatics of [28]) while the part involving normal cones gives a rougher estimate. The reason is that, contrary to earlier publications related to the abstract approach, normal cones, rather than subdifferentials, were chosen in [28] as original objects. As a result the cones that appear in the exact statement of [28] are necessarily weak*-closed. Thus, in the case of a "subdifferentially generated normal structure" the cones that appear in [28] are weak* closures of the cones that appear in the part (b) of Theorem 12.

We next consider a more special scheme which includes a set $Q \subset X$, not assumed to be closed, a bounded linear operator A from X onto another Banach space Y and a point $\overline{y} \in Y$. We shall be interested in conditions that guarantee local separation of $\mathrm{cl}Q$ and $A^{-1}(\overline{y})$ at a certain $\overline{x}$ which belongs to both $\mathrm{cl}Q$ and $A^{-1}(\overline{y})$. An important *simplifying assumption* is that $Q \cap A^{-1}(\overline{y}) = \emptyset$.

[16] It is not clear whether under the assumptions of part (a) of the Theorem we can replace normal cones by the subdifferentials of the distance functions.

By Theorem 12 the only condition we need to prove the ε-separation theorem in this case is that $2\overline{x}$ is a boundary point of $\mathrm{cl}\,Q + A^{-1}(\overline{y})$. This is obviously the same as $\overline{x}$ being a boundary point of $\mathrm{cl}\,Q + \mathrm{Ker}\,A$.

Proposition 13. *A sufficient condition for $\overline{x}$ to be a boundary point of $\mathrm{cl}\,Q +$ Ker A is that there is a sequence $(v_k) \subset Y$ converging to zero such that for all k.*

$$v_k + A(\mathrm{cl}\,Q) \subset A(Q). \tag{$*$}$$

Proof. Indeed, in this case $\overline{y} - v_k \notin A(\mathrm{cl}\,Q)$ for otherwise we would have $\overline{y} \in A(Q)$, that is $Q \cap A^{-1}(\overline{y}) \neq \emptyset$ contrary to the simplifying assumption. As A is onto, there is a sequence $(u_n) \subset X$ such that $Au_n = v_n$ and $\|u_k\| \leq K\|v_n\| \to 0$ for some sufficiently large K. Then $\overline{x} - v_n \notin \mathrm{cl}\,Q + \mathrm{Ker}\,A$ for otherwise we would have $\overline{y} - v_n \in A(\mathrm{cl}\,Q)$. □

We also observe that since A is onto (and by (P4)) the normal cone to Ker A at zero is the annihilator of Ker A. Combining now the proposition with Theorem 12, we get

Proposition 14. *Consider a set $Q \subset X$ and a linear bounded mapping A from X onto another Banach space Y. We assume that $\overline{x} \in \mathrm{cl}\,Q$ is such that $\overline{y} = A\overline{x} \notin A(Q)$ and the qualification condition $(*)$ holds:*

(a) If ∂ is a subdifferential trusted on X, then for any $\varepsilon > 0$ there are $x \in Q$ with $\|x - \overline{x}\| < \varepsilon$ and a nonzero $x^* \in N(\mathrm{cl}\,Q, x) \cap (\mathrm{Ker}\,A)^{\perp} + \varepsilon B$.
(b) If in addition ∂ is a robust subdifferential and $\mathrm{cl}\,Q$ is compactly epi-Lipschitz near $\overline{x}$, then both $\partial d(\cdot, Q)(\overline{x})$ and $N(\mathrm{cl}\,Q, \overline{x})$ contain nonzero vectors belonging to $(\mathrm{Ker}\,A)^{\perp}$.

Remark 1. As by (P2) the value of any subdifferential at a point is determined by the restriction of the function to arbitrarily small neighborhood of the point, we can replace in $(*)$ and all our argument afterwards $\mathrm{cl}\,Q$ by $(\mathrm{cl}\,Q) \bigcap (\overline{x} + \varepsilon B)$.

2. Both assumptions, that $A(\mathrm{cl}\,Q)$ is compactly epi-Lipschitz and $(*)$ say that Q must be sufficiently massive. In particular both are satisfied if $A(\mathrm{cl}\,Q)$ is epi-Lipschitz (that is if the set C in the definition of compact epi-Lipschitzness is a singleton).[17]

4. The second theorem of welfare economics

The standard model of welfare economics (we do not include public goods for simplicity) contains:

---

[17] In fact the assumption that the preference set is epi-Lipschitz was used as a qualification condition in the proof of a second welfare theorem in [3].

- A space of commodities X (which we assume Banach)
- n consumers with consumer sets $X_i \subset X$ and preference (set-valued) maps $P_i(x)$ from X_i into itself
- m producers with production sets $Y_j \subset X$
- Vector $w \in X$ of aggregate endowment

We assume that $\text{cl}P_i(x) \subset X_i$ and $x \in (\text{cl}P_i(x)) \backslash P_i(x)$ for every $x \in X_i$ for which $P_i(x) \neq \emptyset$.[18]

An *allocation* is an element of X^{n+m}. An allocation $\xi = (x_1, \ldots, x_n, y_1, \ldots, y_m)$ is *feasible* if $x_i \in X_i$ for every consumer, $y_j \in Y_j$ for all $j = 1, \ldots, m$ and

$$\sum_{i=1}^{n} x_i - \sum_{j=1}^{m} y_j = w. \tag{8}$$

A feasible allocation $\bar{\xi} = (\overline{x}_1, \ldots, \overline{x}_n, \overline{y}_1, \ldots, \overline{y}_m)$ is *Pareto optimal* if for any other feasible allocation ξ either $x_i \notin P(\overline{x}_i)$ for all i or $x_i \notin \text{cl}P_i(\overline{x}_i)$ for some i. If for any other feasible allocation $x_i \notin P(\overline{x}_i)$ for some i, then it is said that $\bar{\xi}$ is a *weak Pareto optimum*.

Given a subdifferential ∂, we can define a *price equilibrium* as a pair $(\bar{\xi}, p)$ such that $\bar{\xi}$ is a feasible allocation, $0 \neq p \in X^*$ and the following two relations hold:

$$-p \in N(\text{cl}P_i(\overline{x}_i), \overline{x}_i), \quad i = 1, \ldots, n;$$

$$p \in N(\text{cl}Y_j, \bar{y}_j), \quad j = 1, \ldots, m.$$

It is also possible to consider an *ε-price equilibrium* as a pair $(\bar{\xi}, p)$, where as above, $\bar{\xi}$ is a feasible allocation and $p \neq 0$, such that the inclusions

$$-p \in N(\text{cl}P_i(\bar{x_i}), x_i) + \varepsilon B, \quad i = 1, \ldots, n;$$

$$p \in N(\text{cl}Y_j, y_j) + \varepsilon B, \quad j = 1, \ldots, m,$$

hold for some $x_i \in \text{cl}P_i(\overline{x}_i)$, $y_j \in \text{cl}Y_j$ such that $\|x_i - \overline{x}_i\| < \varepsilon$, $\|y_j - \overline{y}_j\| < \varepsilon$. All versions of the second theorem of welfare economics give conditions which guarantee that Pareto optimality in one or another sense imply the existence of equilibrium prices.

We can get such conditions for our model as Pareto efficiency can be easily reduced to the scheme of the previous section. Indeed, let Z be the product of $n + m$ copies of X. Fix a feasible allocation $\bar{\xi}$ and set

[18] Nothing will change in the argument to follow if we assume that preferences of each consumer depend on the choices of the others. In other words we can assume that P_i is a mapping from $X_1 \times \cdots \times X_n$ into X_i. The assumption in this case assumes the form $x_i \in \text{cl}P_i(x_1, \ldots, x_n) \backslash P(x_1, \ldots, x_n)$.

$$\mathcal{P}_i = \mathrm{cl}P_1(\overline{x}_1)\times\cdots\times\mathrm{cl}P_{i-1}(\overline{x}_{i-1})\times P_i(\overline{x}_i)\times\mathrm{cl}P_{i+1}(\overline{x}_{i+1})\times\cdots\times\mathrm{cl}P_n(\overline{x}_n),$$

$$Q = \Big(\bigcup_{i=1}^{n}\mathcal{P}_i\Big)\times\prod_{j=1}^{m}Y_j.$$

Then $\bar{\xi}$ is Pareto optimal if and only if Q does not meet the set of allocations $\xi = (x_1, \ldots, x_n, y_1, \ldots, y_m)$ satisfying (8).

Likewise, if we set

$$\widetilde{\mathcal{P}} = P_1(\overline{x}_1)\times\cdots\times P_n(\overline{x}_n),$$

$$\widetilde{Q} = \widetilde{\mathcal{P}}\times\prod_{j=1}^{m}Y_j,$$

then $\bar{\xi}$ is weakly Pareto optimal if and only if $\widetilde{Q}$ does not meet the set of allocations $\xi = (x_1, \ldots, x_n, y_1, \ldots, y_m)$ satisfying (8).

Set

$$A\xi = \sum_{i=1}^{n}x_i - \sum_{j=1}^{m}y_j.$$

Than A is a linear bounded operator from Z into X which is obviously onto and the set of allocations satisfying (8) is precisely $A^{-1}(w)$. We have

$$\mathrm{cl}Q = \mathrm{cl}\widetilde{Q} = \Big(\prod_{i=1}^{m}\mathrm{cl}P_i(\overline{x}_i)\Big)\times\Big(\prod_{j=1}^{m}\mathrm{cl}Y_j\Big) \tag{9}$$

so $\bar{\xi}\in\mathrm{cl}Q$ and, on the other hand, no allocation satisfying $A\xi = w$ can belong to either Q or $\widetilde{Q}$. This is precisely the case considered in the concluding part the previous section.

Taking into account the first remark at the end of the previous section, we can restate condition $(*)$ as follows: there are $\varepsilon > 0$ and $u_k \to 0$ $(u_k \in X)$ such that

$$\begin{aligned} u_k + \sum_i(\mathrm{cl}P_i(\overline{x}_i))\bigcap(\overline{x}_i + \varepsilon B) - \sum_J \mathrm{cl}Y_j\bigcap(\overline{y}_j + \varepsilon B) \\ \subset \bigcup_k(P_k(\overline{x}_k) + \sum_{i\neq k}\mathrm{cl}P_i(\overline{x}_i)) - \sum_j Y_j \end{aligned} \tag{$**$}$$

in case of Pareto optimality, or such that

$$u_k+\sum_i(\mathrm{cl}P_i(\overline{x}_i))\bigcap(\overline{x}_i+\varepsilon B)-\sum_J\mathrm{cl}Y_j\bigcap(\overline{y}_j+\varepsilon B)\subset\sum_i P_i(\overline{x}_i)-\sum_j Y_j \tag{$\widetilde{**}$}$$

in case of weak Pareto optimality.

The final observations we have to do are:

(a) As A is onto, the annihilator of Ker A coincides with Im A^* which is the collection of vectors $\eta = (x^*, \ldots, x^*, -x^*, \ldots, -x^*)$ (first n components with plus and the last m components with minus) when x^* runs through X^*.
(b) Taking into account the product structure of Q, we can easily see that $\eta \in N(\mathrm{cl}Q, \xi)$ is the same as $x^* \in N(\mathrm{cl}P_i(\overline{x}_i), x_i)$ and $-x^* \in N(\mathrm{cl}Y_j, y_j)$ for all i and j, so setting $p = -x^*$, we get the desired inclusions.

Thus, we can conclude by stating the following theorem.

Theorem 15. *If $\bar{\xi}$ is Pareto (resp. weak Pareto) optimal and the qualification condition $(**)$ (resp. $(\widetilde{**})$) holds, then for any $\varepsilon > 0$ there is a $p \neq 0$ such that $(\bar{\xi}, p)$ is an ε-price equilibrium with prices associated with a subdifferential trusted on X^{n+m}.*

If, moreover, one of the sets $\mathrm{cl}P_i(\overline{x}_i)$ is compactly epi-Lipschitz at $\overline{x}_i$ or one of the sets $\mathrm{cl}Y_j$ is compactly epi-Lipschitz at y_j and the prices are taken from normal cones associated with a tight and robust subdifferential trusted on X^{n+m}, then there is a nonzero $p \in X^*$ such that $(\bar{\xi}, p)$ is a price equilibrium.

Proof. In view of the second observation above, the first statement is an immediate consequence of Proposition 14(a). We cannot directly apply Proposition 14 to justify the second part of the theorem (because the set $\mathrm{cl}Q$ in (10) need not be compactly epi-Lipschitz under the assumptions). However $\mathrm{cl}Q$ is a product of several sets one of which is compactly epi-Lipschitz and we have the same vectors in normal cones to each of the sets. So the limiting process similar to that used, e.g., in the proof of Proposition 5 applied to the compactly epi-Lipschitz component set in leads to the desired result. □

Remark. In addition to the differences with [21,28] discussed in the previous section, the qualification condition $(**)$ differs from that in [21, 28] where it was assumed that for some k and $u_n \to 0$

$$\begin{aligned} u_n + \sum_i (\mathrm{cl}P_i(\overline{x}_i)) \bigcap (\overline{x}_i + \varepsilon B) - \sum_J \mathrm{cl}Y_j \bigcap (\overline{y}_j + \varepsilon B) \\ \subset P_k(\overline{x}_k) + \sum_{i \neq k} \mathrm{cl}P_i(\overline{x}_i)) - \sum_j Y_j. \end{aligned} \tag{10}$$

We emphasize that $(**)$ not just more symmetric than (10) but actually weaker as is seen from the following simple example.

Example. Let $X = I\!R^2$,

$$P_1 = \{a = (\alpha_1, \alpha_2) : \alpha_1\alpha_2 = 0 \quad \& \quad \text{either} \quad \alpha_1 \geq 0 \quad \text{or} \quad 0 < \alpha_2 \neq 2^{-k}, \; k = 1, 2, \ldots\},$$

$$P_2 = \{a = (\alpha_1, \alpha_2) : \alpha_1\alpha_2 = 0 \quad \& \quad \text{either} \quad \alpha_1 \leq 0 \quad \text{or} \quad 0 < \alpha_2 \neq 2^{-k}, \; k = 1, 2, \ldots\}.$$

Then

$$\mathrm{cl}P_1 + \mathrm{cl}P_2 = \{a = (\alpha_1, \alpha_2) : \quad \alpha_2 \geq 0\};$$

$$\mathrm{cl}P_1 + P_2 = (\mathrm{cl}P_1 + \mathrm{cl}P_2) \setminus \{a = (\alpha_1, \alpha_2) : \alpha_1 > 0, \; \alpha_2 = 2^{-k}, k = 1, 2, \ldots\};$$

$$P_1 + \mathrm{cl}P_2 = (\mathrm{cl}P_1 + \mathrm{cl}P_2) \setminus \{a = (\alpha_1, \alpha_2) : \alpha_1 < 0, \; \alpha_2 = 2^{-k}, k = 1, 2, \ldots\}.$$

Thus $a + \mathrm{cl}P_1 + \mathrm{cl}P_2 \not\subset P_i + \mathrm{cl}P_{3-i}$ for any $a \in I\!R^2$ and either $i = 1$ or $i = 2$ but

$$(0, \beta) + \mathrm{cl}P_1 + \mathrm{cl}P_2 \subset (P_1 + \mathrm{cl}P_2) \bigcup (\mathrm{cl}P_1 + P_2)$$

whenever $\beta > 0$.

References

1. Aussel, D., Corvellec, J.-N., Lassonde, M.: Mean value property and subdifferential criteria for lower semicontinuous functions. Trans. Am. Math. Soc. **347**, 4147–4161 (1995)
2. Aussel, D., Corvellec, J.-N., Lassonde, M.: Nonsmooth constrained optimization and multidirectional mean value inequalities. SIAM J. Optimization **9**, 690–706 (1999)
3. Bonnisseau, J.-M., Cornet, B.: Valuation equilibrium and Pareto optimum in nonconvex economies. J. Math. Econ. **17**, 293–308 (1988)
4. Borwein, D., Borwein, J.M., Wang, X.: Approximate subgradient and coderivatives in $I\!R^n$, Set-valued Anal. **4**, 375–398 (1996)
5. Borwein, J.M., Joffre, A.: Nonconvex separation theorem in Banach spaces. J. Oper. Res. Appl. Math. **48**, 169–180 (1998)
6. Borwein, J.M., Lucet, Y., Mordukhovich, B.S.: Compactly epi-Lipschitzian convex sets and functions in normed spaces. J. Convex Anal. **7**, 375–393 (2000)
7. Borwein, J.M., Strojwas, H.: Tangential approximations. Nonlinear Anal. Theory Methods Appl. **9**, 1347–1366 (1985)
8. Borwein, J.M., Wang, X.: Lipschitz functions with maximal Clarke subdifferentials are generic. Proc. Am. Math. Soc. **128**, 3221–3229 (2000)

9. Borwein, J.M., Zhu, J.: Techniques of variational analysis. CMS Books in Mathematics, vol. 20. Berlin: Springer 2006
10. Cornet, B.: The second welfare theorem in non-convex economies. CORE discussion paper 8630 (1986)
11. Correa, R., Joffré, A., Thibault, L.: Subdifferential monotonicity as characterization of convex functions. Numer. Funct. Ana. Optimization **15**, 1167–1183 (1994)
12. Fabian, M.: Subdifferentiability and trustworthiness in light of the new variational principle of Borwein and Preiss. Acta Univ. Carolinae **30**, 51–56 (1989)
13. Hamano, T.: On the non-existence of the marginal cost price equilibrium and the Ioffe normal cone. Z. Nationalökonomie **50**, 47–53 (1989)
14. Ioffe, A.D.: Sous-différentielles approchées des fonctions numériques. C. R. Acad. Sci. Paris **292** (1981), 675–678
15. Ioffe, A.D.: On subdifferentiability spaces. Ann. N.Y. Acad. Sci. **410**, 107–121 (1983)
16. Ioffe, A.D.: Approximate subdifferentials and applications 2. Mathematika **33**, 111–128 (1986)
17. Ioffe, A.D.: On the local surjection property. Nonlinear Anal. Theory Methods Appl. **11**, 565–592 (1987)
18. Ioffe, A.D.: Fuzzy principles and characterization of trustworthiness. Set-valued Anal. **6**, 265–276 (1998)
19. Ioffe, A.D.: Codirectional compactness, metric regularity and subdifferential calculus. In: Thera, M. (ed.): Constructive, experimental and nonlinear analysis, CMS Conference Proceeding, vol. 27, pp. 123–165 (2000)
20. Ioffe, A.D.: Metric regularity and subdifferential calculus. Uspehi Mat. Nauk **55**(3), 103–162 (2000) (in Russian), English translation: Russian Math. Surveys **55**(3), 501–558 (2000)
21. Joffre, A.: A second welfare theorem in nonconvex economies. In: Thera, M. (ed.): Constructive, experimental and nonlinear analysis, CMS Conference Proceeding, vol. 27, pp. 175–184 (2000)
22. Katriel, G.: Are the approximate and the Clarke subgradients generically equal? J. Math. Anal. Appl. **193**, 588–593 (1995)
23. Khan, M.A.: Ioffe's normal cone and foundations of welfare economics. The infinite dimensional theory. J. Math. Anal. Appl. **161**, 284–298 (1991)
24. Khan, M.A.: The Mordukhovich normal cone and foundations of welfare economics. J. Public Econ. Theory **1**, 309–338 (1999)
25. Khan, M.A., Vohra, R.: An extension of the second welfare theorem to economies with non-convexities and public goods. Q. J. Econ. **102**, 223–245 (1987)
26. Lassonde, M.: First order rules for nonsmooth constrained optimization. Nonlinear Anal. Theory Methods Appl. **44** (2001), 1031–1056
27. Mordukhovich, B.S.: Metric approximations and necessary conditions for optimality for general classes of nonsmooth optimization problems. Dokl. Acad. Nauk SSSR **254** (1980), 1072–1076
28. Mordukhovich, B.S.: Abstract extremal principle with applications to wellfare economics. J. Math. Anal. Appl. **251**, 187–216 (2000)
29. Mordukhovich, B.S.: Variational analysis and generalized differentiation. Berlin: Springer 2005

30. Penot, J.-P.: The compatibility with order of some subdifferentials. Positivity **6**, 413–432 (2002)
31. Rockafellar, R.T.: Maximal monotone relations and the second derivatives of nonsmooth functions. Ann. Inst. H. Poincaré. Analyse Non-Linéaire **2**, 167–184 (1985)
32. Zhu, Q.J.: The equivalence of several basic theorems for subdifferentials. Set-valued Anal. **6**, 171–185 (1998)

Adv. Math. Econ. 12, 97–127 (2009)

Advances in
MATHEMATICAL
ECONOMICS

Smooth feasible solutions to a dual Monge–Kantorovich problem with applications to best approximation and utility theory in mathematical economics

Vladimir L. Levin*

Central Economics and Mathematics Institute of the Russian Academy of Sciences, Nakhimovskii Prospect 47, 117418 Moscow, Russia
(e-mail: vl_levin@cemi.rssi.ru)

Received: January 21, 2008
Revised: October 9, 2008

JEL classification: C65

Mathematics Subject Classification (2000): 46N10, 41A50, 91B16

Abstract. Given a (closed or open) subset X in $\mathbb{R}^n$, which is stable with respect to shifts in positive directions, we consider inequalities $u(x) - u(y) \leq c(x, y), x, y \in X$, and for a wide class of functions c on $X \times X$, derive a smooth solution to these inequalities from a Lebesgue measurable one. Applications are given to a best approximation problem and to several problems of mathematical economics relating to preferences that admit smooth (or Lipschitz continuous) utility functions, smooth-utility-rational choice, and smooth representations of interval orders.

Key words: axioms of revealed preference, dual Monge–Kantorovich problem, exact solutions to a best approximation problem, Lipschitz continuous and smooth utility functions, preference, representations of interval orders, smooth-utility-rational choice, strengthened acyclicity assumption

* Supported in part by Russian Foundation for Basic Research (grant 07-01-00048) and by Russian Leading Scientific School Support Programme (grant NSh-929.2008.6).

DOI: 10.1007/978-4-431-92935-2_4,

1. Introduction

This paper is concerned with the existence of smooth feasible solutions to dual Monge–Kantorovich problem with given marginal difference on some particular subsets X in $\mathbb{R}^n$. We develop a method that enables us to derive smooth solutions from Lebesgue measurable ones. This method was already used in [35–37] in connection with some problems of best approximation theory and of utility theory. In the present paper, we consider it in general setting and give further applications.[1]

Let X be a separable metrizable topological space. Given a cost function $c : X \times X \to \mathbb{R} \cup \{+\infty\}$ and two positive finite Borel measures σ_1 and σ_2 on X with $\sigma_1 X = \sigma_2 X$, the Monge–Kantorovich mass transportation problem (MKP) with a cost function c and a marginal difference $\rho = \sigma_1 - \sigma_2$ is to minimize the functional

$$c(\mu) := \int_{X\times X} c(x, y)\, \mu(d(x, y))$$

over the set of positive Borel measures μ on $X \times X$ satisfying $\pi_1\mu - \pi_2\mu = \sigma_1 - \sigma_2$ where $\pi_1\mu$ and $\pi_2\mu$ are the marginals of μ: for every Borel set $B \subset X$, $\pi_1\mu(B) = \mu(B \times X)$, $\pi_2\mu(B) = \mu(X \times B)$. It is an infinite linear program, and the dual problem is to maximize the functional

$$\rho(u) := \int_X u(x)\, \rho(dx)$$

over the constraint set $Q(c)$ of bounded continuous functions $u : X \to \mathbb{R}$ satisfying

$$u(x) - u(y) \le c(x, y) \tag{1}$$

for all $x, y \in X$. Every $u \in Q(c)$ may be considered thus as a feasible solution to this dual linear program.

For the first time, MKP was posed by Kantorovich, who studied duality of two problems in the case that (X, d) is a metric compact space and $c = d$; see [11–15]. In that case, $Q(c)$ is the set $Lip_1(X, d)$ of Lipschitz continuous functions on (X, d) with the Lipschitz constant $L \le 1$, and the above-posed mass transportation problem is equivalent to a different variant of MKP, with given marginals [14, 15]. The latter consists in minimizing $c(\mu)$ subject to $\pi_1\mu = \sigma_1$, $\pi_2\mu = \sigma_2$, and it is a relaxation of the Monge "excavation and embankments" problem [42].

Duality for both variants of MKP with arbitrary continuous cost functions on (not necessarily metrizable) compact topological spaces is studied since

[1] Some results of this paper are announced without proofs in [38].

1974; see [17, 18, 20].[2] Notice that the term itself, *Monge–Kantorovich problem*, has appeared in 1970s (see [17, 46]) in connection with both variants of MKP.[3] In [22,25,26,31,39],[4] more general (topological and non-topological) spaces X were considered and duality theory for both variants of MKP with a general (discontinuous) cost function was developed.

In this paper, we don't deal with the Monge–Kantorovich duality as such. Properties of the dual constraint set $Q(c)$ and especially conditions for it to be non-empty is the only thing that will be needed to us. Also we will consider the set $Q_0(c)$ of all functions $u : X \to \mathbb{R}$ satisfying (1) and the set $Q(c; \mathcal{L}^\infty(X))$ of bounded Lebesgue measurable functions satisfying (1).[5] Properties of these and similar sets and conditions for them to be non-empty were studied earlier in connection with various generalizations and applications of MKP (see [23, 26–29, 32, 33, 35, 36]).

An important role in study of such sets is played by reduced cost functions [19, 20, 39]. Given a cost function $c : X \times X \to \mathbb{R} \cup \{+\infty\}$, the *reduced cost function* c_* is defined as follows:

$$c_*(x, y) := \min\left(c(x, y), \inf_m \inf_{x^1,\dots,x^m} \sum_{i=1}^{m+1} c(x^{i-1}, x^i)\right), \tag{2}$$

where $x^0 = x$, $x^{m+1} = y$. Clearly, it turns into

$$\begin{aligned} c_*(x, y) :&= \inf_m \inf\left\{\sum_{i=1}^{m+1} c(x^{i-1}, x^i) : x^i \in X, x^0 = x, x^{m+1} = y\right\} \\ &= \lim_{m\to\infty} \inf\left\{\sum_{i=1}^{m+1} c(x^{i-1}, x^i) : x^i \in X, x^0 = x, x^{m+1} = y\right\} \end{aligned} \tag{3}$$

when c vanishes on the diagonal: $c(x, x) = 0 \quad \forall x \in X$. Clearly, $c_* \le c$ and c_* satisfies the triangle inequality: for every $x, y, z \in X$,

$$c_*(x, y) + c_*(y, z) \ge c_*(x, z)$$

---

[2] In general case, two variants of MKP, with a given marginal difference and with given marginals, are not equivalent.

[3] For the first time, this word combination as a title of a paper has appeared in [19, 20].

[4] Also see [44, Chap. 4] where some results of [22, 23, 25, 26, 39] are presented.

[5] Here, $\mathcal{L}^\infty(X)$ stands for the Banach space of bounded Lebesgue measurable functions (Lebesgue equivalent functions are not identified) with the uniform norm $\|u\|_{\mathcal{L}^\infty(X)} = \sup_{x\in X} |u(x)|$. The classical Lebesgue space $L^\infty(X)$ is naturally isometric to its factor-space: $L^\infty(X) = \mathcal{L}^\infty(X)/\mathcal{N}_0$ where $\mathcal{N}_0$ is a subspace in $\mathcal{L}^\infty(X)$ consisting of Lebesgue negligible functions.

(we assume, by definition, that $+\infty + (-\infty) = +\infty$). Also, it follows from the above definition that: (1) $Q(c) = Q(c_*)$, (2) if c_* is bounded continuous and vanishes on the diagonal then $Q(c)$ is non-empty and $c_*(x, y) = \sup_{u \in Q(c)}(u(x) - u(y))$. Similar facts hold for $Q_0(c)$ and $Q(c; \mathcal{L}^\infty(X))$; see [35, 36] for details.

The paper consists of five sections. In §2 we suppose that $X \subset \mathbb{R}^n$ is closed or open and stable with respect to shifts in positive directions (i.e. $x \in X,\ z \in \mathbb{R}^n_+ \Rightarrow x + z \in X$). We prove a theorem on the existence of smooth functions in $Q(c)$ for some particular class of cost functions c. The rest of the paper is devoted to applications of this existence theorem in approximation theory and in utility theory.

In §3, we deal with the following best approximation problem [35, 36]. Given a function $f \in C_b(X \times X)$, one has to approximate it by functions h_u from the subspace

$$H = \{h_u(x, y) = u(x) - u(y) : u \in C_b(X)\} \subset C_b(X \times X),$$

where C_b stands for the Banach space of bounded continuous real-valued functions on the corresponding topological space. The optimal value of this problem is thus

$$m(f; H) := \inf_{h_u \in H} \|f - h_u\| = \inf_{u \in C_b(X)} \sup_{x, y \in X} |f(x, y) - u(x) + u(y)|,$$

and u proves to be an exact solution to the problem if and only if $u \in Q(\varphi)$ where $\varphi = \min(f(x, y), -f(y, x)) + m(f; h)$ [36, Lemma 1]. Basing on this fact, along with relation $Q(\varphi; \mathcal{L}^\infty(X)) \neq \varnothing$ (see [36, Lemma 2]), and applying the theorem of §2, we generalize our previous results [36, Theorems 3 and 4] on the existence of smooth exact solutions to the best approximation problem.

§4 is devoted to several aspects of utility theory. Given a separable metric space (X, d), by a preference on it we mean any binary relation $\preceq$ (in general, neither transitivity nor reflexivity of $\preceq$ is required). According with the Debreu theorem [5, 6], any closed total preorder $\preceq$ is generated by a continuous utility function. In [21, 23, 24] the existence of continuous utility functions was established for several classes of closed non-total preorders. More general (non-total and non-transitive) preferences that admit d-Lipschitz continuous utility functions were completely characterized in [28] in terms of some strengthened acyclicity assumption. In §4.1 we obtain further results in that direction including a jointly Lipschitz continuous utility theorem for a varying preference $\preceq_\omega$ depending on a parameter ω.

In §4.2, we deal with preferences on subsets of $\mathbb{R}^n$. Conditions for the existence of a smooth utility function based on manifold theory may be found in [41][6] in the case that X is open in $\mathbb{R}^n$ while $\preceq$ is a locally non-satiated closed total preorder. In [37] we have proved the existence of smooth utility functions for a class of closed (non-total) preorders on subsets $X \subset \mathbb{R}^n$ that are stable with respect to shifts in positive directions. This class of preorders is given by the condition that adding one and the same positive vector to each of two comparable alternatives cannot affect the preference relation between them. For $X = \mathbb{R}^n$ a close class of total preorders was considered earlier in connection with social choice problems; see [9, 43] and references therein. Also, in [37] we have proved the existence of universal smooth utilities for preferences depending on a parameter. Basing on the existence theorem from §2, we now extend the approach of [37] to a broader class of preferences and prove the existence of smooth utility functions (and smooth joint utilities) u satisfying $\|\nabla u(x)\| \leq 1, x \in X$.

In §4.3, we deal with rationalizable choice functions. Suppose that $\mathcal{M}$ is a family of non-empty subsets in a separable metric space (X, d), and in each $M \in \mathcal{M}$ a certain subset $\gamma(M) \subset M$ is chosen. The problem is to find conditions on a choice function γ that ensure the existence of utility function $u : X \to \mathbb{R}$ that has nice properties (such as continuity, smoothness, monotonicity, concavity and so on) and rationalizes the choice:

$$\gamma(M) = \{x \in M : u(x) = \max_{y \in M} u(y)\}, \quad M \in \mathcal{M}.$$

Originally, the rational choice problem appeared in demand theory in form of consumer's choice [4, 10]. In this setting, $X \subset \mathbb{R}^n_+$ is a commodity space, and $\mathcal{M} = \{M_{p,I} : p \in \mathbb{R}^n_+, I \in \mathbb{R}_+\}$, where p is the price vector, I is the consumer's wealth, and $M_{p,I} = \{x \in X : px \leq I\}$ is the consumer's budget set. Later, various aspects of general rational choice theory were developed by many authors; see, e.g. [16, 45]. An important role here is played by intensifications of the Houthakker strong axiom of revealed preference.[7] Following [28, Corollary 2], we give a criterion for a choice function to be d-Lipschitz-utility-rational. We show further that:

(a) If X is closed or open in $\mathbb{R}^n$, γ satisfies the strengthened axiom of revealed preference, and X, $\mathcal{M}$, γ are stable with respect to shifts in positive directions,[8] then γ is smooth-utility-rational;

---

[6] Also see [2, 7, 8].

[7] As is shown in [28, 34], various versions of the strong axiom of revealed preference mean the validity of some strengthened acyclicity assumption, which, in turn, may be formulated as the inequality $c_*(x, x) \geq 0$, $x \in X$, where c_* is the reduced cost function associated with an appropriate cost function c.

[8] That is, for each $z \in \mathbb{R}^n_+$, $x \in X \Rightarrow (x + z) \in X$ and $M \in \mathcal{M} \Rightarrow [M + z \in \mathcal{M}, \gamma(M + z) \supseteq \gamma(M) + z]$.

(b) If, in addition, $X = \mathbb{R}^n$, $\mathcal{M}$, and γ are stable with respect to shifts by any $z \in \mathbb{R}^n$, and there is a closed convex set $M \in \mathcal{M}$ with non-empty interior and smooth boundary, then γ can be rationalized by a linear function.

§4.4 is devoted to representations of interval orders on a (closed or open) set $X \subset \mathbb{R}^n$ satisfying $X = X + \mathbb{R}^n_+$. We consider an interval order $\succ$ satisfying

$$x \succ y \Leftrightarrow (x + z) \succ (y + z)$$

for each $z \in \mathbb{R}^n_+$, and show that for this class of interval orders, the existence of Lebesgue measurable representations and of smooth ones are equivalent.

§5 is a conclusion.

2. An existence theorem

In what follows, X is a closed (or open) subset in $\mathbb{R}^n$ satisfying $X = X + \mathbb{R}^n_+$ (that is $x \in X$, $z \in \mathbb{R}^n_+$ implies $x + z \in X$), $c : X \times X \to \mathbb{R} \cup \{+\infty\}$ is a Lebesgue measurable bounded below function,

$$Q_0(c) = \{u \in \mathbb{R}^X : u(x) - u(y) \leq c(x, y) \quad \text{for all } x, y \in X\},$$

and

$$Q(c) = Q_0(c) \cap C_b(X),$$

where $C_b(X)$ is the space of all bounded continuous real-valued functions on X.

In this section, we give a sufficient condition for the existence of smooth functions in $Q(c)$.

Let $C^\infty(X) = \bigcap_{r=1}^{\infty} C^r(X)$ where $C^r(X)$ is the class of all r times continuously differentiable real-valued functions on X: $u \in C^r(X)$ if and only if for every $x = (x_1, \ldots, x_n) \in int\, X$ all the partial derivatives $\frac{\partial^k u(x)}{\partial x_1^{k_1} \cdots \partial x_n^{k_n}}$, $k \leq r$, $k_1 + \cdots + k_n = k$, exist and each of them is uniquely continued with preserving continuity to the whole of X.

As is established in [26] (see also [30, 34]), if $c \in C^1(X \times X)$ and $c(x, x) = 0$ for all $x \in X$ then either $Q_0(c)$ is empty or $Q_0(c) = \{u + \alpha : \alpha \in \mathbb{R}\}$, where $u \in C^1(X)$ is a unique, up to a constant term, function satisfying

$$\nabla u(x) = -\nabla_y c(x, y)|_{y=x}, \quad x \in X.$$

Also in these papers conditions on c are given, separately necessary ones and sufficient ones, for $Q_0(c)$ to be non-empty. In contrast to this, in the following theorem $Q_0(c)$ is supposed to be non-empty, and although it may be rather extensive, the existence of a smooth function in it is non-trivial.

Theorem 2.1. *Suppose there is a bounded Lebesgue measurable function u on X satisfying (1), and for every $x, y \in X$ the inequality holds true*

$$\int_0^\infty \cdots \int_0^\infty c(x+z, y+z)\eta(-z)\,dz_1 \cdots dz_n \le c(x, y), \tag{4}$$

where

$$\eta(z) = a_n \prod_{i=1}^{n} h(z_i), \; z = (z_1, \ldots, z_n),$$

$$h(t) = \begin{cases} 0 & \text{for } t \ge 0, \\ \exp(t - \frac{1}{t^2}) & \text{for } t < 0, \end{cases}$$

$$a_n = \left(\int_0^\infty h(-t)\,dt\right)^{-n};$$

then there is a function $v \in Q(c) \cap C^\infty(X)$. Moreover, $u(X) \subset (0, 1)$ implies $v(X) \subset (0, 1)$, and if u is non-decreasing[9] *then v is non-decreasing, too. Also, if X is convex and u is concave (or convex) then one can find $v \in Q(c) \cap C^\infty(X)$ with the same properties.*

Proof. We extend c to the whole of $\mathbb{R}^n \times \mathbb{R}^n$ by setting $c(x, y) = +\infty$ for $(x, y) \notin X \times X$. Now, given a function $u \in \mathcal{L}^\infty(X) \cap Q_0(c)$, we extend it to the whole of $\mathbb{R}^n$ by setting $u(x) = 0$ for $x \notin X$ and observe that so extended function satisfies (1) whenever $(x, y) \in \mathbb{R}^n \times \mathbb{R}^n$. Let us define a function $\Phi(u)$ on $\mathbb{R}^n$ to be the convolution of u and η: for every $x = (x_1, \ldots, x_n) \in \mathbb{R}^n$,

$$\begin{aligned}\Phi(u)(x) := (u * \eta)(x) &= \int_{\mathbb{R}^n} u(x - z)\eta(z)\,dz_1 \cdots dz_n \\ &= \int_{\mathbb{R}^n} u(z)\eta(x - z)\,dz_1 \cdots dz_n.\end{aligned} \tag{5}$$

Since $\eta \in C^\infty(\mathbb{R}^n)$, it follows from (5) that $\Phi(u) \in C^\infty(\mathbb{R}^n)$, and since $\eta(-z) = 0$ for $z \notin \mathbb{R}^n_+$, we get

$$\Phi(u)(x) = \int_{\mathbb{R}^n_+} u(x + z)\eta(-z)\,dz_1 \cdots dz_n. \tag{6}$$

Now, multiplying the inequality

$$u(x + z) - u(y + z) \le c(x + z, y + z), \quad z \in \mathbb{R}^n_+$$

---

[9] That is, $x \le y$ implies $u(x) \le u(y)$, where $x \le y$ means $x_i \le y_i$, $i = 1, \ldots, n$.

by $\eta(-z)$, along with subsequent integrating by the Lebesgue measure on $\mathbb{R}^n_+$, yields

$$\Phi(u)(x) - \Phi(u)(y) \leq \int_{\mathbb{R}^n_+} c(x+z, y+z)\eta(-z)\, dz_1 \cdots dz_n. \qquad (7)$$

We define v to be the restriction of $\Phi(u)$ onto X. Taking into account (4), we derive from (7) that $v \in C^\infty(X) \cap Q_0(c)$.

If $u(X) \subset (0, 1)$ then $v(X) = \Phi(u)(X) \subset (0, 1)$ because of the equality $\int_{\mathbb{R}^n} \eta(z) dz_1 \cdots dz_n = \int_{\mathbb{R}^n_+} \eta(-z)\, dz_1 \cdots dz_n = 1$. If u is non-decreasing then $u(x+z) \leq u(y+z)$ whenever $x \leq y$, $z \in \mathbb{R}^n_+$, and $v(x) \leq v(y)$ by (6). Finally, if X is convex and u is concave (resp. convex) then, by (6), $\Phi(u)$ is concave (resp. convex), as well. □

Remark 2.1 Inequality (4) is obviously satisfied with the equality sign when $c(x, y) = g(x - y)$.

Remark 2.2 Clearly (4) is satisfied when $c(x+z, y+z) \leq c(x, y)$ for all $x, y \in X$, $z \in \mathbb{R}^n_+$. In particular, it is a case where c is non-increasing in (x, y). Moreover, non-increase of the functions on $\mathbb{R}^n_+$, $z \mapsto c(x+z, y+z)$, whenever $x, y \in X$ is sufficient for (4) to be satisfied. Also, (4) is satisfied when $c(x, y) = g(x, y, x - y)$ where $g : X \times X \times \mathbb{R}^n \to \mathbb{R} \cup \{+\infty\}$ and the function $z \mapsto g(x+z, y+z, x-y)$, is non-increasing on $\mathbb{R}^n_+$ whenever $x, y \in X$.

Remark 2.3 A bounded Lebesgue measurable function on X satisfying (1) exists in any of the following cases: (a) (cf. [26, Theorem 9.2]) c satisfies the triangle inequality, vanishes on the diagonal, and is Borel measurable (or its Lebesgue sublevel sets $L(c; \alpha) = \{(x, y) \in X \times X : c(x, y) \leq \alpha\}$, $\alpha \in \mathbb{R}$, are Souslin); (b) (cf. [35, Proposition 11] or [27, Lemma 2]) c_* is bounded above, Borel measurable, and $c_*(x, x) > -\infty$ for all $x \in X$ (or, what is the same, for all positive integers l and all cycles $x^0, \ldots, x^{l-1}, x^l = x_0$ in X, the inequality holds $\sum_{i=1}^{l} c(x^{i-1}, x^i) \geq 0$). Yet one (trivial) case is that c is non-negative.

Remark 2.4 Theorem 2.1 remains true with the same proof when η is an arbitrary $C^\infty(\mathbb{R}^n)$-smooth non-negative function that equals 0 outside $\mathbb{R}^n_-$ and satisfies $\int_{\mathbb{R}^n_+} \eta(-z)\, dz_1 \cdots dz_n = 1$.

3. An application to approximation theory

In this section we deal with the following best approximation problem. Given a closed subset $X \subseteq \mathbb{R}^n$, a subspace H in $C_b(X \times X)$,

$$H := \{h_u(x, y) = u(x) - u(y) : u \in C_b(X)\},$$

and a function $f \in C_b(X \times X)$, one has to find the optimal value

$$m(f; H) := \inf_{h_u \in H} \|f - h_u\| = \inf_{u \in C_b(X)} \sup_{x,y \in X} |f(x, y) - u(x) + u(y)|. \quad (8)$$

Here, given a topological space Y, $C_b(Y)$ denotes the Banach space of bounded continuous real-valued functions on it with the standard uniform norm $\|u\| = \sup_{y \in Y} |u(y)|$.

Definition 3.1. We say a function $u \in C_b(X)$ is an *exact solution* to the best approximation problem (8), if infimum in (8) is attained at it:

$$m(f; H) = \sup_{x,y \in X} |f(x, y) - u(x) + u(y)|.$$

Let us consider the cost function

$$\varphi(x, y) = c(x, y) + m(f; H), \quad (9)$$

where

$$c(x, y) = \min(f(x, y), -f(y, x)). \quad (10)$$

The following two lemmas are particular cases of Lemmas 1 and 2 in [36], where more general spaces X are considered.

Lemma 3.1. *$m(f; H) = \inf\{\alpha \in \mathbb{R}_+ : Q(c + \alpha) \neq \varnothing)\}$, and a function u is an exact solution to (8) if and only if $u \in Q(\varphi)$.*

Lemma 3.2. *$Q(\varphi; \mathcal{L}^\infty(X)) \neq \varnothing$.*

In the proof of Lemma 3.2 the existence of strong lifting of $\mathcal{L}^\infty(X)$ is substantially used; see [36] for details.

The next theorem generalizes Theorem 4 in [36] and Theorem 16 in [35][10] where some sufficient conditions were given for f to be as in the theorem.

Theorem 3.1. *1. Suppose X satisfies $X = X + \mathbb{R}^n_+$ and the function c, as given by (10), satisfies (4); then there exists a function $v \in C^\infty(X)$ which is an exact solution to problem (8).*

2. Suppose that either f is non-positive and satisfies (4) or f is non-negative and $(-f)$ satisfies (4); then c satisfies (4).

[10] See also the first statement of Theorem 3 in [36].

Proof. 1. By Lemma 3.2, $Q(\varphi; \mathcal{L}^\infty(X)) \neq \varnothing$. Since c satisfies inequality (4), the function φ, as given by (9), satisfies it as well. Now, from Theorem 2.1 it follows that there is a function $v \in Q(\varphi) \cap C^\infty(X)$, and applying Lemma 3.1 completes the proof.

2. If f is non-positive then $c(x, y) = f(x, y)$, and if f is non-negative then $c(x, y) = -f(y, x)$, and in both cases the result follows. □

4. Applications to utility theory

4.1. Preferences admitting Lipschitz continuous utility functions

Let X be a metric space with a distance d. Its elements may be considered as states of some system. By a (original) *preference* on X we mean an arbitrary binary relation $\preceq$ (reflexivity and transitivity of $\preceq$ are not supposed): given two states $x, y \in X$, we say that y is preferred to x if $x \preceq y$. We say that y is strictly preferred to x and write it as $x \prec y$ if $x \preceq y$, $\neg(y \preceq x)$.[11]

Besides the original preference $\preceq$ on X, we will consider a revealed (extended) one, $\preceq_*$. It is defined as follows. Given $x, y \in X$, we denote by $T(x, y)$ the set of all chains (finite trajectories) $\tau = (x^1 \to x^2 \to \cdots \to x^m)$ in X leading from x to y ($m = m(\tau)$, $x^1 = x$, $x^m = y$). Every $\tau \in T(x, y)$ is appraised by

$$e(\tau) = \sum_{k=1}^{m} c(x^k, x^{k+1}) = \sum_{k \in J(\tau)} d(x^k, x^{k+1}), \tag{11}$$

where, for any $z, z' \in X$,

$$c(z, z') := \begin{cases} 0 & \text{if } \ z \preceq z', \\ d(z, z') & \text{otherwise,} \end{cases} \tag{12}$$

$J(\tau) = \{k < m = m(\tau) : \neg(x^k \preceq x^{k+1})\}$. A chain $\tau \in T(x, y)$ is considered thus as a trajectory $x = x^1 \to x^2 \to \cdots \to x^m = y$ that starts at x and finishes at y. It comprises $m - 1$ elementary fragments $x^k \to x^{k+1}$, $k = 1, \ldots, m - 1$, and each fragment either improves the state ($x^k \preceq x^{k+1}$) or is a jump aside ($\neg(x^k \preceq x^{k+1})$). The value $e(\tau)$ may be treated as a total payment for moving along the trajectory provided that a displacement $x^k \to x^{k+1}$ improving the state is free while a jump fee equals the distance between the corresponding states, x^k and x^{k+1}. We define

$$x \preceq_* y \Leftrightarrow \inf_{\tau \in T(x,y)} e(\tau) = 0. \tag{13}$$

[11] Writing $\neg(y \preceq x)$ means that $y \preceq x$ fails.

Remark 4.1 (cf. [28, Lemma 1]). Say $\tau \in T(x, y)$ is *regular* if it is of the form $y^0 \to x^1 \to y^1 \to x^2 \to \cdots \to x^m \to y^m \to x^{m+1}$ where $x^k \preceq y^k$, $k = 1, \ldots, m$, $y^0 = x$, $x^{m+1} = y$. Since d satisfies the triangle inequality, it is profitable to replace two neighboring jumps $x^k \to x^{k+1}$ and $x^{k+1} \to x^{k+2}$ with the single one $x^k \to x^{k+2}$, and we derive from (11) that it suffices to take only regular τ in (13). Thus,

$$x \preceq_* y \Leftrightarrow \inf_{\tau \in T_{reg}(x,y)} e(\tau) = 0,$$

where $T_{reg}(x, y)$ is the subset in $T(x, y)$ consisting of regular τ.

It follows from (11), (12), (13) that $\preceq_*$ is a preorder (a reflexive and transitive binary relation) on X. Clearly $x \preceq y \Rightarrow x \preceq_* y$.

Remark 4.2 Notice that

$$\inf_{\tau \in T(x,y)} e(\tau) = \inf_{\tau \in T_{reg}(x,y)} e(\tau) = c_*(x, y), \tag{14}$$

where c_* is the reduced cost function (see (2)) for the cost function c given by (12). The definition of $\preceq_*$, as given by (13), may be then rewritten as

$$x \preceq_* y \Leftrightarrow c_*(x, y) = 0. \tag{15}$$

The preference $\preceq_*$ generates the corresponding strict preference $\prec_*$,

$$x \prec_* y \Leftrightarrow (x \preceq_* y, \neg(y \preceq_* x)).$$

The next result is an immediate consequence of (11), (13), (15).

Lemma 4.1. *The following conditions are equivalent: (a)* $x \prec y \Rightarrow x \prec_* y$, *(b) if* $x \prec y$ *then there is a number* $\delta = \delta(x, y) > 0$ *such that* $e(\tau) > \delta$ *for every (for every regular)* $\tau \in T(y, x)$, *(c)* $x \prec y \Rightarrow c_*(y, x) > 0$.

Definition 4.1. Given a preference $\preceq$ on X, a function $u : X \to \mathbb{R}$ is called a *utility function* for it if for any $x, y \in X$ two implications hold as follows:

$$x \preceq y \Rightarrow u(x) \leq u(y),$$

$$x \prec y \Rightarrow u(x) < u(y).$$

Remark 4.3 Condition (b) of Lemma 4.1 strengthens the acyclicity assumption: if $x \prec y$ then no $\tau = (y = x^1 \to x^2 \to \cdots \to x^m = x) \in T(y, x)$ can exist with $x^k \preceq x^{k+1}$, $k = 1, \ldots, m-1$. Obviously, this acyclicity assumption is necessary for the existence of an utility function for $\preceq$. But it is not sufficient: a simplest counter-example is the standard lexicographical order on $\mathbb{R}^2$ as $\preceq$.

Remark 4.4 An equivalent formulation of the acyclicity assumption is as follows: if $x \prec y$ then $e(\tau) > 0$ for every $\tau \in T(y, x)$.

Definition 4.2. Say a preference $\preceq$ satisfies the *strengthened acyclicity assumption* if statement (b) of Lemma 4.1 holds true, that is for every $x \prec y$ there is a number $\delta = \delta(x, y) > 0$ such that $e(\tau) > \delta$ for all $\tau \in T(y, x)$.

The next lemma says that replacing a given distance by an equivalent one can affect neither the revealed preference $\preceq_*$ nor the strengthened acyclicity assumption.

Lemma 4.2. *Let d^1 and d^2 be equivalent distances on X, i.e. there are positive constants A, B such that $Ad^2(x, y) \le d^1(x, y) \le Bd^2(x, y)$ for all $x, y \in X$. Consider two cost functions, c^1 and c^2, that answer d^1 and d^2 according to (12); then for any $x, y \in X$ the equivalence holds true*

$$c_*^1(x, y) = 0 \Leftrightarrow c_*^2(x, y) = 0,$$

and both the preorder $\preceq_*$ (see (13) or (15)) and the strengthened acyclicity assumption don't depend on what of two distances is used.

Proof. For any $x, y \in X$ we consider two functions on $T(y, x)$, e^1 and e^2, given by (11) and responding to c^1 and c^2 respectively. Clearly, one has $Ac^2(x, y) \le c^1(x, y) \le Bc^2(x, y)$; therefore, $Ac_*^2(x, y) \le c_*^1(x, y) \le Bc_*^2(x, y)$ and, for every $\tau \in T(y, x)$, $Ae^2(\tau) \le e^1(\tau) \le Be^2(\tau)$, and the result follows. □

Definition 4.3. Given a metric space (X, d), a function $u : X \to \mathbb{R}$ is called *d-Lipschitz continuous* if $|u(x) - u(y)| \le Ld(x, y)$ for all $x, y \in X$ where $L > 0$. The class of functions satisfying this inequality will be denoted as $Lip_L(X, d)$.

Clearly, $Lip_L(X, d) = Lip_1(X, Ld)$, that is one can assume $L = 1$ by passing to an equivalent distance.

We shall need the following simple lemma.

Lemma 4.3. *For any $a, b, c \in \mathbb{R}_+$, one has*

$$a - b \le c \Rightarrow \frac{a}{1+a} - \frac{b}{1+b} \le \frac{c}{1+c}, \tag{16}$$

and for any $a, b \in \mathbb{R}$,

$$a \le b \Leftrightarrow \frac{a}{1+|a|} \le \frac{b}{1+|b|}, \quad a < b \Leftrightarrow \frac{a}{1+|a|} < \frac{b}{1+|b|}. \tag{17}$$

The next result is a direct consequence of Lemma 4.3.

Corollary 4.1. *If $u : X \to \mathbb{R}$ is a non-negative utility function for $\preceq$ and $u \in Lip_1(X, d)$, then the function $v = \frac{u}{1+u}$ has the same properties as u, and $v(X) \subset [0, 1]$.*

Theorem 4.1 (cf. [28, Theorem 1]). *Suppose that $\preceq$ is a preference on a separable metric space (X, d). The following statements are then equivalent: (a) there exists a (non-negative) d-Lipschitz continuous utility function for $\preceq$; (b) $\preceq$ satisfies the strengthened acyclicity assumption.*

Proof. (a)⇒(b) Suppose u is a d-Lipschitz continuous utility function for $\preceq$. We will assume by passing, if needed, to $L^{-1}u$ that $u \in Lip_1(X, d)$. Then, by (12), $u \in Q_0(c)$. If now $x \prec y$, then $\delta(x, y) := u(y) - u(x) > 0$, and we get, for every $\tau = (y = x^1, x^2, \dots, x^m = x) \in T(y, x)$,

$$e(\tau) = \sum_{k=1}^{m-1} c(x^k, x^{k+1}) \geq \sum_{k=1}^{m-1} (u(x^k) - u(x^{k+1})) = u(y) - u(x) = \delta(x, y) > 0.$$

(b)⇒(a) Since, by implication (b)⇒(a) of Lemma 4.1, $x \prec y \Rightarrow x \prec_* y$, every utility function for $\preceq_*$ will be a utility function for $\preceq$. Therefore, it suffices to present a (non-negative) d-Lipschitz continuous utility function for $\preceq_*$. Let us consider the function

$$u(x) = \sum_{k=1}^{\infty} \frac{1}{2^k} \frac{c_*(x, x^k)}{1 + c_*(x, x^k)},$$

where the sequence (x^k) is dense in X. Since c_* satisfies the triangle inequality, one has $c_*(x, x^k) - c_*(y, x^k) \leq c_*(x, y)$, $k = 1, 2, \dots$. Suppose $x \preceq_* y$, then, by (15), $c_*(x, y) = 0$, and we get $c_*(x, x^k) \leq c_*(y, x^k)$, $k = 1, 2, \dots$. Now, taking into account equivalence (17) from Lemma 4.3, one gets $u(x) \leq u(y)$. Furthermore, if $x \prec y$, then $c_*(y, x) > 0$ by Lemma 4.1, and applying the triangle inequality yields

$$-d(x, x^k) \leq -c_*(x, x^k) \leq c_*(y, x) - c_*(y, x^k) \leq c_*(x^k, x) \leq d(x^k, x). \tag{18}$$

Let us chose a subsequence (x^{k_n}) that tends to x; then

$$\lim_{n \to \infty} d(x, x^{k_n}) = \lim_{n \to \infty} d(x^{k_n}, x) = 0,$$

and we derive from (18) that

$$\lim_{n \to \infty} c_*(x, x^{k_n})) = 0, \tag{19}$$

$$\lim_{n \to \infty} c_*(y, x^{k_n}) = c_*(y, x)) > 0. \tag{20}$$

We see from (19), (20) that $c_*(x, x^{k_n}) < c_*(y, x^{k_n})$ for large n, and since $c_*(x, x^k) \le c_*(y, x^k)$ for all k, we derive from (17) that $u(x) < u(y)$.

It remains to show that u is d-Lipschitz continuous. We have $c_*(x, x^k) - c_*(y, x^k) \le c_*(x, y) \le c(x, y) \le d(x, y)$ for any $x, y \in X$, and applying implication (16) from Lemma 4.3 with $a = c_*(x, x^k)$, $b = c_*(y, x^k)$, and $c = d(x, y)$ yields

$$\frac{c_*(x, x^k)}{1 + c_*(x, x^k)} - \frac{c_*(y, x^k)}{1 + c_*(y, x^k)} \le \frac{d(x, y)}{1 + d(x, y)}.$$

This implies $u(x) - u(y) \le \frac{d(x,y)}{1+d(x,y)} \le d(x, y)$, that is $u \in Lip_1(X, d)$. □

Corollary 4.2. *Suppose $\preceq$ is a preference on a separable metrizable space X, the following statements are then equivalent: (a) there exists a (non-negative bounded) continuous utility function for $\preceq$; (b) there exists a bounded distance*[12] *d on X such that d determines topology of X and $\preceq$ satisfies the strengthened acyclicity assumption with respect to d.*

Proof. (a)⇒(b) Suppose u is a continuous utility function for $\preceq$. We will assume by passing, if needed, to $\frac{1}{2} + \frac{1}{2}\frac{u}{1+|u|}$ that u is non-negative and bounded. Let d_1 be an arbitrary distance that determines topology of X, and

$$d(x, y) := |u(x) - u(y)| + \frac{d_1(x, y)}{1 + d_1(x, y)}.$$

Clearly, $u \in Lip_1(X, d)$, and d is a bounded distance determining topology of X. Statement (b) follows then from Theorem 4.1.

(b)⇒(a) This follows directly from Theorem 4.1. □

Theorem 4.2. *Suppose that Ω is a metrizable topological space, (X, d_X) is a separable metric space, and for every $\omega \in \Omega$ a preference $\preceq_\omega$ is given on X. Let d be a distance on $\Omega \times X$ consistent with the product topology and satisfying $d((\omega, x), (\omega, y)) = d_X(x, y)$ for all $\omega \in \Omega$, $x, y \in X$. The following statements are then equivalent: (a) there exists a function $u : \Omega \times X \to [0, 1]$ such that $u \in Lip_1(\Omega \times X, d)$ and, for every $\omega \in \Omega$, $u(\omega, \cdot)$ belongs to $Lip_1(X, d_X)$ and is a utility function for $\preceq_\omega$; (b) the preference $\preceq$ on $\Omega \times X$, determined by*

$$(\omega, x) \preceq (\omega', y) \Leftrightarrow \omega = \omega',\ x \preceq_\omega y, \tag{21}$$

satisfies the strengthened acyclicity assumption.

---

[12] A distance d is called bounded if there is $C > 0$ such that $d(x, y) \le C$ for all $x, y \in X$.

Remark 4.5 Obviously, if $\preceq$ satisfies the strengthened acyclicity assumption then, for every $\omega \in \Omega$, $\preceq_\omega$ satisfies it, too.

Proof. (a)$\Rightarrow$(b) It follows from the definition of the preference $\preceq$ on $\Omega \times X$ (see (21)) that u is a utility function for $\preceq$. Then $u(\omega, x) - u(\omega', y) \leq 0$ if $(\omega, x) \preceq (\omega', y)$, and since $u(\omega, x) - u(\omega', y) \leq d((\omega, x), (\omega', y))$ for all $(\omega, x), (\omega', y) \in \Omega \times X$, one gets $u(\omega, x) - u(\omega', y) \leq c((\omega, x), (\omega', y))$ for all $(\omega, x), (\omega', y) \in \Omega \times X$, where

$$c((\omega, x), (\omega', y)) := \begin{cases} 0 & \text{if } \omega = \omega',\ x \preceq_\omega y, \\ d((\omega, x), (\omega', y)) & \text{otherwise.} \end{cases} \tag{22}$$

If now $(\omega, x) \prec (\omega', y)$ then $\omega = \omega'$ and $x \prec_\omega y$, hence $u(\omega, x) < u(\omega, y)$. Then, for $\delta(x, y) := u(\omega, y) - u(\omega, x) > 0$ and any chain (trajectory) in $\Omega \times X$ leading from $(\omega, y) = (\omega^1, x^1)$ to $(\omega, x) = (\omega^m, x^m)$, $\tau = ((\omega^1, x^1) \to (\omega^2, x^2) \to \cdots \to (\omega^m, x^m))$, one has

$$\begin{aligned} e(\tau) &= \sum_{k=1}^{m-1} c((\omega^k, x^k), (\omega^{k+1}, x^{k+1})) \geq \sum_{k=1}^{m-1} \left(u(\omega^k, x^k) - u(\omega^{k+1}, x^{k+1})\right) \\ &= u(\omega, y) - u(\omega, x) = \delta(x, y), \end{aligned}$$

and the strengthened acyclicity assumption is thus established.[13]

(b)$\Rightarrow$(a) Consider on $(\Omega \times X) \times (\Omega \times X)$ the cost function c as given by (22) and the corresponding reduced cost function c_*, take in X a dense countable set $\{x^1, x^2, \cdots\}$, and let

$$u(\omega, x) := \sum_{k=1}^{\infty} \frac{c_*((\omega, x), (\omega, x^k))}{2^k \left(1 + c_*((\omega, x), (\omega, x^k))\right)}. \tag{23}$$

Obviously, $u(X) \subset [0, 1]$. Since c_* satisfies the triangle inequality, one has

$$c_*((\omega, x), (\omega, x^k)) - c_*((\omega', y), (\omega', x^k)) \leq c_*((\omega, x), (\omega', y)).$$

Now, taking into account (16) and arguing as in the proof of Theorem 4.1, (b)$\Rightarrow$(a), one gets

$$\begin{aligned} u(\omega, x) - u(\omega', y) &\leq \sum_{k=1}^{\infty} \frac{c_*((\omega, x), (\omega', y))}{2^k (1 + c_*((\omega, x), (\omega', y)))} \\ &= \frac{c_*((\omega, x), (\omega', y))}{1 + c_*((\omega, x), (\omega', y))}, \end{aligned} \tag{24}$$

---

13 When Ω is separable, the validity of this assumption follows immediately from Theorem 4.1.

and as $c_* \leq c \leq d$, the inequality holds

$$u(\omega, x) - u(\omega', y) \leq \frac{d((\omega, x), (\omega', y))}{1 + d((\omega, x), (\omega', y))} \leq d((\omega, x), (\omega', y))$$

that is $u \in Lip_1(\Omega \times X, d)$ hence $u(\omega, \cdot) \in Lip_1(X, d_X)$. It remains to show that $u(\omega, \cdot)$ is a utility function for $\preceq_\omega$. Let $x \preceq_\omega y$, then $c((\omega, x), (\omega, y)) = 0$; therefore,

$$c_*((\omega, x), (\omega, x^k)) - c_*((\omega, y), (\omega, x^k)) \leq c_*((\omega, x), (\omega, y)) = 0,$$

and we get from (23), along with (17), that $u(\omega, x) \leq u(\omega, y)$. Suppose now that $x \prec_\omega y$, then, by Lemma 4.1, $c_*((\omega, y), (\omega, x)) > 0$. Let us chose a subsequence (x^{k_n}) that tends to x, then $\lim_{n\to\infty} d_X(x, x^{k_n}) = \lim_{n\to\infty} d_X(x^{k_n}, x) = 0$, and applying the triangle inequality gives

$$\begin{aligned} -d_X(x, x^k) &\leq -c_*((\omega, x), (\omega, x^k)) \leq c_*((\omega, y), (\omega, x)) - c_*((\omega, y), (\omega, x^k)) \\ &\leq c_*((\omega, x^k), (\omega, x)) \leq d_X(x^k, x). \end{aligned}$$

It follows that

$$\lim_{n\to\infty} c_*((\omega, x), (\omega, x^{k_n})) = 0, \tag{25}$$

$$\lim_{n\to\infty} c_*((\omega, y), (\omega, x^{k_n})) = c_*((\omega, y), (\omega, x)) > 0, \tag{26}$$

and since $c_*((\omega, x), (\omega, x^k)) \leq c_*((\omega, y), (\omega, x^k))$ for all k, we derive from (25), (26), along with (17), that $u(\omega, x) < u(\omega, y)$. □

Remark 4.6 A similar result on a jointly continuous representation for closed preorders $\preceq_\omega$ was obtained earlier in [21, 26]. For the case of closed total preorders, see also [40].

4.2. Preferences admitting smooth utility functions

In this subsection, we deal with preferences on a subset X of $\mathbb{R}^n$. In what follows, $d_X(x, y) = \|x - y\|$ where $\|\cdot\|$ stands for the Euclidean norm.

Theorem 4.3. *Suppose X is closed or open and satisfies $X + \mathbb{R}^n_+ = X$, $\preceq$ is a preference on X satisfying both the strengthened acyclicity assumption and the implication*

$$x \preceq y \Rightarrow (x + z) \preceq (y + z), \quad \forall z \in \mathbb{R}^n_+; \tag{27}$$

then there is a utility function v for $\preceq$ such that $v \in C^\infty(X)$ and $\|\nabla v(x)\| \leq 1$ for all $x \in X$. If, in addition, $\preceq$ is monotone, i.e. $x \leq y$ implies $x \preceq y$, then v is non-decreasing.

Proof. By Theorem 4.1 and Corollary 4.1, there is a d_X-Lipschitz continuous utility function u for $\preceq$ such that $u(X) \subset (0, 1)$ and $u \in Lip_1(X, d_X)$. Taking into account (27), along with the equality $d_X(x, y) = \|x - y\|$, we see that $c(x + z, y + z) \leq c(x, y)$ whenever $x, y \in X$, $z \in \mathbb{R}^n_+$. It follows from Remark 2.2 that assumption (4) of Theorem 2.1 is satisfied, and applying the theorem gives us a function $v \in Q(c) \cap C^\infty(X)$ such that $v(X) \subset (0, 1)$. Moreover, as follows from the proof of Theorem 2.1, one can take $v = \Phi(u)|_X$. Since by (12), $c(x, y) \leq d_X(x, y)$, one has $Q(c) \subset Lip_1(X, d_X)$; therefore, $v \in Lip_1(X, d_X)$, and as v is smooth, this may be rewritten as $\|\nabla v(x)\| \leq 1$.

Let us show that v is a utility function for $\preceq$. Suppose that $x \preceq y$, then $x + z \preceq y + z$ for all $z \in \mathbb{R}^n_+$, hence $u(x + z) \leq u(y + z)$, and (6) implies $v(x) = \Phi(u)(x) \leq \Phi(u)(y) = v(y)$. If now $x \prec y$ then $u(x) < u(y)$, and since u is continuous, there is $\delta > 0$ such that $u(x + z) < u(y + z)$ whenever $z \in \mathbb{R}^n_+$, $\|z\| < \delta$. Let $B = \{z = (z_1, \dots, z_n) \in \mathbb{R}^n_+ : \|z\| < \delta\}$. Taking into account that $u(x + z) \leq u(y + z)$ for all $z \in \mathbb{R}^n_+$, it follows

$$\int_B u(x + z)\eta(-z)\, dz_1 \cdots dz_n < \int_B u(y + z)\eta(-z)\, dz_1 \cdots dz_n,$$

$$\int_{\mathbb{R}^n_+ \setminus B} u(x + z)\eta(-z)\, dz_1 \cdots dz_n \leq \int_{\mathbb{R}^n_+ \setminus B} u(y + z)\eta(-z)\, dz_1 \cdots dz_n,$$

and we deduce from (6) that $v(x) = \Phi(u)(x) < \Phi(u)(y) = v(y)$, that is v is a utility function. Finally, notice that for a monotone preference, non-decrease of an utility function is obvious. □

Theorem 4.4. *Suppose that $X + \mathbb{R}^n_+ = X$, Ω is a metrizable topological space, d is a distance on $\Omega \times X$ such as in Theorem 4.2, for every $\omega \in \Omega$ a preference $\preceq_\omega$ satisfying (27) is given on X, and condition (b) of Theorem 4.2 is fulfilled. Then there exists a function $v : \Omega \times X \to \mathbb{R}$ such that: (i) $v \in Lip_1(\Omega \times X, d)$; (ii) for every $\omega \in \Omega$, $v(\omega, \cdot)$ is a utility function for $\preceq_\omega$, $v(\omega, \cdot) \in C^\infty(X)$, and $\|\nabla_x v(\omega, x)\| \leq 1$, $x \in X$.*[14] *If all $\preceq_\omega$ are monotone then all $v(\omega, \cdot)$ are non-decreasing.*

Remark 4.7 A similar result is given in [37] for the case where all $\preceq_\omega$ are preorders.

Proof. By Theorem 4.2, there is a function $u : \Omega \times X \to (0, 1)$ such that $u \in Lip_1(\Omega \times X, d)$ and, for every $\omega \in \Omega$, $u(\omega, \cdot)$ belongs to $Lip_1(X, d_X)$ and is a utility function for $\preceq_\omega$. We define a function $v : \Omega \times X \to (0, 1)$,

$$v(\omega, x) := \Phi(u(\omega, \cdot))(x) = \int_{\mathbb{R}^n_+} u(\omega, x + z)\eta(-z)\, dz_1 \cdots dz_n,$$

[14] $\nabla_x v(\omega, x) := (\partial v(\omega, x)/\partial x_1, \dots, \partial v(\omega, x)/\partial x_n)$.

and arguing as in the proof of Theorem 4.3, convince ourselves that the statement of the theorem holds true. □

Remark 4.8 Both Theorems, 4.3 and 4.4, remain true for $d_X(x, y) = \|x - y\|$ where $\|\cdot\|$ is an arbitrary (non-Euclidean) norm, if one replaces $\|\nabla v(x)\| \leq 1$ (resp. $\|\nabla_x v(\omega, x)\| \leq 1$) with $\|\nabla v(x)\|_* \leq 1$ (resp. $\|\nabla_x v(\omega, x)\|_* \leq 1$) where $\|\cdot\|_*$ is the dual norm.

4.3. Applications to rational choice problem

Let $\mathcal{M}$ be a family of non-empty subsets in a separable metric space (X, d), and suppose that for every $M \in \mathcal{M}$ a certain non-empty subset $\gamma(M) \subset M$ is chosen.

Definition 4.4. A choice function γ is called *utility-rational* if there is a real-valued function u on X such that, for every $M \in \mathcal{M}$,

$$\gamma(M) = \{x \in M : u(x) = \max_{y \in M} u(y)\}. \tag{28}$$

In such a case, one says that u *rationalizes* γ. If, in addition, u is d-Lipschitz continuous or X is a domain in $\mathbb{R}^n$ and u is smooth (C^r), we will say that γ is *d-Lipschitz-utility-rational* or *C^r-smooth-utility-rational.*

Definition 4.5. Say a trajectory $z^0 \to z^1 \to \cdots \to z^m$ in X is *improving* if there are sets $M_i \in \mathcal{M}$, $i = 0, 1, \ldots, m + 1$ such that $z^i \in \gamma(M_i) \cap M_{i+1}$, $i = 0, 1, \ldots, m$.

As is well-known, if γ is utility-rational then it satisfies the *strong axiom of revealed preference*: no improving trajectory $z^0 \to z^1 \to \cdots \to z^m$ can exist in X with $z^0 \in \gamma(M)$ and $z^m \in M \setminus \gamma(M)$, where $M_0 = M_{m+1} = M$. The same assumption for $m = 1$ only is known as the *weak axiom of revealed preference*: no $M, M_1 \in \mathcal{M}$, $z^0 \in \gamma(M) \cap M_1$, $z^1 \in (M \setminus \gamma(M)) \cap \gamma(M_1)$ can exist.

Definition 4.6. We say that γ satisfies the *strengthened axiom of revealed preference*, if for every $M \in \mathcal{M}$, every $x \in M \setminus \gamma(M)$, and every $y \in \gamma(M)$, there exists $\delta = \delta(M, x, y) > 0$ such that given a trajectory $y = y^0 \to x^1 \to y^1 \to \cdots \to x^m \to y^m \to x^{m+1} = x$ with $x^k \in M_k$, $y^k \in \gamma(M_k)$, $M_k \in \mathcal{M}$, $k = 1, \ldots, m$, one has

$$\sum_{k=1}^{m+1} d(y^{k-1}, x^k) \geq \delta. \tag{29}$$

If (29) holds for $m = 1$ only (that is, $d(y, x^1) + d(y^1, x) \geq \delta$ whenever $M, M_1 \in \mathcal{M}$, $x \in M \setminus \gamma(M)$, $x^1 \in M_1$, $y^1 \in \gamma(M_1)$, $y \in \gamma(M)$), we will say that γ satisfies the *strengthened weak axiom of revealed preference.*

Remark 4.9 Given a trajectory $z^0 \to z^1 \to \cdots \to z^m$ where $z^0 \in \gamma(M), z^m \in M \setminus \gamma(M)$, $z^k \in M_{k+1} \cap \gamma(M_k)$, $k = 0, 1, \ldots, m$, and $M_0 = M_{m+1} = M$, one can associate it with the trajectory $y = y^0 \to x^1 \to y^1 \to \cdots \to x^m \to y^m \to x^{m+1} = x$ where $y^0 = x^1 = z^0$, $y^1 = x^2 = z^1, \ldots, y^m = x^{m+1} = z^m = x$. Since $x^k \in M_k$, $y^k \in \gamma(M_k)$ $(k = 1, \ldots, m)$, and $d(y^{k-1}, x^k) = 0$ $(k = 1, \ldots, m+1)$, (29) fails. It follows that the strengthened axiom of revealed preference implies the strong axiom of revealed preference, and the strengthened weak axiom of revealed preference implies the weak axiom of revealed preference.

Lemma 4.4. *The strengthened weak axiom of revealed preference implies that each $\gamma(M)$ is closed in M.*

Proof. Indeed, otherwise there are $x \in M \setminus \gamma(M)$ and a sequence $(z^1, z^2, \ldots) \subset \gamma(M)$ such that $\lim_{k\to\infty} d(x, z^k) = 0$. But this contradicts (29) for $m = 1$, $M_1 = M$, $y = y^0 = x^1 = z^1$, and $y^1 = x^2 = z^k$, where k is large enough. □

Given a choice function γ, we associate it with a preference $\preceq_\gamma$ as follows:

$$x \preceq_\gamma y \Leftrightarrow [x = y \text{ or } \exists M \in \mathcal{M} : x \in M, \; y \in \gamma(M)].$$

Lemma 4.5. *The strengthened axiom of revealed preference for γ implies the strengthened acyclicity assumption for $\preceq_\gamma$.*

Proof. This follows easily from definitions if one takes into account that $x \prec_\gamma y \Rightarrow [\exists M \in \mathcal{M} : x \in M \setminus \gamma(M), \; y \in \gamma(M)]$. □

Lemma 4.6. *Suppose (28) holds, so that γ is utility-rational with a rationalizing function u, then*

$$x \prec_\gamma y \Leftrightarrow [\exists M \in \mathcal{M} : x \in M \setminus \gamma(M), \; y \in \gamma(M)],$$

and u is a utility function for $\preceq_\gamma$.

Proof. Clearly $x \preceq_\gamma y \Leftrightarrow u(x) \le u(y)$. Suppose $x \prec_\gamma y$; then, by the definition of $\preceq_\gamma$, there is a set $M \in \mathcal{M}$ such that $x \in M \setminus \gamma(M)$, $y \in \gamma(M)$. If now $x \in M \setminus \gamma(M)$, $y \in \gamma(M)$ for some $M \in \mathcal{M}$ then, by (28), $u(x) < u(y)$. It follows that no set $M' \in \mathcal{M}$ can exist with the property $y \in M'$, $x \in \gamma(M')$, hence $x \prec_\gamma y$, and u is a utility function for $\preceq_\gamma$. □

The next result is an easy consequence of Theorem 4.1 for the preference $\preceq_\gamma$ if one takes into account Lemmas 4.5 and 4.6.

Theorem 4.5. ([28, Corollary 2]). *The following statements are equivalent: (a) γ is d-Lipschitz-utility-rational; (b) γ satisfies the strengthened axiom of revealed preference.*

Theorem 4.6. *Suppose that X is closed or open in $\mathbb{R}^n$, $X + \mathbb{R}^n_+ = X$, a family $\mathcal{M}$ satisfies*

$$M \in \mathcal{M},\ z \in \mathbb{R}^n_+ \Rightarrow z + M \in \mathcal{M}, \tag{30}$$

a choice function γ satisfies the strengthened axiom of revealed preference, and

$$\gamma(z + M) \supseteq z + \gamma(M), \quad M \in \mathcal{M}, \quad z \in \mathbb{R}^n_+; \tag{31}$$

then there is a function $u \in C^\infty(X)$ that rationalizes γ and satisfies the inequality $\|\nabla u(x)\| \leq 1$, $x \in X$.

Proof. Taking into account that (31) implies (27) for $\preceq_\gamma$, this is a direct consequence of Theorem 4.3 along with Lemma 4.5. □

In the sequel, we will strengthen conditions (30) and (31) as follows:

$$M \in \mathcal{M},\ z \in \mathbb{R}^n,\ z + M \subset X \Rightarrow z + M \in \mathcal{M}, \tag{32}$$

$$M \in \mathcal{M},\ z \in \mathbb{R}^n,\ z + M \in \mathcal{M} \Rightarrow \gamma(z + M) = z + \gamma(M). \tag{33}$$

Notice that (33) may be rewritten equivalently as

$$M \in \mathcal{M},\ z \in \mathbb{R}^n,\ z + M \in \mathcal{M} \Rightarrow \gamma(z + M) \supseteq z + \gamma(M). \tag{34}$$

Indeed, if $M \in \mathcal{M}$ and $z + M \in \mathcal{M}$ then $M = -z + (z + M)$, and (34) implies $\gamma(M) \supseteq -z + \gamma(z + M) \supseteq -z + z + \gamma(M) = \gamma(M)$; therefore, $\gamma(z + M) = z + \gamma(M)$.

Remark 4.10 Suppose $X = \mathbb{R}^n$, $\mathcal{M}$ satisfies (32), and (31) holds with the equality sign, then (33) is satisfied. Indeed, given $M \in \mathcal{M}$ and $z \in \mathbb{R}^n$, we find $z^0 \in \mathbb{R}^n_+$, such that $(z^0 + z) \in \mathbb{R}^n_+$, and take $M_0 = -z^0 + M$. Then $M_0 \in \mathcal{M}$, $M = z^0 + M_0$, $z + M = (z + z^0) + M_0$, and (31) implies $\gamma(M) = z^0 + \gamma(M_0)$, $\gamma(z + M) = z + z^0 + \gamma(M_0) = z + \gamma(M)$.

We now show that if $X = \mathbb{R}^n$ and conditions (32), (33) are satisfied then in the strengthened axiom of revealed preference (see Definition 4.6) it suffices to consider a particular class of trajectories as follows.

Definition 4.7. Given $M \in \mathcal{M}$, $x \in M \setminus \gamma(M)$, and $y \in \gamma(M)$, we say a trajectory $y = y^0 \to x^1 \to y^1 \to \cdots \to x^m \to y^m \to x^{m+1} = x$ is *strongly regular* if

$$x^{k+1} = y^k \in M_{k+1} \cap \gamma(M_k), \quad k = 0, 1, \ldots, m-1$$

and $y^m \in \gamma(M_m)$, where $M_1, \ldots, M_m \in \mathcal{M}$ and $M_0 = M$. Clearly, for such a trajectory one has $\sum_1^{m+1} d(y^{k-1}, x^k) = d(y^m, x)$.

Lemma 4.7. *Suppose* $X = \mathbb{R}^n$ *and conditions (32), (33) are satisfied, the following statements are then equivalent: (a) the strengthened axiom of revealed preference holds; (b) for every* $M \in \mathcal{M}$, *every* $x \in M \setminus \gamma(M)$, *and every* $y \in \gamma(M)$ *there is a number* $\delta = \delta(M, x, y) > 0$ *such that* $d(y^m, x) \geq \delta$ *whenever* $y = y^0 \to x^1 \to y^1 \to \cdots \to x^m \to y^m \to x^{m+1} = x$ *is a strongly regular trajectory.*

Proof. It suffices to show that $(b) \Rightarrow (a)$. To this end, take $M \in \mathcal{M}$, $x \in M \setminus \gamma(M)$, $y \in \gamma(M)$, and consider an arbitrary trajectory

$$y = y^0 \to x^1 \to y^1 \to \cdots \to x^m \to y^m \to x^{m+1} = x$$

with $x^k \in M_k$, $y^k \in \gamma(M_k)$, $k = 1, \ldots, m$. The result will follow if we find a strongly regular trajectory

$$y = \overline{y}^0 \to \overline{x}^1 \to \overline{y}^1 \to \cdots \to \overline{x}^m \to \overline{y}^m \to x \tag{35}$$

satisfying $\sum\limits_{k=1}^{m+1} d(y^{k-1}, x^k) \geq d(\overline{y}^m, x)$. We define $\overline{y}^k = \overline{x}^{k+1} = z^k$ for $k = 1, \ldots, m-1$ and $\overline{y}^m = z^m$, where $z^0 = y^0 = y$ and $z^k = \sum\limits_{j=0}^{k} y^j - \sum\limits_{j=1}^{k} x^j$, $k = 1, \ldots, m$. Since $x^1 \in M_1$ and $y = y^0 \in \gamma(M)$, we have $z^0 = y^0 = x^1 + (y^0 - x^1) \in \gamma(M) \cap (M_1 + y^0 - x^1)$. Similarly, since $y^k \in \gamma(M_k)$, $z^k = y^k + \sum_{j=1}^{k}(y^{j-1} - x^j) \in \gamma(M_k) + \sum_{j=1}^{k}(y^{j-1} - x^j)$, and since $x^{k+1} \in M_{k+1}$, $z^k = x^{k+1} + \sum_{j=1}^{k+1}(y^{j-1} - x^j) \in M_{k+1} + \sum_{j=1}^{k+1}(y^{j-1} - x^j)$. We derive from (33)

$$z^k \in \gamma(\overline{M}_k) \cap \overline{M}_{k+1}, \quad k = 0, 1, \ldots, m-1,$$

where $\overline{M}_0 = M$ and

$$\overline{M}_k = M_k + \sum_{j=1}^{k}(y^{j-1} - x^j) \in \mathcal{M}, \quad k = 1, \ldots, m.$$

It follows that trajectory (35) is strongly regular, and since $d(\overline{y}^m, x) = d(z^m, x) = \| \sum\limits_{j=1}^{m+1} (y^{j-1} - x^j) \| \leq \sum\limits_{j=1}^{m+1} \|y^{j-1} - x^j\| = \sum\limits_{j=1}^{m+1} d(y^{j-1}, x^j)$, the proof is complete. □

Theorem 4.7. *Suppose* $X = X + \mathbb{R}^n_+$, *conditions (32), (33) are satisfied, and there exist* $M_0 \in \mathcal{M}$ *and* $n+1$ *points in* $\gamma(M_0)$, $y, y^1, y^2, \ldots, y^n$, *such that the interior of* $M_0 \setminus \gamma(M_0)$ *is non-empty and the vectors* $y^1 - y, y^2 - y, \ldots, y^n - y$ *are linearly independent; then the strong axiom of revealed preference fails to be true.*

Proof. First suppose that $X = \mathbb{R}^n$. Given $x \in M_0 \setminus \gamma(M_0)$, one has a representation $x - y = \sum_{i=1}^{n} \alpha_i (y^i - y)$, where the coefficients α_i are uniquely determined. Moreover, since the interior of $M_0 \setminus \gamma(M_0)$ is non-empty, we can find x in $M_0 \setminus \gamma(M_0)$ for which all α_i are rational, so that $\alpha_i = \frac{p_i}{q}$ where $q \geq 1$ and $p_i, i = 1, \ldots, n$, are integers. Suppose for the sake of definiteness, that there are both positive and negative p_i,[15] and by passing, if needed, to a new enumeration, assume $p_i > 0$ for $1 \leq i \leq r$, $p_i < 0$ for $r + 1 \leq i \leq m$, and $p_i = 0$ for $m + 1 \leq i \leq n$ where $1 \leq r < m \leq n$. We get

$$x = y + \sum_{i=1}^{m} p_i (y^i - y) + (q - 1)(y - x). \tag{36}$$

By letting $p_0 := 0$, $M_0(0) := M_0$, we define the sets

$$M_i(1) = \begin{cases} M_{i-1}(p_{i-1}) + y^i - y & \text{for } 1 \leq i \leq r, \\ M_{i-1}(|p_{i-1}|) + y - y^i & \text{for } r + 1 \leq i \leq m, \\ M_{i-1}(|p_{i-1}|) + y - x & \text{for } i = m + 1, \end{cases}$$

and for $j > 1$,

$$M_i(j) = \begin{cases} M_i(j-1) + y^i - y & \text{for } 1 \leq i \leq r, \\ M_i(j-1) + y - y^i & \text{for } r < i \leq m, \\ M_i(j-1) + y - x & \text{for } i = m + 1. \end{cases}$$

All these sets are shifts of M_0:

$$M_i(j) = M_0 + z^i(j), \tag{37}$$

where

$$z^1(j) = j(y^1 - y), \quad 1 \leq j \leq p_1,$$

$$z^i(j) = \begin{cases} \sum_{k<i} p_k (y^k - y) + j(y^i - y) & \text{for } 1 \leq j \leq p_i, \ 1 < i \leq r, \\ \sum_{k<i} p_k (y^k - y) + j(y - y^i) & \text{for } 1 \leq j \leq |p_i|, \ r + 1 \leq i \leq m, \\ \sum_{k<i} p_k (y^k - y) + j(y - x) & \text{for } 1 \leq j \leq q - 1, \ i = m + 1. \end{cases}$$

Taking into account (32), (33), it follows from (37) that

$$\gamma(M_i(j)) = \gamma(M_0) + z^i(j) \quad \forall (i, j). \tag{38}$$

Let us set

$$y^i(j) = y + z^i(j)$$

[15] The case that all p_i are non-negative or all of them are non-positive is examined similarly.

for $1 \le i \le m$, $1 \le j \le |p_i|$ and for $i = m+1$, $1 \le j \le q-1$. It follows from (38) that $y^i(j) \in \gamma(M_i(j))$ for all i, j, and if $i \le r$ then $y^i(1) = y + z^i(1) = y + z^{i-1}(p_{i-1}) + y^i - y = y^i + z^{i-1}(p_{i-1}) \in \gamma(M_{i-1}(p_{i-1}))$ (for $i = 1$ one has $y^1(1) = y + z^1(1) = y^1 \in \gamma(M_0)$) and, for $1 < j \le p_i$, $y^i(j) = y + z^i(j) = y^i + z^i(j-1) \in \gamma(M_i(j-1))$. Further, since $z^r(p_r) + y - y^{r+1} = z^{r+1}(1)$, we have $y^r(p_r) = y + z^r(p_r) = y^{r+1} + z^{r+1}(1) \in \gamma(M_{r+1}(1))$ hence $y^r(p_r) \in \gamma(M_r(p_r)) \cap \gamma(M_{r+1}(1))$. Similarly, for each i, $r+1 \le i \le m$, $y^i(|p_i|) = y + z^i(|p_i|) = y^{i+1} + z^{i+1}(1) \in \gamma(M_i(|p_i|)) \cap \gamma(M_{i+1}(1))$, and for $1 \le j < |p_i|$, $y^i(j) = y + z^i(j) = y^i + z^i(j) + y - y^i = y^i + z^i(j+1) \in \gamma(M_i(j+1))$ hence $y^i(j) \in \gamma(M_i(j)) \cap \gamma(M_i(j+1))$. Also, taking into account the equalities $z^{m+1}(1) = z^m(|p_m|) + y - x$ and $z^{m+1}(j+1) = z^{m+1}(j) + y - x$ for $1 \le j < q-1$, we get $y^m(|p_m|) = y + z^m(|p_m|) = x + z^{m+1}(1) \in M_0 + z^{m+1}(1) = M_{m+1}(1)$ hence $y^m(|p_m|) \in \gamma(M_m(|p_m|)) \cap M_{m+1}(1)$, and $y^{m+1}(j) = y + z^{m+1}(j) = x + z^{m+1}(j+1) \in \gamma(M_{m+1}(j)) \cap M_{m+1}(j+1)$, $1 \le j < q-1$. Finally, by (38), $y^{m+1}(q-1) \in \gamma(M_{m+1}(q-1))$. We obtain thus a trajectory

$$\begin{aligned} y &\to y^1(1) \to y^1(2) \to \cdots \to y^1(p_1) \to y^2(1) \to y^2(2) \to \cdots \\ &\to y^2(p_2) \to y^3(1) \to \cdots \to y^r(p_r) \to y^{r+1}(1) \to y^{r+1}(2) \to \cdots \\ &\to y^{r+1}(|p_{r+1}|) \to y^{r+2}(1) \to \cdots \to y^{r+2}(|p_{r+2}|) \to \cdots \\ &\to y^m(|p_m|) \to y^{m+1}(1) \to \cdots \to y^{m+1}(q-1), \end{aligned}$$

which is improving and leads from y to $y^{m+1}(q-1)$, and since, by (36), $y^{m+1}(q-1) = y + z^{m+1}(q-1) = x$, the strong axiom of revealed preference fails to be true.

Thus, for $X = \mathbb{R}^n$, the proof is complete. If now X is a proper subset in $\mathbb{R}^n$, the result is derived from here by replacing M_0, $M_i(j)$ with their shifts $M_0 + z^*$, $M_i(j) + z^*$ where $z^* \in \mathbb{R}^n_+$ is taken from the condition that all these shifts are contained in X. □

Theorem 4.8. *Suppose that $X = X + \mathbb{R}^n_+$, $\mathcal{M}$ satisfies (32) and consists of closed convex sets, $\gamma(M) \ne M$ for every $M \in \mathcal{M}$, and a choice function γ satisfies both the strengthened weak axiom of revealed preference and condition (33); then, for every $M \in \mathcal{M}$, $\gamma(M)$ is a closed convex subset in the boundary of M, and for each $t \in \mathbb{R}$ an implication holds*

$$[x, y \in \gamma(M), (1-t)x + ty \in M] \Rightarrow (1-t)x + ty \in \gamma(M). \tag{39}$$

Proof. Let us fix a point $x \in M \setminus \gamma(M)$. If $y \in \gamma(M)$ is an interior point of M then there exists $\varepsilon > 0$ such that the ε-ball with center at y is contained in M. Let us fix $0 < \varepsilon < \|x - y\|$ and take $0 < \delta < \frac{\varepsilon}{\|x-y\|}$, $1 - \delta < t < 1$,

$x(t) = (1-t)x + ty$, and $M_1 = (x(t) - y) + M$. We have $x(t) - y = (1-t)(x-y)$, hence $\|x(t) - y\| < \varepsilon$ and $x(t) = y + (x(t) - y) \in \gamma(M_1)$. Further, since $\|x(t) - y\| < \varepsilon$, one has $2y - x(t) = y - (x(t) - y) \in M$ and $y = (x(t) - y) + (2y - x(t)) \in M_1$. We get a trajectory $y \to x(t)$ where $y \in \gamma(M)$, $x(t) \in M \setminus \gamma(M)$, and $x(t) \in \gamma(M_1)$, what is a contradiction with the weak axiom of revealed preference. Thus, we have established that each $\gamma(M)$ consists of boundary points. Also, $\gamma(M)$ is closed by Lemma 4.4.

Let us show that $\gamma(M)$ is convex. Suppose that $x, y \in \gamma(M)$ but $x(t) = (1-t)x + ty \notin \gamma(M)$ for some $0 < t < 1$. We consider the straight line passing through x and y, $L = \{(1-t)x + ty : t \in \mathbb{R}\}$, and taking into account that $\gamma(M)$ is closed, we will assume that $x, y \in \gamma(M) \cap L$ are chosen in such a way that $x(t) \notin \gamma(M)$ for all $0 < t < 1$. Fix such a t, which is close to 1, and consider $M_1 = x(t) - y + M$, $x^1 = x(t)$, and $y^1 = x - y + x(t)$. Here, we suppose, without loss of generality, that $M_1 \subset X$, otherwise we find a vector $z \in \mathbb{R}^n_+$ such that $z + x(t) - y \in \mathbb{R}^n_+$, hence $z + x(t) - y + M \subset X$, and consider $z + M$ in place of M. Then $x^1 \in M_1$, $y^1 \in \gamma(M_1)$, and since $d(y, x^1) + d(y^1, x) = \|y - x(t)\| + \|x(t) - y\| = 2(1-t)\|y - x\|$ becomes arbitrarily small when t is close enough to 1, we obtain a contradiction with the strengthened weak axiom of revealed preference.

It remains to prove (39). Since $\gamma(M)$ is closed, the values $t_{\min} = \min\{t \in \mathbb{R} : (1-t)x + ty \in \gamma(M)\} \le 0$ and $t_{\max} = \max\{t \in \mathbb{R} : (1-t)x + ty \in \gamma(M)\} \ge 1$ are well-defined. Clearly, (39) will be established if we show that $x(t) = (1-t)x(t_{\min}) + tx(t_{\max}) \notin M$ for $t \in \mathbb{R} \setminus [t_{\min}, t_{\max}]$. Suppose $x(t) \in M$ for some $t > t_{\max}$. We can assume that t is close to $t_{\max}$ hence $x(t)$ is close to $x(t_{\max})$. We consider $M_1 = x(t) - x(t_{\max}) + M$ and suppose that $M_1 \subset X$; otherwise we will pass from M to $M + z$ where $z \in \mathbb{R}_+$ is chosen from the condition that $z + x(t) - x(t_{\max}) \in \mathbb{R}_+$. Let us take a trajectory $y^* \to x^1 \to y^1 \to x^*$, where $x^* = x^1 = y^1 = x(t)$, $y^* = x(t_{\max})$, and notice that $x^* \in M \setminus \gamma(M)$, $y^* \in \gamma(M)$, $x^1 \in \gamma(M_1)$, $y^1 \in \gamma(M_1)$. Since $d(y^1, x^*) = 0$ and $d(y^*, x^1) = \|x(t_{\max}) - x(t)\|$ becomes arbitrarily small when t is close enough to $t_{\max}$, we obtain a contradiction with the strengthened weak axiom of revealed preference. Similarly, if $t < t_{\min}$ is close enough to $t_{\min}$ and $x(t) \in M$ then, arguing as above, we again get a contradiction with the strengthened weak axiom of revealed preference for $M_1 = x(t) - x(t_{\min}) + M$, $x^* = x^1 = y^1 = x(t)$, $y^* = x(t_{\min})$. □

As follows from Theorems 4.7 and 4.8, conditions (32), (33) are strong enough, especially in combination with axioms of revealed preference. Let us consider three examples.

Example 4.1. Suppose $\mathcal{M}$ consists of all compact convex sets in X, and $\gamma(M)$ is given by (28), where $u(x) = a \cdot x$ is any non-zero linear function. Obviously (32), (33) are satisfied. Also, by Theorem 4.5, the strengthened axiom of revealed preference is satisfied, too.

Example 4.2. (For the sake of simplicity, we suppose $X = \mathbb{R}^n$.) Fix any $y^* \neq 0$ in X and consider $\mathcal{M} = \{M_* + z : z \in X\}$ and $\gamma(M_* + z) = \gamma(M_*) + z$ for every $z \in X$, where $M_* = \{0, y^*\}$ and $\gamma(M_*) = \{y^*\}$. Obviously, (32) and (33) are satisfied. Let us show that the strengthened axiom of revealed preference is satisfied, too. Suppose $M = M_0 \in \mathcal{M}$, $x \in M \setminus \gamma(M)$, $y \in \gamma(M)$, and let $y = y^0 \to x^1 \to y^1 \to \cdots \to x^m \to y^m \to x$ be a strongly regular trajectory leading from y to x. Then $x^{k+1} = y^k \in M_{k+1} \cap \gamma(M_k)$, $k = 0, 1, \ldots, m-1$, and $y^m \in \gamma(M_m)$ where $M_k = M_* + z^k \in \mathcal{M}$, $k = 0, 1, \ldots, m$. Since $x \in M_0 \setminus \gamma(M_0)$ and $M_* \setminus \gamma(M_*) = \{0\}$, we get $z^0 = x$. Similarly, $y^m \in \gamma(M_m)$ implies $y^m = y^* + z^m$, and $y^k \in M_{k+1} \cap \gamma(M_k)$ for $k = 0, 1, \ldots, m-1$ implies (a) $z^k = y^k - y^*$ and (b) either $y^k = z^{k+1}$ (this is the case $y^k \in M_{k+1} \setminus \gamma(M_{k+1})$) or $y^k = y^* + z^{k+1}$ (this is the case $y^k \in \gamma(M_{k+1})$). It follows that, for each $k = 0, 1, \ldots, m-1$, $z^{k+1} - z^k$ is equal y^* or 0; therefore, $z^m = z^0 + \sum_{k=0}^{m-1}(z^{k+1} - z^k) = x + m_1 y^*$, and $y^m = y^* + z^m = x + (m_1 + 1)y^*$, where $m_1 \leq m$. Hence $d(y^m, x) \geq (m_1 + 1)\|y^*\| \geq \|y^*\|$ and, by Lemma 4.7, the strengthened axiom of revealed preference is satisfied. (This follows also from Theorem 4.5, if one takes into account that γ is rationalized by any linear function $u(x) = a \cdot x$ satisfying $a \cdot y^* > 0$.)

Example 4.3. Suppose $X = \mathbb{R}^n$, consider the vectors $e^1 = (1, 0, \ldots, 0)$, $e^2 = (0, 1, \ldots, 0), \ldots, e^n = (0, 0, \ldots, 1)$, $x = (x_1, x_2, \ldots, x_n)$, and define $M_0 = \{0, e^1, e^2, \ldots, e^n, x\}$, $\mathcal{M} = \{M_0 + z : z \in \mathbb{R}^n\}$, $\gamma(M_0) = \{0, e^1, e^2, \ldots, e^n\}$, $\gamma(M_0 + z) = \gamma(M_0) + z$. Obviously, (32) and (33) are satisfied. It follows easily from Lemma 4.7 that the strengthened axiom of revealed preference fails if, and only if, for every $\varepsilon > 0$, there exist integers $q \geq 1, p_1, \ldots, p_n$ such that $|qx_i + p_i| < \varepsilon$, $i = 1, \ldots, n$.[16]

Theorem 4.9. *Suppose $X = \mathbb{R}^n$, $\mathcal{M}$ satisfies (32), γ satisfies both (33) and the strengthened axiom of revealed preference, and there is a closed domain*[17] *$M \in \mathcal{M}$ with a smooth boundary containing $\gamma(M)$; then for every function $u \in C^\infty(\mathbb{R}^n)$ rationalizing γ and satisfying $\|\nabla u(x)\| \leq 1$*[18] *there exist a vector of unit length $a = (a_1, \ldots, a_n) \in \mathbb{R}^n$ and a function $\lambda \in C^\infty(\mathbb{R}^n)$, $0 < \lambda \leq 1$, such that*

$$a_i \frac{\partial \lambda(x)}{\partial x_j} = a_j \frac{\partial \lambda(x)}{\partial x_i}, \quad x \in \mathbb{R}^n, \quad i, j \in \{1, \ldots, n\}, \tag{40}$$

---

[16] It seems plausible that this condition is satisfied for all $x \in \mathbb{R}^n$, otherwise one would have an example of a C^∞-smooth-utility-rational choice function γ that satisfies (33) but cannot be rationalized by a linear function.

[17] A closed domain is a closed set that coincides with the closure of its interior.

[18] The existence of such functions follows from Theorem 4.6.

and

$$\nabla u(x) = \lambda(x)a, \quad x \in \mathbb{R}^n. \tag{41}$$

Furthermore, a and λ are uniquely determined by u as follows:

$$\lambda(x) = \|\nabla u(x)\|, \quad a = \frac{\nabla u(x)}{\|\nabla u(x)\|} \quad \forall x \in \mathbb{R}^n, \tag{42}$$

and the linear function $u_1(x) = a \cdot x$ rationalizes γ as well.

Proof. Let y^* be any point in $\gamma(M)$, then y^* is a boundary point of M, and since the boundary of M is smooth, the normal to it at y^* is well defined. Moreover, it follows from (33) and (32) that each $x \in \mathbb{R}^n$ belongs to the set $\gamma(M + x - y^*)$ hence is a boundary point of $M + x - y^*$, and the normal to the boundary of $M + x - y^*$ at x does not depend on x. We take a to be the unit normal vector at y^*, which is directed outside M. Every $x \in \mathbb{R}^n$ lies on two smooth surfaces, the boundary of $M + x - y^*$ and the surface $\{z : u(z) = u(x)\}$, and, since u rationalizes γ, both the surfaces have the same tangent hyperplane at x. Then there is a coefficient $\lambda(x) > 0$ such that $\nabla u(x) = \lambda(x)a$. Moreover, since $u \in C^\infty(\mathbb{R}^n)$, $\|\nabla u(x)\| \leq 1$, it follows that $\lambda \in C^\infty(\mathbb{R}^n)$, $\lambda(x) \leq 1$, and (41) is thus established. Notice also that (40) and (42) are direct consequences of (41).

The proof will be completed if we show that an equivalence holds as follows:

$$u(x) \leq u(y) \Leftrightarrow a \cdot x \leq a \cdot y. \tag{43}$$

Notice that if there exists a smooth function $h : \mathbb{R} \to \mathbb{R}$ such that

$$\lambda(x) = \frac{dh(t)}{dt}|_{t=a \cdot x}, \quad x \in \mathbb{R}^n, \tag{44}$$

then h is increasing and $u(x) = h(a \cdot x) + const$, therefore, (43) holds. Let us prove the existence of such a function h. We assume, for the sake of definiteness, that $a_1 \neq 0$, and pass from $x = (x_1, \ldots, x_n)$ to new variables $y = (y_1, \ldots, y_n) = Ax$, where $y_1 = a_1x_1 + a_2x_2 + \cdots + a_nx_n$, $y_k = x_k$ $(k = 2, \ldots, n)$. Let $y = Ax$, and $\mu(y) := \lambda(A^{-1}(y)) = \lambda(x)$. One has

$$\frac{\partial \lambda}{\partial x_1} = \frac{\partial \mu}{\partial y_1} a_1, \quad \frac{\partial \lambda}{\partial x_k} = \frac{\partial \mu}{\partial y_1} a_k + \frac{\partial \mu}{\partial y_k} \quad (k = 2, \ldots, n);$$

and by taking into account (40), we derive from here

$$\frac{\partial \mu}{\partial y_k} = \frac{\partial \lambda}{\partial x_k} - \frac{a_k}{a_1} \frac{\partial \lambda}{\partial x_1} = 0 \quad \forall k \neq 1.$$

It follows that $\mu(y)$ depends on y_1 only, i.e. $\lambda(x)$ is a function of $a \cdot x$; then there is a smooth function $\lambda_0 : \mathbb{R} \to (0, 1]$ such that $\lambda(x) = \lambda_0(a \cdot x)$, and (44) is satisfied for h being a primitive function of λ_0. □

Corollary 4.3. *Suppose $X = \mathbb{R}^n$, $\mathcal{M}$ satisfies (32), γ satisfies both (33) and the strengthened axiom of revealed preference, and there is a closed convex set $M_* \in \mathcal{M}$ with non-empty interior and smooth boundary; then there is a linear function rationalizing γ.*

Proof. Taking into account that the interior of M_* is non-empty, the strengthened axiom of revealed preference implies $\gamma(M_*) \neq M_*$. Let $\mathcal{M}_1 := \{M_* + z : z \in \mathbb{R}^n\}$. Since $\mathcal{M}_1 \subset \mathcal{M}$, γ satisfies the strengthened axiom of revealed preference with respect to $\mathcal{M}_1$; then, by Theorem 4.8, the boundary of M_* contains $\gamma(M_*)$, and applying Theorem 4.9 concludes the proof. □

Remark 4.11 The proof of Theorem 4.9 is similar to that of Theorem 3.2 in [37] where the existence of a linear utility function is established for a class of closed total preorders on X. I would like to eliminate an annoying defect slipped in the proof of Theorem 3.2 in [37]. It relates to the boundary of the set $M_\varepsilon(y^*) = \{x \in X : x \preceq y^*\} \cap B_\varepsilon(y^*)$. It is said in [37, p. 101] that the boundary of $M_\varepsilon(y^*)$ is $\{x : u(x) = u(y^*)\} \cap B_\varepsilon(y^*)$. Of course, this is nonsense. In fact, the boundary of $M_\varepsilon(y^*)$ consists of two pieces, viz. $\{x : u(x) = u(y^*), \|x - y^*\| < \varepsilon\}$ and $\{x \in M_\varepsilon(y^*) : \|x - y^*\| = \varepsilon\}$. Nevertheless, the theorem is correct and its proof, as given in [37], holds true taking into account that, for $y \in int\, X$, $M_\varepsilon(y)$ is the shift of $M_\varepsilon(y^*)$, $y \in \{x : u(x) = u(y), \|x - y\| < \varepsilon\}$ is a boundary point of $M_\varepsilon(y)$, and the boundary of $M_\varepsilon(y)$ is smooth near y.

4.4. On a class of interval orders admitting smooth representations

Definition 4.8. Recall (see, e.g. [2, Chap. 6]) that a binary relation $\succ$ on a set X is called an *interval order* if it is asymmetric ($x \succ y \Rightarrow \neg(y \succ x)$) and satisfies the following condition:

$$(x \succ y \text{ and } x' \succ y') \Rightarrow (x \succ y' \text{ or } x' \succ y).$$

Given an interval order $\succ$, one can associate it with a preference $\preceq$ as follows: $x \preceq y \Leftrightarrow \neg(x \succ y)$. Since $\succ$ is asymmetric, one has

$$x \succ y \Rightarrow y \preceq x.$$

It follows from Definition 4.8 that $\succ$ is transitive; however generally $\preceq$ is not such.

Definition 4.9. Given an interval order $\succ$, a pair (u, v) of real-valued functions on X is called its *representation* if, for any $x, y \in X$, an equivalence holds as follows:

$$x \succ y \Leftrightarrow u(x) > v(y). \tag{45}$$

Clearly, (45) implies

$$x \preceq y \Leftrightarrow u(x) \leq v(y). \tag{46}$$

In what follows, X is supposed to be a subset in $\mathbb{R}^n$ which is stable with respect to shifts in positive directions and either closed or open. A representation (u, v) of $\succ$ is called *Lebesgue measurable* (resp. *continuous, smooth*) if both the functions, u and v, are Lebesgue measurable (resp. continuous, smooth). In the next theorem we describe a class of interval orders on X for which the existence of Lebesgue measurable and of smooth representations are equivalent.

Theorem 4.10. *Suppose X is closed or open and satisfies $X = X + \mathbb{R}^n_+$, and $\succ$ is an interval order on X such that, for every $z \in \mathbb{R}^n_+$, an equivalence holds as follows:*

$$x \succ y \Leftrightarrow (x + z) \succ (y + z). \tag{47}$$

If $\succ$ has a Lebesgue measurable representation then there is a representation (u, v) such that $u, v \in C^\infty(X)$ and $u(X) \subset (0, 1)$, $v(X) \subset (0, 1)$.

Proof. Let (u_0, v_0) be a Lebesgue measurable representation of $\succ$. Taking into account Lemma 4.3 and passing, if needed, from u_0, v_0 to $\frac{1}{2} + \frac{1}{2}\frac{u_0}{1+|u_0|}$, $\frac{1}{2} + \frac{1}{2}\frac{v_0}{1+|v_0|}$, we will assume that $u_0, v_0 \in \mathcal{L}^\infty(X)$ and $u_0(X) \subset (0, 1)$, $v_0(X) \subset (0, 1)$. Let us define $u = \Phi(u_0)$, $v = \Phi(v_0)$ where Φ is given by (6); then $u, v \in C^\infty(X)$, and $u(X) \subset (0, 1)$, $v(X) \subset (0, 1)$. Furthermore, if $x \succ y$ then, by (47), $(x + z) \succ (y + z)$ for all $z \in \mathbb{R}^n_+$, hence $u_0(x + z) > v_0(y + z)$, and we derive from (6) that $u(x) > v(y)$. If now $x \succ y$ fails then $x \preceq y$, and taking into account (46) along with (47) and (6), it follows that $u(x) \leq v(y)$. It follows that $x \succ y \Leftrightarrow u(x) > v(y)$, and (u, v) is thus a C^∞-smooth representation of $\succ$. □

Remark 4.12 Clearly, (47) is equivalent to

$$x \preceq y \Leftrightarrow (x + z) \preceq (y + z) \quad \forall z \in \mathbb{R}^n_+,$$

which is a strengthening of (27).

Remark 4.13 A sufficient condition for an interval order on a connected separable topological space to have a representation (u, v) such that u is lower semi-continuous and v is upper semi-continuous may be found in [1] (see also [2, Theorem 6.4.5]). A criterion for an interval order on a connected topological space to have a continuous representation is given in [3] (see also [2, Theorem 6.5.5]). By combining Theorem 4.10 with these theorems, one can obtain sufficient conditions for the existence of smooth representations. We omit precise formulations of the corresponding results.

5. Conclusion

In this paper, sufficient conditions were obtained for the existence of a smooth feasible solution to a dual Monge–Kantorovich problem with a fixed marginal difference on a closed or open subset X in $\mathbb{R}^n$ which is stable with respect to shifts in positive directions. Based on the existence theorem, a united method is developed for solving various problems in approximation theory and mathematical economics. Among other things, the following results were obtained.

We have considered a problem of best approximating a bounded continuous function on $X \times X$ by differences of the form $u(x) - u(y)$ and we have given a condition for the existence of a smooth exact solution to it.

We have proved the existence of a smooth utility function for a (generally non-reflexive and non-transitive) preference relation on X satisfying the strengthened acyclicity assumption and the condition that adding one and the same positive vector to each of two comparable alternatives cannot affect the preference relation between them. A similar result (the existence of a smooth joint utility) is obtained for a class of preferences depending on a parameter.

We have studied a general rational choice problem on a family of subsets of X, and we have given conditions for the existence of a linear (or smooth) utility function rationalizing the choice. These conditions are a strengthened axiom of revealed preference and a translation invariance requirement (or some its weakening).

We have proved that for an interval order $\succ$ on X satisfying $x \succ y \Leftrightarrow (x+z) \succ (y+z)$ whenever $z \in \mathbb{R}^n_+$ the existence of a smooth representation and of a Lebesgue measurable one are equivalent.

References

1. Bridges, D.S.: Numerical representation of interval orders on a topological space. J. Econ. Theory **38**, 160–166 (1986)
2. Bridges, D.S., Mehta, G.B.: Representations of preference orderings. Lecture Notes in Economics and Mathematical Systems, vol. 422. Berlin: Springer 1995
3. Chateauneuf, A.: Continuous representation of a preference relation on a connected topological space. J. Math. Econ. **16**, 139–146 (1987)
4. Chipman, J.C., Hurwicz, L., Richter, M.K., Sonnenschein, H. (eds.): Preferences, utility and demand. New York: Harcourt Brace Jovanovich 1971
5. Debreu, G.: Representation of a preference ordering by a numerical function. In: Thrall, R. et al. (eds.): Decision processes. New York: Wiley 1954, pp. 159–165
6. Debreu, G.: Continuity properties of Paretian utility. Intern. Econ. Rev. **5**, 285–293 (1964)

7. Debreu, G.: Smooth preferences. Econometrica **40**, 603–615 (1972)
8. Debreu, G.: Smooth preferences: a corrigendum. Econometrica **44**, 831–832 (1976)
9. Gevers, L.: On interpersonal comparability and social welfare orderings. Econometrica **47**, 75–89 (1979)
10. Houthakker, H.S.: Revealed preference and the utility function. Economica **17**, 159–174 (1950)
11. Kantorovich, L.V.: On mass transfer. Dokl. Acad. Nauk SSSR **37**(7–8), 199–201 (1942) (in Russian)
12. Kantorovich, L.V.: On a problem of Monge. Usp. Matem. Nauk **3**(2), 225–226 (1948) (in Russian)
13. Kantorovich, L.V., Akilov, G.P.: Functional analysis. Moscow: Nauka 1984 (in Russian)
14. Kantorovich, L.V., Rubinshtein, G.S.: On a function space and some extremal problems. Dokl. Acad. Nauk SSSR **115**, 1058–1061 (1957) (in Russian)
15. Kantorovich, L.V., Rubinshtein, G.S.: On a space of completely additive functions. Vestnik Leningrad Univ. **13**(7), 52–59 (1958) (in Russian)
16. Kim, T., Richter, M.K.: Nontransitive-nontotal consumer theory. J. Econ. Theory **38**, 324–363 (1986)
17. Levin, V.L.: Duality and approximation in the mass transfer problem. In: Mityagin, B.S. (ed.): Mathematical economics and functional analysis. Moscow: Nauka 1974, pp. 94–108 (in Russian)
18. Levin, V.L.: On the problem of mass transfer. Soviet Math. Dokl. **16**, 1349–1353 (1975)
19. Levin, V.L.: Duality theorems in the Monge–Kantorovich problem. Usp. Matem. Nauk **32**(3), 171–172 (1977) (in Russian)
20. Levin, V.L.: The Monge–Kantorovich mass transfer problem. In: Efimov, B.A. (ed.): Methods of functional analysis in mathematical economics. Moscow: Nauka, 1978, pp. 23–55 (in Russian)
21. Levin, V.L.: A continuous utility theorem for closed preorders on a σ-compact metrizable space. Soviet Math. Dokl. **28**(3), 715–718 (1983)
22. Levin, V.L.: The problem of mass transfer in a topological space, and probability measures having given marginal measures on the product of two spaces. Soviet Math. Dokl. **29**(3), 638–643 (1984)
23. Levin, V.L.: Functionally closed preorders and strong stochastic dominance. Soviet Math. Dokl. **32**(1), 22–26 (1985)
24. Levin, V.L.: Extremal problems with probability measures, functionally closed preorders and strong stochastic dominance. In: Arkin, V.I., Shiraev, A., Wets, R. (eds.): Stochastic optimization. Lecture Notes in Control and Information Sciences, vol. 81. Berlin: Springer 1986, pp. 435–447
25. Levin, V.L.: Measurable selections of multivalued mappings and the mass transfer problem. Soviet Math. Dokl. **35**(1), 178–183 (1987)
26. Levin, V.L.: General Monge–Kantorovich problem and its applications in measure theory and mathematical economics. In: Leifman, L.J. (ed.): Functional analysis, optimization, and mathematical economics (A collection of papers dedicated to memory of L.V.Kantorovich). Oxford: Oxford University Press 1990, pp. 141–176

27. Levin, V.L.: A formula for the optimal value of the Monge–Kantorovich problem with a smooth cost function and a characterization of cyclically monotone maps. Mat. Sbornik **181**(12), 1694–1709 (1990) (in Russian); English translation in: Math. USSR-Sb. **71**, 533–548 (1992)
28. Levin, V.L.: Some applications of set-valued mappings in mathematical economics. J. Math. Econ. **20**, 69–87 (1991)
29. Levin, V.L.: A superlinear multifunction arising in connection with mass transfer problems. Set-Valued Anal. **4**, 41–65 (1996)
30. Levin, V.L.: Reduced cost functions and their applications. J. Math. Econ. **28**, 155–186 (1997)
31. Levin, V.L.: On duality theory for non-topological variants of the mass transfer problem. Sb. Math. **188**(4), 571–602 (1997) (English translation)
32. Levin, V.L.: Abstract cyclical monotonicity and Monge solutions for the general Monge–Kantorovich problem. Set-Valued Anal. **7**, 7–32 (1999)
33. Levin, V.L.: The Monge–Kantorovich problems and stochastic preference relations. Adv. Math. Econ. **3**, 97–124 (2001)
34. Levin, V.L.: A method in demand analysis connected with the Monge–Kantorovich problem. Adv. Math. Econ. **7**, 47–93 (2005)
35. Levin, V.L.: Abstract convexity and the Monge–Kantorovich duality. In: Konnov, I.V., Luc, D.T., Rubinov, A.M. (eds.): Generalized convexity and related topics. Lecture Notes in Economics and Mathematical Systems, vol. 583. Berlin: Springer 2006, pp. 33–72
36. Levin, V.L.: Best approximation problems relating to Monge–Kantorovich duality. Sb. Math. **197**(9), 1353–1364 (2006)
37. Levin, V.L.: On preference relations that admit smooth utility functions. Adv. Math. Econ. **11**, 95–104 (2008)
38. Levin, V.L.: Smooth feasible solutions to a dual Monge–Kantorovich problem and their application to the best approximation and mathematical economics problems. Dokl. Math. **77**(2), 281–283 (2008)
39. Levin, V.L., Milyutin, A.A.: The problem of mass transfer with a discontinuous cost function and a mass statement of the duality problem for convex extremal problems. Russian Math. Surveys **34**, 1–78 (1979) (English translation)
40. Mas-Colell, A.: On the continuous representation of preorders. Intern. Econ. Rev. **18**, 509–513 (1977)
41. Mas-Colell, A.: The theory of general economic equilibrium: a differentiable approach. London: Cambridge University Press 1985
42. Monge, G.: Mémoire sur la théorie des déblais et de remblais. In: Histoire de l'Académie Royale des Sciences de Paris, avec les Mémoires de Mathématique et de Physique pour la même année, 1781, pp. 666–704
43. Neuefeind, W., Trockel, W.: Continuous linear representations for binary relations. Econ. Theory **6**, 351–356 (1995)
44. Rachev, S.T., Rüschendorf, L.: Mass transportation problems, Vol. 1: Theory, Vol. 2: Applications. Berlin: Springer 1998
45. Richter, M.K.: Duality and rationality. J. Econ. Theory **20**, 131–181 (1979)
46. Sudakov, V.N.: Geometric problems in the theory of infinite-dimensional probability distributions. Proc. Steklov Inst. Math. **141**, 1–178 (1979); translated from the Russian: Trudy Mat. Inst. Steklov **141** (1976)

Adv. Math. Econ. 12, 129–152 (2009)

Advances in MATHEMATICAL ECONOMICS

Optimal growth rate in random trade time

Koichi Matsumoto*

Department of Economic Engineering, Faculty of Economics, Kyushu University
6-19-1 Hakozaki Higashi-ku, Fukuoka-shi, Fukuoka 812-8581, Japan
(e-mail: k-matsu@en.kyushu-u.ac.jp)

Received: March 28, 2008
Revised: September 3, 2008

JEL classification: G11

Mathematics Subject Classification (2000): 91B28, 91B16, 91B70

Abstract. We study the optimal growth rate in the market where there are a saving asset and a low liquid risky asset. In this paper the low liquid asset can be traded at random trade times. We show the optimal growth rate both with finite time horizon and with infinite time horizon. And we find an optimal strategy. Further we discuss the convergence of the optimal growth rate and the optimal strategy as the time horizon goes to infinity.

Key words: liquidity, optimal growth rate, optimal strategy

1. Introduction

Liquidity effects are analyzed by many kinds of model. One of most familiar models is a model of transaction costs (see Leland [8], Davis and Norman [4], Boyle and Vorst [1], Kusuoka [7], Kabanov [6]). Price impact and execution delay are studied by Subramanian and Jarrow [14] and stochastic supply curve is discussed by Cetin, Jarrow and Protter [2]. In these models, there is no restriction on trade times. On the other hand, there are some studies where the liquidity is represented by restrictions on trade times. A discrete trade time model is studied by Rogers [12] and further random trade time model

* I would like to thank Prof. Sigeo Kusuoka for helpful discussions and comments. I wish to thank an anonymous referee for careful reading and for many valuable comments. This research was partially supported by the Ministry of Education, Science, Sports and Culture, Grant-in-Aid for Young Scientists (B), 19740051.

S. Kusuoka, T. Maruyama (eds.), *Advances in Mathematical Economics Volume 12*,
DOI: 10.1007/978-4-431-92935-2_5,

is studied by Rogers and Zane [13], Matsumoto [9, 10]. They consider some classical Merton wealth and consumption problems and analyze the liquidity effects on optimal strategies.

In this paper we study the optimal growth rate in a random trade time model. Here trade times are exponentially distributed. An investor wants to maximize the expected growth rate by trading a saving account and a risky asset. This is a kind of classical wealth problem. In a continuous trade times model, Merton [11] studies this problem and shows that the investor should invest a constant proportion of wealth in the risky asset. We consider the liquidity effects in comparison to Merton's result. We are interested in both the finite time horizon problem and the infinite time horizon problem. The finite time horizon problem is essentially studied in Matsumoto [10] and then our study is mainly devoted to the infinite time horizon problem. The optimal growth rate can be solved in an explicit form. And we find an optimal strategy which attains the optimal growth rate. Further we study the convergence problem between finite time horizon and infinite time horizon.

This paper is organized as follows. §2 provides the model and the problems. §3 shows the optimal growth rate and an optimal strategy. §4 discusses the convergence problem. §5 explains an asymptotic expansion of the optimal strategy and analyzes the liquidity effect on the optimal growth rate. Finally we conclude the paper in §6.

2. Model and problem

Let $(\Omega, \mathcal{F}, P, \{\mathcal{F}_t; t \geq 0\})$ be a filtered probability space satisfying the usual conditions. Under P, $\{B(t); t \geq 0, B(0) = 0\}$ is an $\{\mathcal{F}_t\}$-Brownian motion and $\{Q(t); t \geq 0, Q(0) = 0\}$ is an $\{\mathcal{F}_t\}$-Poisson process independent of $B(t)$, with intensity λ. Also we denote the first jump time of $Q(t)$ by τ.

We assume the same model of a financial market as Matsumoto [10], that is, an investor trades one safety asset and one low liquid risky asset whose prices follow

$$d\beta(t) = r\beta(t)dt, \quad \beta(0) = 1,$$

$$dS(t) = \mu S(t)dt + \sigma S(t)dB(t), \quad S(0) = S_0,$$

where S_0, r, μ and σ are positive constants. Let $W(t)$ be his total wealth and let $X(t)$ be the fraction of total wealth invested in the risky asset. Set $W(0) = w > 0$ and $X(0) = x$ $(0 \leq x \leq 1)$. He tries to trade assets in order to change the fraction $X(t)$ to $v(t)$ but he succeeds only at jump times of $Q(t)$. Also he must not sell the risky asset short, nor borrow to buy the risky asset. That is, v belong to the admissible processes defined by

$$\mathcal{V}_0 = \{v | v \text{ is predictable and } 0 \leq v(t) \leq 1 \text{ for } t \geq 0\}.$$

v is his control variable and then we call v a strategy. When we emphasize that $W(t)$ and $X(t)$ depend on w, x and v, we write $W^{w,x,v}(t)$, $X^{x,v}(t)$. We can show

$$dW^{w,x,v}(t) = W(t-)((\mu - r)X(t-) + r)dt + W(t-)X(t-)\sigma dB(t), \quad (1)$$

$$\begin{aligned} dX^{x,v}(t) &= X(t-)(1 - X(t-))(\mu - r - \sigma^2 X(t-))dt \\ &\quad + X(t-)(1 - X(t-))\sigma dB(t) + (v(t) - X(t-))dQ(t). \quad (2) \end{aligned}$$

Please see Matsumoto [10] for the details.

In this study we discuss two types of optimization problems:

1. Finite time horizon problem: For $T > 0$, the optimal growth rate is defined by

$$\xi_T^\lambda(x) = \sup_{v \in \mathcal{V}_0} \frac{1}{T} E\left[\log \frac{W^{w,x,v}(T)}{w}\right].$$

We want to solve $\xi_T^\lambda(x)$ and find an optimal strategy which attains $\xi_T^\lambda(x)$.
2. Infinite time horizon problem: The optimal growth rate is defined by

$$\xi_\infty^\lambda(x) = \sup_{v \in \mathcal{V}_0} \liminf_{T \to \infty} \frac{1}{T} E\left[\log \frac{W^{w,x,v}(T)}{w}\right].$$

We want to solve $\xi_\infty^\lambda(x)$ and find an optimal strategy which attains $\xi_\infty^\lambda(x)$.

When the risky asset is completely liquid, namely, in the case of $\lambda = \infty$, similar problems are studied by Merton [11], Grossman and Zhou [5], Cvitanic and Karatzas [3], etc. We use Merton's result as a benchmark. Merton's growth rate $\xi_T^\infty(x)$ and Merton's strategy $v_T^\infty(t)$ are given by

$$\xi_T^\infty(x) = r + \frac{(\mu - r)^2}{2\sigma^2}, \quad 0 \leq T \leq \infty,$$

$$v_T^\infty(t) = x_0, \quad 0 \leq t \leq T \leq \infty,$$

where

$$x_0 = \frac{\mu - r}{\sigma^2}.$$

Since $\xi_T^\infty(x)$, $v_T^\infty(t)$ are independent of x, t, T, we abbreviate $\xi_T^\infty(x)$, $v_T^\infty(t)$ to ξ^∞, v^∞, respectively. Also we assume Merton's strategy is in (0, 1), that is,

$$0 < x_0 < 1$$

throughout this paper. This assumption is not essential and can be removed easily.

3. Optimal growth rate and optimal strategy

First we show the result in the finite time horizon problem. Since the similar problem is considered in Matsumoto [10], we review the result without the proof.

Theorem 3.1. *The optimal growth rate is given by*

$$\xi_T^\lambda(x) = r + \frac{J^\lambda(T, x)}{T},$$

where

$$J^\lambda(T, x) = \frac{1}{\lambda} E[f_0(Y^x(\tau))\mathbf{1}_{\{\tau \le T\}}] + \int_0^T \sup_{0 \le y \le 1} E[f_0(Y^y(\tau))\mathbf{1}_{\{\tau \le s\}}]ds,$$

$$f_0(y) = (\mu - r)y - \frac{1}{2}\sigma^2 y^2,$$

$$Y^y(t) = \frac{yS(t)/S_0}{yS(t)/S_0 + (1-y)\beta(t)}.$$

The strategy $v_T^\lambda(t)$ given by

$$v_T^\lambda(t) \in \operatorname*{argsup}_{0 \le x \le 1} E[f_0(Y^x(\tau))\mathbf{1}_{\{\tau \le T-t\}}]$$

is an optimal strategy. Specially if λ is sufficiently large, the optimal strategy is unique.

Next we show the result in the infinite time horizon problem. This theorem is the main result in this section.

Theorem 3.2. *The optimal growth rate is given by*

$$\xi_\infty^\lambda(x) = r + \sup_{0 \le y \le 1} E[f_0(Y^y(\tau))].$$

The strategy $v_\infty^\lambda(t)$ given by

$$v_\infty^\lambda(t) \in \operatorname*{argsup}_{0 \le x \le 1} E[f_0(Y^x(\tau))]$$

is an optimal strategy.

$v_\infty^\lambda(t)$ can be time homogeneous and then we denote $v_\infty^\lambda(t)$ by a constant, v_∞^λ.

Remark 3.1 In this case, the optimal growth rate does not depend on x, which is different from the result with finite time horizon. In a short term investment of the low liquid asset, the initial position is important but the investor can overcome a disadvantage of the initial position in a long term investment.

We prepare some lemmas for giving the proof of the main theorem. For $0 \le x \le 1$, let

$$A_\infty^\lambda(x) = \frac{1}{\lambda}\left(E[f_0(Y^x(\tau))] - \sup_{0\le y\le 1} E[f_0(Y^y(\tau))]\right)$$

and let

$$\hat{\xi} = r + \sup_{0\le y\le 1} E[f_0(Y^y(\tau))].$$

By the definition of $Y^x(t)$, we have

$$0 \le Y^x(t) \le 1 \tag{3}$$

and

$$\begin{aligned} Y^x(t) &= H_0^x(\tilde{S}(t)),\\ \frac{\partial Y^x(t)}{\partial x} &= H_1^x(\tilde{S}(t)),\\ \frac{\partial^2 Y^x(t)}{\partial x^2} &= -2H_2^x(\tilde{S}(t)), \end{aligned}$$

where

$$\begin{aligned} \tilde{S}(t) &= \frac{S(t)}{S_0\beta(t)} = \exp\left(\left(\mu - r - \frac{1}{2}\sigma^2\right)t + \sigma B(t)\right),\\ H_0^x(s) &= \frac{xs}{xs+1-x},\\ H_1^x(s) &= \frac{s}{(xs+1-x)^2},\\ H_2^x(s) &= \frac{s(s-1)}{(xs+1-x)^3}. \end{aligned}$$

Lemma 3.1. *For any* $0 < x < 1$, *we have*

$$\left|\frac{\partial Y^x(t)}{\partial x}\right| \le \frac{1}{4x(1-x)}, \tag{4}$$

$$\left|\frac{\partial^2 Y^x(t)}{\partial x^2}\right| \le \max\left\{\frac{1}{x^2}, \frac{1}{(1-x)^2}\right\}. \tag{5}$$

Proof. It is sufficient to show $H_1^x(s)$ and $H_2^x(s)$ satisfy the lemma's inequalities. Since $H_1^x(s)$ is a non-negative function in $(0, \infty)$ and it has an absolute maximum at $s = (1-x)/x$, we have

$$|H_1^x(s)| \le \left| H_1^x\left(\frac{1-x}{x}\right)\right| = \frac{1}{4x(1-x)}$$

and then (4) follows. Next we set

$$\alpha_1 = \frac{1-\sqrt{1-x(1-x)}}{x},$$
$$\alpha_2 = \frac{1+\sqrt{1-x(1-x)}}{x}.$$

We can show that $H_2^x(s)$ has an absolute minimum at $s = \alpha_1$ and an absolute maximum at $s = \alpha_2$. We have

$$H_2^x(\alpha_1) = -\frac{1}{27}\frac{H_3(x)^3}{H_4(x)}\frac{1}{(1-x)^2},$$
$$H_2^x(\alpha_2) = \frac{H_4(x)}{H_3(x)^3}\frac{1}{x^2},$$

where

$$H_3(x) = 2 - x + \sqrt{1-x(1-x)},$$
$$H_4(x) = \left(1+\sqrt{1-x(1-x)}\right)\left(1-x+\sqrt{1-x(1-x)}\right).$$

Since $H_3(x)$ and $H_4(x)$ are positive and decreasing functions in [0, 1], we have

$$|H_2^x(s)| \le \max\left\{\frac{1}{27}\frac{H_3(0)^3}{H_4(1)}\frac{1}{(1-x)^2}, \frac{H_4(0)}{H_3(1)^3}\frac{1}{x^2}\right\}$$
$$= \frac{1}{2}\max\left\{\frac{1}{(1-x)^2}, \frac{1}{x^2}\right\}.$$

By this inequality, (5) follows. □

Lemma 3.2. *For* $0 < x < 1$*, we have*

$$\frac{dA_\infty^\lambda(x)}{dx} = \frac{1}{\lambda}E\left[\left(\mu - r - \sigma^2 Y^x(\tau)\right)\frac{\partial Y^x(\tau)}{\partial x}\right], \tag{6}$$

$$\frac{d^2A_\infty^\lambda(x)}{dx^2} = \frac{1}{\lambda}E\left[-\sigma^2\left(\frac{\partial Y^x(\tau)}{\partial x}\right)^2 + \left(\mu - r - \sigma^2 Y^x(\tau)\right)\frac{\partial^2 Y^x(\tau)}{\partial x^2}\right]. \tag{7}$$

And there exist some constants C_1 and C_2 such that

$$\left|\frac{dA_\infty^\lambda(x)}{dx}x(1-x)\right| \le C_1, \tag{8}$$

$$\left|\frac{d^2A_\infty^\lambda(x)}{dx^2}x^2(1-x)^2\right| \le C_2 \tag{9}$$

for all $0 < x < 1$.

Proof. From Lemma 3.1, $\partial Y^x(t)/\partial x$ and $\partial^2 Y^x(t)/\partial x^2$ are bounded in some neighborhood of x. By (3), using the mean value theorem and the bounded convergence theorem, (6) and (7) can be obtained.

By Lemma 3.1, we have

$$\left|\frac{\partial Y^x(t)}{\partial x}x(1-x)\right| \le \frac{1}{4},$$

$$\left|\frac{\partial^2 Y^x(t)}{\partial x^2}x^2(1-x)^2\right| \le 1.$$

From (3), (6) and (7), we get (8) and (9). □

Here we define $\mu_0 : [0,1]\times[0,1] \to \boldsymbol{R}$ and $\sigma_0 : [0,1] \to \boldsymbol{R}$ by

$$\mu_0(x,v) = \begin{cases} f_0(x) + r - \hat{\xi} + \lambda\left(A_\infty^\lambda(v) - A_\infty^\lambda(x)\right), & x = 0, 1, \\ f_0(x) + r - \hat{\xi} + \dfrac{dA_\infty^\lambda(x)}{dx}x(1-x)(\mu - r - \sigma^2 x) \\ \quad + \dfrac{1}{2}\dfrac{d^2A_\infty^\lambda(x)}{dx^2}x^2(1-x)^2\sigma^2 \\ \quad + \lambda\left(A_\infty^\lambda(v) - A_\infty^\lambda(x)\right), & 0 < x < 1, \end{cases}$$

$$\sigma_0(x) = \begin{cases} 0, & x = 0, 1, \\ \dfrac{dA_\infty^\lambda(x)}{dx}x(1-x)\sigma, & 0 < x < 1. \end{cases}$$

Lemma 3.3. *For all* $0 \le x \le 1$, μ_0 *satisfies*

$$\sup_{0\le v\le 1} \mu_0(x,v) = 0.$$

Proof. Assume that $0 < x < 1$ and let us introduce

$$Z(t) = A_\infty^\lambda(Y^y(t))e^{-\lambda t} + \int_0^t e^{-\lambda s}(f_0(Y^y(s)) + r - \hat{\xi})ds.$$

Since

$$
\begin{aligned}
A^{\lambda}_{\infty}(Y^y(t))e^{-\lambda t} &= E\left[\int_0^{\infty} e^{-\lambda(t+s)} f_0(Y^y(s))ds\right]\Big|_{y=Y^y(t)} + \frac{e^{-\lambda t}}{\lambda}(r-\hat{\xi})\\
&= E\left[\int_0^{\infty} e^{-\lambda(t+s)} f_0(Y^y(t+s))ds|\mathcal{F}_t\right] + \int_t^{\infty} e^{-\lambda s}(r-\hat{\xi})ds\\
&= E\left[\int_t^{\infty} e^{-\lambda s}(f_0(Y^y(s)) + r - \hat{\xi})ds|\mathcal{F}_t\right],
\end{aligned}
$$

we have

$$
Z(t) = E\left[\int_0^{\infty} e^{-\lambda s}(f_0(Y^y(s)) + r - \hat{\xi})ds|\mathcal{F}_t\right].
$$

By Itô's formula, we have

$$
dY^y(t) = Y^y(t)(1-Y^y(t))(\mu - r - \sigma^2 Y^y(t))dt + Y^y(t)(1-Y^y(t))\sigma dB(t).
$$

Also we have

$$
\begin{aligned}
\sup_{0\le v\le 1} \mu_0(x,v) = f_0(x) + r - \hat{\xi} + \frac{dA^{\lambda}_{\infty}(x)}{dx}x(1-x)(\mu - r - \sigma^2 x)\\
+\frac{1}{2}\frac{d^2A^{\lambda}_{\infty}(x)}{dx^2}x^2(1-x)^2\sigma^2 - \lambda A^{\lambda}_{\infty}(x)
\end{aligned}
$$

since

$$
\sup_{0\le v\le 1} A^{\lambda}_{\infty}(v) = 0.
$$

Using Itô's formula again, we get

$$
dZ(t) = \sup_{0\le v\le 1} e^{-\lambda t}\mu_0(Y^y(t), v)dt + e^{-\lambda t}\sigma_0(Y^y(t))dB(t).
$$

Because $e^{-\lambda t} > 0$, $Z(t)$ is a martingale and $\{Y^y(t)|0 < y < 1\} = (0,1)$ a.s. for any $t > 0$, we get

$$
\sup_{0\le v\le 1} \mu_0(x,v) = 0
$$

for all $0 < x < 1$.

It remains to show the case of $x = 0, 1$. In this case, $Y^x(t) = Y^x(0)$ for all $t > 0$. And then we have

$$
\begin{aligned}
\sup_{0\le v\le 1} \mu_0(x,v) &= f_0(x) + r - \hat{\xi} - \lambda A^{\lambda}_{\infty}(x)\\
&= f_0(x) + r - \hat{\xi} - \left(f_0(x) - \sup_{0\le y\le 1} E[f_0(Y^y(\tau))]\right)\\
&= 0.
\end{aligned}
$$

□

Lemma 3.4. *For $w > 0$ and $0 \le x \le 1$, let*

$$I(w,x) = \log w + A_\infty^\lambda(x).$$

Then

$$E\left[\frac{I(W^{w,x,v}(T), X^{x,v}(T)) - I(w,x)}{T}\right] \le \hat{\xi} \tag{10}$$

for any $v \in \mathcal{V}_0$. Specially if $v = v_\infty^\lambda$, the equality holds.

Proof. From (1) and (2), using Itô's formula, we have

$$\begin{aligned}
&E[I(W^{w,x,v}(T), X^{x,v}(T)) - \hat{\xi}T] - I(w,x)\\
&= E\left[\int_0^T \mu_0(X^{x,v}(t-), v(t))dt\right]\\
&\quad + E\left[\int_0^T \left(X^{x,v}(t-)\sigma + \sigma_0(X^{x,v}(t-))\right) dB(t)\right]\\
&\quad + E\left[\int_0^T (A_\infty^\lambda(v(t)) - A_\infty^\lambda(X^{x,v}(t-)))(dQ(t) - \lambda dt)\right].
\end{aligned}$$

By Lemma 3.2, the second and the third terms are 0. By Lemma 3.3, we have

$$E[I(W^{w,x,v}(T), X^{x,v}(T)) - \hat{\xi}T] - I(w,x) \le 0.$$

Specially if $v = v_\infty^\lambda$, the equality holds. Therefore we have our assertion. □

Lemma 3.5. *There exists some constant C such that*

$$|I(w,x) - \log w| \le C\frac{1}{\lambda}$$

for all $w > 0$ and $0 \le x \le 1$.

Proof. Since f_0 is a quadratic function, we have from (3)

$$\min\{f_0(0), f_0(1)\} \le f_0(Y^x(\tau)) \le \sup_{0\le y\le 1} f_0(y) = \frac{(\mu - r)^2}{2\sigma^2}. \tag{11}$$

Therefore we get

$$\begin{aligned}
|I(w,x) - \log w| = |A_\infty^\lambda(x)| &= \frac{\sup_{0\le y\le 1} E[f_0(Y^y(\tau))] - E[f_0(Y^x(\tau))]}{\lambda}\\
&\le \frac{1}{\lambda}\left(\frac{(\mu - r)^2}{2\sigma^2} - \min\{f_0(0), f_0(1)\}\right).
\end{aligned}$$

□

Proof of Theorem 3.2. By Lemma 3.5 there exists C such that

$$-\frac{C}{\lambda}+\log W^{w,x,v}(T)\le I(W^{w,x,v}(T),X^{x,v}(T))\le\frac{C}{\lambda}+\log W^{w,x,v}(T) \tag{12}$$

for any $v\in\mathcal{V}_0$. And we have

$$\begin{aligned}
&\sup_{v\in\mathcal{V}_0}\liminf_{T\to\infty}E\left[-\frac{C}{\lambda T}+\frac{1}{T}\log\frac{W^{w,x,v}(T)}{w}\right]\\
&\le\sup_{v\in\mathcal{V}_0}\liminf_{T\to\infty}E\left[\frac{I(W^{w,x,v}(T),X^{x,v}(T))-\log w}{T}\right]\\
&\le\sup_{v\in\mathcal{V}_0}\liminf_{T\to\infty}\frac{I(w,x)-\log w+\hat{\xi}T}{T}\\
&\le\sup_{v\in\mathcal{V}_0}\liminf_{T\to\infty}C\frac{1}{\lambda T}+\hat{\xi}=\hat{\xi}.
\end{aligned}$$

The second inequality follows by (10) and the last inequality follows by Lemma 3.5. Therefore we get

$$\sup_{v\in\mathcal{V}_0}\liminf_{T\to\infty}\frac{1}{T}E\left[\log\frac{W^{w,x,v}(T)}{w}\right]\le\hat{\xi}.$$

By Lemma 3.4 we have

$$E[I(W^{w,x,v_\infty^\lambda}(T),X^{x,v_\infty^\lambda}(T))]=I(w,x)+\hat{\xi}T.$$

By (12), we have

$$\begin{aligned}
&\liminf_{T\to\infty}E\left[\frac{C}{\lambda T}+\frac{1}{T}\log\frac{W^{w,x,v_\infty^\lambda}(T)}{w}\right]\\
&\ge\liminf_{T\to\infty}E\left[\frac{I(W^{w,x,v_\infty^\lambda}(T),X^{x,v_\infty^\lambda}(T))-\log w}{T}\right]\\
&=\liminf_{T\to\infty}\frac{I(w,x)-\log w+\hat{\xi}T}{T}\\
&\ge\liminf_{T\to\infty}-\frac{C}{\lambda T}+\hat{\xi}=\hat{\xi}.
\end{aligned}$$

Then we get

$$\liminf_{T\to\infty}\frac{1}{T}E\left[\log\frac{W^{w,x,v_\infty^\lambda}(T)}{w}\right]\ge\hat{\xi}.$$

Therefore we obtain

$$\liminf_{T\to\infty}\frac{1}{T}E\left[\log\frac{W^{w,x,v}(T)}{w}\right]\le\hat{\xi}=\liminf_{T\to\infty}\frac{1}{T}E\left[\log\frac{W^{w,x,v_{\infty}^{\lambda}}(T)}{w}\right]$$

for all $v\in\mathcal{V}_0$. Then $\hat{\xi}$ is the optimal growth rate and v_{∞}^{λ} is an optimal strategy. This completes the proof. □

4. Convergence problem as $T\to\infty$

In the finite time horizon case, the optimal strategy can be unique. On the other hand, it is not guaranteed in the infinite time horizon case. In this section we consider the convergence problem as the time horizon goes to infinity and show that v_{∞}^{λ} is a special optimal strategy. Here are the main theorems in this section.

Theorem 4.1. *The optimal growth rate satisfies*

$$\lim_{T\to\infty}\xi_T^{\lambda}(x)=\xi_{\infty}^{\lambda}(x).$$

Theorem 4.2. *If λ is sufficiently large, v_T^{λ}, v_{∞}^{λ} are unique and satisfies*

$$\lim_{T\to\infty}v_T^{\lambda}(t)=v_{\infty}^{\lambda}.$$

Remark 4.1 *By Theorem 4.1, it is reasonable to consider that the limit of the optimal strategy with finite horizon is a natural optimal strategy with infinite time horizon. And Theorem 4.2 shows that v_{∞}^{λ} is the natural optimal strategy.*

First we set

$$g_T^{\lambda}(x)=E[f_0(Y^x(\tau))\mathbf{1}_{\{\tau\le T\}}],$$
$$g_{\infty}^{\lambda}(x)=E[f_0(Y^x(\tau))].$$

Lemma 4.1. *We have*

$$\lim_{T\to\infty}\sup_{0\le x\le 1}|g_T^{\lambda}(x)-g_{\infty}^{\lambda}(x)|=0$$

and

$$\lim_{T\to\infty}\sup_{0\le x\le 1}g_T^{\lambda}(x)=\sup_{0\le x\le 1}g_{\infty}^{\lambda}(x).$$

Proof. Set

$$C_{f_0} = \max\left\{|f_0(0)|, |f_0(1)|, \frac{(\mu - r)^2}{2\sigma^2}\right\}.$$

From (11), we get

$$\sup_{0\le x\le 1} |g_T^\lambda(x) - g_\infty^\lambda(x)| \le E[\sup_{0\le x\le 1} |f_0(Y^x(\tau))|\mathbf{1}_{\{\tau>T\}}] \le C_{f_0} P[\tau > T].$$

Since

$$g_T^\lambda(x) = E[f_0(Y^x(\tau))] - E[f_0(Y^x(\tau))\mathbf{1}_{\{\tau>T\}}],$$

we have from (11)

$$g_T^\lambda(x) \ge E[f_0(Y^x(\tau))] - \frac{(\mu - r)^2}{2\sigma^2} P[\tau > T]$$

$$g_T^\lambda(x) \le E[f_0(Y^x(\tau))] - \min\{f_0(0), f_0(1)\}\, P[\tau > T].$$

Then we get

$$\sup_{0\le x\le 1} g_T^\lambda(x) \ge \sup_{0\le x\le 1} g_\infty^\lambda(x) - \frac{(\mu - r)^2}{2\sigma^2} P[\tau > T],$$

$$\sup_{0\le x\le 1} g_T^\lambda(x) \le \sup_{0\le x\le 1} g_\infty^\lambda(x) - \min\{f_0(0), f_0(1)\}\, P[\tau > T].$$

Therefore we have

$$\left|\sup_{0\le x\le 1} g_T^\lambda(x) - \sup_{0\le x\le 1} g_\infty^\lambda(x)\right| \le C_{f_0} P[\tau > T].$$

Since

$$\lim_{T\to\infty} P[\tau > T] = \lim_{T\to\infty} e^{-\lambda T} = 0, \tag{13}$$

we get the desired results. □

Proof of Theorem 4.1. By Theorem 3.1 and the boundedness of $f_0(Y^x(\tau))$, we have

$$
\begin{aligned}
\lim_{T\to\infty} \xi_T^\lambda(x) &= r + \lim_{T\to\infty} \frac{J^\lambda(T,x)}{T} \\
&= r + \lim_{T\to\infty} \frac{1}{T}\left(\frac{1}{\lambda}E[f_0(Y^x(\tau))\mathbf{1}_{\{\tau\le T\}}]\right. \\
&\qquad \left. + \int_0^T \sup_{0\le y\le 1} E[f_0(Y^y(\tau))\mathbf{1}_{\{\tau\le s\}}]ds\right) \\
&= r + \lim_{T\to\infty} \frac{1}{T}\int_0^T \sup_{0\le y\le 1} g_s^\lambda(y)ds \\
&= r + \lim_{T\to\infty} \sup_{0\le y\le 1} g_T^\lambda(y).
\end{aligned}
$$

By Lemma 4.1, the result follows. □

Lemma 4.2. *Suppose that $n_1 \in \mathbf{Z}, n_2 \in \mathbf{N} \cup \{0\}$. Let*

$$
\lambda_0(n) = n\left(\mu - r + \frac{n-1}{2}\sigma^2\right).
$$

If $\lambda \ge 1 + \lambda_0(n_1) \vee \lambda_0(n_1 - n_2)$, we have

$$
E\left[\frac{\tilde{S}(\tau)^{n_1}}{(x\tilde{S}(\tau)+1-x)^{n_2}}\right] \le 1 + \lambda_0(n_1) \vee \lambda_0(n_1-n_2), \quad 0 \le x \le 1. \tag{14}
$$

Proof. Set $n \in \mathbf{Z}$. From $0 < x_0 < 1$, $\lambda_0(n)$ is non-negative. If $\lambda > \lambda_0(n)$, we have

$$
\begin{aligned}
E[\tilde{S}(\tau)^n] &= E\left[\exp\left(n\left(\mu - r - \frac{1}{2}\sigma^2\right)\tau + n\sigma B(\tau)\right)\right] \\
&= E[\exp(\lambda_0(n)\tau)] \\
&= \frac{\lambda}{\lambda - \lambda_0(n)}.
\end{aligned}
$$

The right-hand side is a decreasing function of λ for $\lambda > \lambda_0(n)$. If $\lambda \ge 1 + \lambda_0(n)$, we have

$$
E[\tilde{S}(\tau)^n] \le 1 + \lambda_0(n)
$$

which is (14) for $n_2 = 0$.

Next, we assume that $n_2 > 0$. Since $\tilde{S}(\tau)$ is positive, we have

$$
\begin{aligned}
\frac{\tilde{S}(\tau)^{n_1}}{(x\tilde{S}(\tau)+1-x)^{n_2}} &\le \min\left\{\frac{\tilde{S}(\tau)^{n_1}}{(1-x)^{n_2}}, \frac{\tilde{S}(\tau)^{n_1}}{(x\tilde{S}(\tau))^{n_2}}\right\} \\
&= \min\left\{\frac{\tilde{S}(\tau)^{n_1}}{(1-x)^{n_2}}, \frac{\tilde{S}(\tau)^{n_1-n_2}}{x^{n_2}}\right\}.
\end{aligned}
$$

If $\lambda \geq 1 + \lambda_0(n_1) \vee \lambda_0(n_1 - n_2)$, we have

$$E\left[\frac{\tilde{S}(\tau)^{n_1}}{(x\tilde{S}(\tau) + 1 - x)^{n_2}}\right] \leq \min\left\{\frac{1}{(1-x)^{n_2}}\frac{\lambda}{\lambda - \lambda_0(n_1)}, \frac{1}{x^{n_2}}\frac{\lambda}{\lambda - \lambda_0(n_1 - n_2)}\right\}$$
$$\leq \left(\left(\frac{\lambda}{\lambda - \lambda_0(n_1)}\right)^{\frac{1}{n_2}} + \left(\frac{\lambda}{\lambda - \lambda_0(n_1 - n_2)}\right)^{\frac{1}{n_2}}\right)^{n_2}$$
$$\leq \left((1 + \lambda_0(n_1))^{\frac{1}{n_2}} + (1 + \lambda_0(n_1 - n_2))^{\frac{1}{n_2}}\right)^{n_2}$$
$$\leq 1 + \lambda_0(n_1) \vee \lambda_0(n_1 - n_2)$$

and this completes the proof. □

Lemma 4.3. *Suppose that*

$$\lambda \geq \max\left\{\mu - r, \sigma^2 - (\mu - r)\right\} + 1.$$

Then we have

$$\frac{dg_T^\lambda(x)}{dx} = E\left[\left(\mu - r - \sigma^2 Y^x(\tau)\right)\frac{\partial Y^x(\tau)}{\partial x}\mathbf{1}_{\{\tau \leq T\}}\right], \tag{15}$$

$$\frac{dg_\infty^\lambda(x)}{dx} = E\left[\left(\mu - r - \sigma^2 Y^x(\tau)\right)\frac{\partial Y^x(\tau)}{\partial x}\right] \tag{16}$$

for $0 \leq x \leq 1$. *Specially they satisfy*

$$\left.\frac{dg_T^\lambda(x)}{dx}\right|_{x=0} > 0, \quad \left.\frac{dg_T^\lambda(x)}{dx}\right|_{x=1} < 0, \tag{17}$$

$$\left.\frac{dg_\infty^\lambda(x)}{dx}\right|_{x=0} > 0, \quad \left.\frac{dg_\infty^\lambda(x)}{dx}\right|_{x=1} < 0. \tag{18}$$

Proof. Because we can prove (15) and (16) for all $\lambda > 0$ and $0 < x < 1$ in the same way as Lemma 3.2, we only have to consider two cases, $x = 0, 1$. Suppose that $s > 0$. For some $0 < \epsilon < 1$, if $0 \leq x < \epsilon < 1$, then

$$\left|H_1^x(s)\right| = \frac{s}{(xs + 1 - x)^2} \leq \frac{s}{(1-x)^2} \leq \frac{s}{(1-\epsilon)^2}$$

and if $0 < 1 - \epsilon < x \leq 1$, then

$$\left|H_1^x(s)\right| \leq \frac{s}{(xs)^2} = \frac{1}{x^2}\frac{1}{s} \leq \frac{1}{(1-\epsilon)^2}\frac{1}{s}.$$

By Lemma 4.2, if $\lambda \geq \max\left\{\mu - r, \sigma^2 - (\mu - r)\right\} + 1$, $\tilde{S}(\tau)$ and $1/\tilde{S}(\tau)$ is integrable and then $\partial Y^x(t)/\partial x$ is integrable. By (3), using the mean value theorem and the dominated convergence theorem, we have

$$\frac{dg_\infty^\lambda(x)}{dx} = E\left[\left(\mu - r - \sigma^2 Y^x(\tau)\right)\frac{\partial Y^x(\tau)}{\partial x}\right]$$

for $x = 0, 1$. Therefore we get

$$\left.\frac{dg_\infty^\lambda(x)}{dx}\right|_{x=0} = (\mu - r)\, E[\tilde{S}(\tau)] > 0,$$

$$\left.\frac{dg_\infty^\lambda(x)}{dx}\right|_{x=1} = \left(\mu - r - \sigma^2\right) E\left[\frac{1}{\tilde{S}(\tau)}\right] < 0,$$

which are (18). Because $\mathbf{1}_{\{\tau \leq T\}}$ does not depend on x and bounded, (17) can be proved in the same way. □

Lemma 4.4. *If λ is sufficiently large, then we have*

$$\frac{d^2 g_T^\lambda(x)}{dx^2} < 0, \tag{19}$$

$$\frac{d^2 g_\infty^\lambda(x)}{dx^2} < 0 \tag{20}$$

for $0 < x < 1$.

Proof. In a similar way to Lemma 3.2, we have

$$\frac{d^2 g_T^\lambda(x)}{dx^2} = E[G(\tilde{S}(\tau))\mathbf{1}_{\{\tau \leq T\}}],$$

where

$$G(s) = -\sigma^2 H_1^x(s)^2 - 2\left(\mu - r - \sigma^2 H_0^x(s)\right) H_2^x(s).$$

Since

$$G(1) = -\sigma^2 < 0,$$

for any $\epsilon_0 > 0$ there exists $\delta_1 > 0$ such that

$$\left|G(\tilde{S}(\tau)) + \sigma^2\right| < \epsilon_0 \tag{21}$$

for all $|\log \tilde{S}(\tau)| \leq \delta_1$. By the integration by parts formula, we get

$$P[|\log \tilde{S}(\tau)| > \delta_1, \tau \leq T] = -P[|\log \tilde{S}(T)| > \delta_1]e^{-\lambda T} + \int_0^T \frac{dP[|\log \tilde{S}(u)| > \delta_1]}{du} e^{-\lambda u} du.$$

Set

$$\tilde{\mu} = \mu - r - \frac{1}{2}\sigma^2.$$

For $u > 0$, we have

$$\begin{aligned}\frac{dP[|\log \tilde{S}(u)| > \delta_1]}{du} &= \frac{\tilde{\mu}}{2\sigma\sqrt{u}}\left(\phi\left(\frac{\delta_1 - \tilde{\mu}u}{\sigma\sqrt{u}}\right) - \phi\left(\frac{-\delta_1 - \tilde{\mu}u}{\sigma\sqrt{u}}\right)\right) \\ &\quad + \frac{\delta_1}{2\sigma u\sqrt{u}}\left(\phi\left(\frac{\delta_1 - \tilde{\mu}u}{\sigma\sqrt{u}}\right) + \phi\left(\frac{-\delta_1 - \tilde{\mu}u}{\sigma\sqrt{u}}\right)\right) \\ &\geq 0,\end{aligned}$$

where ϕ is the standard normal density function. By the monotone convergence theorem, we get

$$\lim_{\lambda \to \infty} P[|\log \tilde{S}(\tau)| > \delta_1, \tau \leq T] = 0. \tag{22}$$

From $\lim_{\lambda \to \infty} P[\tau \leq T] = 1$, we have

$$\lim_{\lambda \to \infty} P[|\log \tilde{S}(\tau)| \leq \delta_1, \tau \leq T] = 1. \tag{23}$$

By the Schwarz inequality, we have

$$\begin{aligned}E[G(\tilde{S}(\tau))\mathbf{1}_{\{|\log \tilde{S}(\tau)| > \delta_1, \tau \leq T\}}]^2 &\leq E[G(\tilde{S}(\tau))^2]E[\mathbf{1}^2_{\{|\log \tilde{S}(\tau)| > \delta_1, \tau \leq T\}}] \\ &= E[G(\tilde{S}(\tau))^2]P[|\log \tilde{S}(\tau)| > \delta_1, \tau \leq T].\end{aligned}$$

Because $G(\tilde{S}(\tau))$ can be represented by the linear combination of

$$x^{n_3}\frac{\tilde{S}(\tau)^{n_1}}{(x\tilde{S}(\tau) + 1 - x)^{n_2}}, \quad n_1, n_2, n_3 \in \mathbf{N} \cup \{0\},$$

$G(\tilde{S}(\tau))^2$ can be represented by the similar linear combination. If λ is sufficiently large, $E[G(\tilde{S}(\tau))^2]$ is bounded by Lemma 4.2 and then from (22) we get

$$\lim_{\lambda \to \infty} E[G(\tilde{S}(\tau))\mathbf{1}_{\{|\log \tilde{S}(\tau)| > \delta_1, \tau \leq T\}}] = 0. \tag{24}$$

By (13), (21), (22), (23) and (24), we obtain

$$\begin{aligned}
&\limsup_{\lambda\to\infty}\left|\frac{d^2 g_T^\lambda(x)}{dx^2}+\sigma^2\right| \\
&= \limsup_{\lambda\to\infty}\Big|\sigma^2 P[\tau > T] + E[\left(G(\tilde{S}(\tau))+\sigma^2\right)\mathbf{1}_{\{|\log\tilde{S}(\tau)|\le\delta_1,\tau\le T\}}] \\
&\quad + E\left[\left(G(\tilde{S}(\tau))+\sigma^2\right)\mathbf{1}_{\{|\log\tilde{S}(\tau)|>\delta_1,\tau\le T\}}\right]\Big| \\
&\le \limsup_{\lambda\to\infty} E\left[\left|G(\tilde{S}(\tau))+\sigma^2\right|\mathbf{1}_{\{|\log\tilde{S}(\tau)|\le\delta_1,\tau\le T\}}\right] \\
&\le \limsup_{\lambda\to\infty}\epsilon_0 P[|\log\tilde{S}(\tau)|\le\delta_1,\tau\le T] = \epsilon_0.
\end{aligned}$$

Since $\sigma^2 > 0$ and ϵ_0 is arbitrary, (19) follows. Also (20) can be proved similarly. □

Lemma 4.5. *Let*

$$x_T^\lambda \in \operatorname*{argsup}_{0\le x\le 1} g_T^\lambda(x), \qquad x_\infty^\lambda \in \operatorname*{argsup}_{0\le x\le 1} g_\infty^\lambda(x).$$

If λ is sufficiently large, x_T^λ, x_∞^λ exist uniquely and satisfy

$$0 < x_T^\lambda < 1, \quad 0 < x_\infty^\lambda < 1,$$
$$\lim_{T\to\infty} x_T^\lambda = x_\infty^\lambda.$$

Proof. By Lemma 4.4, $g_T^\lambda(x)$ is a concave function. If λ is sufficiently large, $g_T^\lambda(x)$ has a unique absolute maximum point for $0 < x < 1$ by (17). Then x_T^λ exists uniquely and satisfies $0 < x_T^\lambda < 1$. In a similar way, x_∞^λ exists uniquely and satisfies $0 < x_\infty^\lambda < 1$.

For any $\epsilon_2 > 0$, set

$$\epsilon_1 = \frac{g_\infty^\lambda(x_\infty^\lambda) - \max\left\{g_\infty^\lambda((x_\infty^\lambda-\epsilon_2)\vee 0),\, g_\infty^\lambda((x_\infty^\lambda+\epsilon_2)\wedge 1)\right\}}{2} > 0.$$

By Lemma 4.1, there exists $T_1 > 0$ such that

$$|g_T^\lambda(x) - g_\infty^\lambda(x)| < \epsilon_1, \quad 0 \le x \le 1$$

for all $T > T_1$. Suppose that $T > T_1$. For $x \in D_{\epsilon_2} := \{x||x - x_\infty^\lambda| > \epsilon_2\} \cap [0,1]$, we have

$$\begin{aligned}
g_T^\lambda(x_\infty^\lambda) - g_T^\lambda(x) &> \left(g_\infty^\lambda(x_\infty^\lambda) - \epsilon_1\right) - \left(g_\infty^\lambda(x) + \epsilon_1\right) \\
&= g_\infty^\lambda(x_\infty^\lambda) - g_\infty^\lambda(x) - 2\epsilon_1.
\end{aligned} \tag{25}$$

Since x^λ_∞ is a unique absolute maximum point and $g^\lambda_\infty(x)$ is a concave function by Lemma 4.4, we have

$$g^\lambda_\infty(x) < \max\{g^\lambda_\infty((x^\lambda_\infty - \epsilon_2) \vee 0), g^\lambda_\infty((x^\lambda_\infty + \epsilon_2) \wedge 1)\}, \quad x \in D_{\epsilon_2}$$

and then (25) is positive. Therefore x^λ_T satisfies $|x^\lambda_T - x^\lambda_\infty| \le \epsilon_2$. Since ϵ_2 is arbitrary, the result follows. □

Proof of Theorem 4.2. By the definition, v^λ_T, v^λ_∞ satisfy

$$v^\lambda_T(t) \in \operatorname*{argsup}_{0\le x\le 1} g^\lambda_{T-t}(x),$$

$$v^\lambda_\infty \in \operatorname*{argsup}_{0\le x\le 1} g^\lambda_\infty(x).$$

The result follows from Lemma 4.5. □

5. Analysis of liquidity effects

It is useful for analyzing liquidity effects to consider asymptotic behavior of the natural optimal strategy and the optimal growth rate. In this section we show the following theorems.

Theorem 5.1. *There exist η_i, $i \in \boldsymbol{N} \cup \{0\}$ such that, for all $n \in \boldsymbol{N} \cup \{0\}$, there exist $C_n > 0$ and $\lambda_n > 0$ satisfying*

$$\left| v^\lambda_\infty - \sum_{i=0}^{n} \frac{\eta_i}{\lambda^i} \right| \le C_n \frac{1}{\lambda^{n+1}}, \qquad \lambda \ge \lambda_n.$$

Specially η_0 and η_1 are given by

$$\eta_0 = x_0,$$
$$\eta_1 = -\sigma^2 x_0(1-x_0)(1-2x_0)\frac{\Gamma(2)}{\Gamma(1)} = -\sigma^2 x_0(1-x_0)(1-2x_0).$$

Here $\Gamma : (0,\infty) \to \boldsymbol{R}$ is the complete gamma function, that is,

$$\Gamma(s) = \int_0^\infty x^{s-1} e^{-x} dx.$$

Remark 5.1 By Theorem 5.1, the first approximation of the optimal strategy can be represented by

$$v^\infty + 2\sigma^2 x_0(1-x_0)\left(x_0 - \frac{1}{2}\right)\frac{1}{\lambda}.$$

The second term can be considered as the main part of the liquidity effect on the optimal strategy. The liquidity effect changes from positive to negative at $x_0 = 1/2$ *as well as in the finite time horizon problem.*

Theorem 5.2. *We have*

$$\xi_\infty^\lambda(x) \to \xi^\infty$$

and

$$\lambda(\xi^\infty - \xi_\infty^\lambda(x)) \to \frac{1}{2}\sigma^4 x_0^2(1-x_0)^2 \tag{26}$$

as $\lambda \to \infty$ *uniformly in* $0 \le x \le 1$.

Remark 5.2 By Theorem 5.2, the optimal growth rate can be approximated by

$$\xi^\infty - \frac{1}{2}\sigma^4 x_0^2(1-x_0)^2\frac{1}{\lambda}$$

Because the first term is Merton's optimal growth rate, the second term is the main liquidity effect on the optimal growth rate. The liquidity effect is the largest at $x_0 = 1/2$.

Similar theorems are proved in the finite time horizon problem in Matsumoto [10]. We prove our theorems by adjusting its method. Let

$$K_0(t,x) = E[f_0(Y^x(t))].$$

By the definition of $g_\infty^\lambda(x)$ we have

$$g_\infty^\lambda(x) = E[K_0(\tau, x)].$$

From Lemma 4.3, if λ is sufficiently large, we have

$$\frac{dg_\infty^\lambda(x)}{dx} = E\left[\frac{\partial K_0(\tau,x)}{\partial x}\right]$$

since we can show

$$\frac{\partial K_0(t,x)}{\partial x} = E\left[\left(\mu - r - \sigma^2 Y^x(t)\right)\frac{\partial Y^x(t)}{\partial x}\right].$$

From Taylor's theorem for $l = 0, 1$ and $N \in \mathbf{N}$, we have

$$\frac{\partial^l K_0(t, x_0+h)}{\partial x^l} = \sum_{n=0}^{N-1}\frac{1}{n!}\sum_{k=0}^{n}\binom{n}{k} t^k h^{n-k} K_{k,n+l-k} + R_N(t,h,l),$$

where

$$R_N(t,h,l) = \sum_{k=0}^{N} \binom{N}{k} t^k h^{N-k} \int_0^1 \frac{(1-s)^{N-1}}{(N-1)!} \frac{\partial^{N+l} K_0(st, x_0+sh)}{\partial t^k \partial x^{N+l-k}} ds,$$

$$K_{i,j} = \frac{\partial^{i+j} K_0(0,x_0)}{\partial t^i \partial x^j}, \quad i,j \in \mathbf{N} \cup \{0\}.$$

Therefore we obtain

$$\frac{d^l g_\infty^\lambda(x_0+h)}{dx^l} = \sum_{n=0}^{N-1} \frac{1}{n!} \sum_{k=0}^{n} \binom{n}{k} h^{n-k} K_{k,n+l-k} \frac{\Gamma(k+1)}{\lambda^k} + S_N(\lambda,h,l) \quad (27)$$

for $l = 0, 1$ where

$$S_N(\lambda,h,l) = E[R_N(\tau,h,l)].$$

Lemma 5.1. *Suppose that* $0 \le x_0+h \le 1$. *For all* $N \in \mathbf{N}$ *and* $l = 0, 1$, *there exist some constants* $C_{N,l} > 0$ *and* $\lambda_{N,l} > 0$ *such that*

$$|S_N(\lambda,h,l)| \le C_{N,l} \sum_{k=0}^{N} |h|^{N-k} \frac{1}{\lambda^k}, \quad \lambda \ge \lambda_{N,l}.$$

Proof. By the Schwarz inequality, we have

$$\left| E\left[\tau^k \int_0^1 \frac{(1-s)^{N-1}}{(N-1)!} \frac{\partial^{N+l} K_0(s\tau, x_0+sh)}{\partial t^k \partial x^{N+l-k}} ds \right] \right|$$

$$\le \frac{1}{(N-1)!} E[\tau^{2k}]^{\frac{1}{2}} E\left[\left(\int_0^1 (1-s)^{N-1} \frac{\partial^{N+l} K_0(s\tau, x_0+sh)}{\partial t^k \partial x^{N+l-k}} ds \right)^2 \right]^{\frac{1}{2}}$$

$$\le \frac{1}{(N-1)!} E[\tau^{2k}]^{\frac{1}{2}} \left(\int_0^1 (1-s)^{2(N-1)} ds \right)^{\frac{1}{2}}$$

$$\times \left(\int_0^1 E\left[\left(\frac{\partial^{N+l} K_0(s\tau, x_0+sh)}{\partial t^k \partial x^{N+l-k}} \right)^2 \right] ds \right)^{\frac{1}{2}}$$

$$= \frac{1}{(N-1)!} \frac{\Gamma(2k+1)^{\frac{1}{2}}}{\lambda^k} \left(\frac{1}{2N-1} \right)^{\frac{1}{2}}$$

$$\times \left(\int_0^1 E\left[\left(\frac{\partial^{N+l} K_0(s\tau, x_0+sh)}{\partial t^k \partial x^{N+l-k}} \right)^2 \right] ds \right)^{\frac{1}{2}}.$$

From Itô's formula, we have

$$\frac{\partial K_0(t,x)}{\partial t} = E[Y^x(t)(1-Y^x(t))(\mu - r - \sigma^2 Y^x(t))^2$$
$$-\frac{1}{2}\sigma^4 Y^x(t)^2(1-Y^x(t))^2].$$

Similarly we can show that for $k \geq 1$ there exists $F_{2k+2} : \boldsymbol{R} \to \boldsymbol{R}$ which is a polynomial of degree $2k+2$ and satisfies

$$\frac{\partial^k K_0(t,x)}{\partial t^k} = E[F_{2k+2}(Y^x(t))].$$

And then $\partial^{N+l} K_0(t,x)/\partial t^k \partial x^{N+l-k}$ is the expectation of linear combinations of

$$x^{n_3} \frac{\tilde{S}(t)^{n_1}}{(x\tilde{S}(t)+1-x)^{n_2}}, \quad 0 \leq n_1, \;\; n_2 \leq N+l+k+2, \;\; 0 \leq n_3 \leq 2k+2.$$

In a similar way to the proof of Lemma 4.2, we can show that there exist some constants $C_{N+l} > 0$ and $\hat{\lambda} > 0$ such that

$$E[\left(\frac{\partial^{N+l} K_0(s\tau, x_0+sh)}{\partial t^k \partial x^{N+l-k}}\right)^2] \leq C_{N+l}, \quad 0 \leq k \leq N, \;\; 0 \leq s \leq 1, \;\; \lambda \geq \hat{\lambda}.$$

Therefore we have

$$|E[R_N(\tau,h,l)]| \leq \sum_{k=0}^{N} \binom{N}{k} |h|^{N-k} \frac{1}{(N-1)!} \frac{\Gamma(2k+1)^{\frac{1}{2}}}{\lambda^k} \left(\frac{1}{2N-1}\right)^{\frac{1}{2}} C_{N+l}.$$

The result follows. □

Substituting $N=2$ and $l=1$ in (27), we have

$$\frac{dg_\infty^\lambda(x_0+h)}{dx} = \Gamma(1)hK_{0,2} + \frac{1}{\lambda}K_{1,1}\Gamma(2) + S_2(\lambda,h,1) \tag{28}$$

since

$$K_{0,j} = 0, \quad j \neq 0,2,$$
$$K_{0,0} = K_0(0,x_0) = \frac{(\mu-r)^2}{2\sigma^2} = \xi^\infty - r,$$
$$K_{0,2} = -\sigma^2,$$
$$K_{1,0} = -\frac{1}{2}\sigma^4 x_0^2(1-x_0)^2,$$
$$K_{1,1} = -\sigma^4 x_0(1-x_0)(1-2x_0).$$

For the details, see Matsumoto [10].

Lemma 5.2. *Let*

$$h_\infty^\lambda = v_\infty^\lambda - x_0.$$

Then there exist $C_1 > 0$ *and* $\lambda_1 > 0$ *satisfying*

$$\left|h_\infty^\lambda\right| \le C_1 \frac{1}{\lambda}, \quad \lambda \ge \lambda_1.$$

Proof. From Theorem 3.2 and (28), h_∞^λ satisfies

$$\Gamma(1) K_{0,2} h_\infty^\lambda + \frac{1}{\lambda} K_{1,1} \Gamma(2) + S_2(\lambda, h_\infty^\lambda, 1) = 0. \tag{29}$$

By Lemma 5.1 there exist some constant $C_{2,1}$ such that

$$|S_2(\lambda, h, 1)| \le C_{2,1} \left(|h|^2 + \frac{|h|}{\lambda} + \frac{1}{\lambda^2} \right) \tag{30}$$

for sufficiently large λ. Also in the same way as Lemma 5.1, we can show that, there exist some constant C such that

$$\left| \frac{\partial S_2(\lambda, h, 1)}{\partial h} \right| \le C \left(|h| + \frac{1}{\lambda} + |h|^2 + \frac{|h|}{\lambda} + \frac{1}{\lambda^2} \right) \tag{31}$$

for sufficiently large λ.

We consider the solution of (29) by the successive approximation as

$$\begin{aligned} h_1 &= -\frac{1}{\lambda} \frac{K_{1,1}\Gamma(2)}{K_{0,2}\Gamma(1)}, && n = 1, \\ h_n &= -\frac{1}{\lambda} \frac{K_{1,1}\Gamma(2)}{K_{0,2}\Gamma(1)} - \frac{S_2(\lambda, h_{n-1}, 1)}{K_{0,2}\Gamma(1)}, && n \ge 2. \end{aligned}$$

From (30) and (31), in a similar way to the proof of Lemma 3.3 of Matsumoto [10], we can show that there exist constants C', C'' such that

$$|h_n| \le C' \frac{1}{\lambda} + C'' \frac{1}{\lambda^2}$$

and $\lim_{n\to\infty} h_n = h_\infty^\lambda$. The result follows. □

Here we consider the same formal power series as Matsumoto [10]. That is, we consider

$$\sum_{j=1}^{\infty} \phi_j^* z^j + \sum_{i=1}^{\infty} \sum_{k=1}^{i} \gamma_{i,k} z^k \left(\sum_{j=1}^{\infty} \phi_j^* z^j \right)^{i-k} = 0$$

for constants $\gamma_{i,k}$, $1 \le k \le i$. We get

$$\phi_j^* = \begin{cases} -\gamma_{1,1}, & j = 1, \\ -P_j(\gamma_{i,k}, \phi_l^* : 1 \le k \le i \le j, l \le j-1), & j \ge 2, \end{cases}$$

where P_j is a polynomial with positive integer coefficients. η_j is given by replacing $\gamma_{i,k}$ in ϕ_j^* by

$$\binom{i}{k} \frac{1}{i!} \frac{K_{k,i-k+1}}{K_{0,2}} \frac{\Gamma(k+1)}{\Gamma(1)}.$$

Proof of Theorem 5.1. We use the mathematical induction. First it holds for $n = 0$ by Lemma 5.2.

Next we suppose that it holds for $n \le N$. If $|h| \le C/\lambda$ for some constant C, there exists some constant $C' > 0$ such that

$$|S_{N+2}(\lambda, h, l)| \le C' \frac{1}{\lambda^{N+2}}$$

for sufficiently large λ by Lemma 5.1. From (27) and Lemma 5.2, we can show that there exist some constant C''

$$\left| \left(v_\infty^\lambda - \sum_{n=0}^{N+1} \frac{\eta_n}{\lambda^n} \right) K_{0,2}\Gamma(1) \right| = \left| \left(h_\infty^\lambda - \sum_{n=1}^{N+1} \frac{\eta_n}{\lambda^n} \right) \sigma^2 \right| \le \frac{C''}{\lambda^{N+2}}$$

for sufficiently large λ in a similar way to the proof of Theorem 2.2 of Matsumoto [10]. The result follows. □

Proof of Theorem 5.2. Substituting $N = 2$ and $l = 0$ in (27), we have

$$\begin{aligned} \xi_\infty^\lambda(x) - r &= g_\infty^\lambda(x_0 + h_\infty^\lambda) \\ &= K_{0,0} + \Gamma(1) h_\infty^\lambda K_{0,1} + \frac{1}{\lambda} K_{1,0}\Gamma(2) + S_2(\lambda, h_\infty^\lambda, 0) \\ &= \xi^\infty - r - \frac{1}{2}\sigma^4 x_0^2 (1 - x_0)^2 \frac{1}{\lambda} + S_2(\lambda, h_\infty^\lambda, 0). \end{aligned}$$

If λ is sufficiently large, we have

$$|S_2(\lambda, h_\infty^\lambda, 0)| \le C \frac{1}{\lambda^2}$$

for some constant C by Lemmas 5.1 and 5.2. The result follows. □

6. Conclusion

In this paper, the optimal growth rate has been studied in a random trade time model. We have established the existence of the optimal growth rate and provided the explicit solution. And we find a natural optimal strategy which is represented as a solution of a simple maximization problem.

Also we have shown the convergence of the optimal growth rate and the optimal strategy as the time horizon goes to infinity. Further we have shown the liquidity effects are related with Merton's optimal strategy by analyzing their asymptotic behavior as the liquidity becomes higher.

References

1. Boyle, P., Vorst, T.: Option replication in discrete time with transaction costs. J. Finance **47**, 271–293 (1992)
2. Cetin, U., Jarrow, R., Protter, P.: Liquidity risk and arbitrage theory. Finance and Stochastics **8**, 311–341 (2004)
3. Cvitanic, J., Karatzas, I.: On portfolio optimization under drawdown control. IMA Volumes in Mathematics and Its Applications **65**, 35–46 (1995)
4. Davis, M.H.A., Norman A.R.: Portfolio selection with transaction costs. Math. Oper. Res. **15**, 676–713 (1990)
5. Grossman, S.J., Zhou, Z.: Optimal investment strategies for controlling drawdowns. Math. Finance **3**, 241–276 (1993)
6. Kabanov, Yu.: Hedging and liquidation under transaction costs in currency markets. Finance and Stochastics **3**, 237–248 (1999)
7. Kusuoka, S.: Limit theorem on option replication cost with transaction costs. Ann. Appl. Probab. **5**, 198–221 (1995)
8. Leland, H.E.: Option pricing and replication with transactions costs. J. Finance **40**, 1283–1301 (1985)
9. Matsumoto, K.: Optimal portfolio of low liquid assets with a power utility function. J. Math. Sci. The University of Tokyo **10**, 687–726 (2003)
10. Matsumoto, K.: Optimal portfolio of low liquid assets with a log–utility function. Finance and Stochastics **10**, 121–145 (2006)
11. Merton, R.C.: Optimum consumption and portfolio rules in a continuous time model. J. Econ. Theory **3**, 373–413 (1971)
12. Rogers, L.C.G.: The relaxed investor and parameter uncertainty. Finance and Stochastics **5**, 131–154 (2001)
13. Rogers, L.C.G., Zane, O.: A simple model of liquidity effects. In: Sandmann, K. et al. (eds.): Advances in finance and stochastics: Essays in honour of Dieter Sondermann. Berlin: Springer 2002, pp. 161–176
14. Subramanian, A., Jarrow, R.: The liquidity discount. Math. Finance **11**, 447–474 (2001)

Adv. Math. Econ. 12, 153–166 (2009)

Advances in
MATHEMATICAL
ECONOMICS

Some properties of distortion risk measures

Hideatsu Tsukahara*

Hideatsu Tsukahara Department of Economics, Seijo University, 6–1–20 Seijo, Setagaya-ku, Tokyo 157-8511, Japan
(e-mail: tsukahar@seijo.ac.jp)

Received: January 16, 2008
Revised: July 17, 2008

JEL classification: C65, G19

Mathematics Subject Classification (2000): 60B05

Abstract. We give a simplified proof of the fact that law invariant convex risk measures automatically have Fatou property, which is first shown by Jouini et al. (Adv. Math. Econ. 9:49–71, 2006). After providing a streamlined proof of Kusuoka's representation theorem of law invariant and comonotonically additive coherent risk measures, we prove that a coherent distortion risk measures preserves some well-known stochastic orders.

Key words: distortion, risk measure, stochastic order

1. Introduction

We first recall the definition of coherence of risk measures according to Artzner et al. [2, 3]. Let $(\Omega, \mathscr{F}, \mathbf{P})$ be a probability space, and $L^\infty = L^\infty(\Omega, \mathscr{F}, \mathbf{P})$ be the set of all $\mathbf{P}$-essentially bounded random variables. In what follows, a random variable X represents the loss, not the value of a financial position.

Definition 1.1. *A coherent risk measure is a functional* $\rho\colon L^\infty \to \mathbb{R}$ *satisfying the following four properties:*

[PO] (positivity): If $X \le 0$*, then* $\rho(X) \le 0$.
[PH] (positive homogeneity): For any $\lambda > 0$, $\rho(\lambda X) = \lambda\rho(X)$.

* The author would like to express his sincere thanks to Freddy Delbaen for his very helpful comments and for making the preprint by Jouini et al. [11] available at the time of writing. He also thanks an anonymous referee for careful reading.

DOI: 10.1007/978-4-431-92935-2_6,

[SA] (subadditivity): $\rho(X+Y) \leq \rho(X) + \rho(Y)$.
[TI] (translation invariance): For any $c \in \mathbb{R}$, $\rho(X+c) = \rho(X) + c$.

For a nice representation theorem, the following continuity property is needed.

[FA] (*Fatou property*): If the X_n are uniformly bounded in absolute value by 1 and $X_n \xrightarrow{\mathbf{P}} X$, then $\rho(X) \leq \liminf \rho(X_n)$.

Delbaen [4] proved that any coherent risk measure with the Fatou property can be represented as

$$\rho(X) = \sup \left\{ \mathbf{E}^{\mathbf{Q}}(X) \colon \mathbf{Q} \in \mathscr{Q} \right\},$$

where $\mathscr{Q}$ is a set of probability measures and each member of $\mathscr{Q}$ is absolutely continuous with respect to $\mathbf{P}$.

Next we need the following definition. For a distribution function F, we define its quantile F^{-1} on $(0, 1)$ by $F^{-1}(u) := \inf\{x \colon F(x) \geq u\}$.

Definition 1.2. *Random variables* $X_1, \dots, X_d$ *are said to be comonotone if one of the following equivalent statements holds:*

(1) For every $i \neq j$, $\big(X_i(\omega) - X_i(\omega')\big)\big(X_j(\omega) - X_j(\omega')\big) \geq 0$ *for* $\mathbf{P} \otimes \mathbf{P}$*-almost all* (ω, ω').
(2) The joint distribution function of $X_1, \dots, X_d$ *is given by the upper Fréchet bound* $F_{X_1}(x_d) \wedge \cdots \wedge F_{X_d}(x_d)$, *where* F_{X_i} *is the marginal distribution function of* X_i *for* $i = 1, \dots, d$.
(3) For $U \sim U(0, 1)$, $(X_1, \dots, X_d)$ *and* $(F_{X_1}^{-1}(U), \dots, F_{X_d}^{-1}(U))$ *have the same distribution.*
(4) There exist a random variable Z *and increasing functions* $f_1, \dots, f_d$ *such that* $(X_1, \dots, X_d)$ *and* $(f_1(Z), \dots, f_d(Z))$ *have the same distribution.*

Note that we define the comonotonicity as a distributional property rather than a property of random variables. See Dhaene et al. [7] for an overview of the concept of comonotonicity in actuarial science and finance.

Now we introduce two more axioms:

[LI] (*law invariance*): For any two random variables X and Y with the same law, we have $\rho(X) = \rho(Y)$.
[CA] (*comonotonic additivity*): $\rho(X+Y) = \rho(X) + \rho(Y)$ if X and Y are comonotone.

It is strongly desirable that we are able to estimate the value of risk measures statistically (as also claimed in [1]), and to this end the law invariance [LI] is necessary. When X and Y are comonotone, they move together in one direction with probability 1, so, as rightly described in Yaari [20], neither of them is a hedge against the other. The comonotonic additivity [CA] then means that for such two risks, we should have additivity instead of subadditivity, which is a very natural requirement.

Recently the concept of convex risk measure has been introduced by Föllmer and Schied [8,9]. A *convex risk measure* is a functional $\rho\colon L^\infty \to \mathbb{R}$ satisfying the translation invariance [TI] and

[MO] (*monotonicity*): If $X \le Y$, then $\rho(X) \le \rho(Y)$.
[CX] (*convexity*): $\rho(\lambda X + (1-\lambda)Y) \le \lambda\rho(X) + (1-\lambda)\rho(Y)$ for $0 \le \lambda \le 1$.

Note that every coherent risk measure is a convex risk measure and that [TI] and [MO] imply (see [8])

$$|\rho(X) - \rho(Y)| \le \|X - Y\|_\infty. \tag{1.1}$$

2. Fatou property and law invariance

Jouini et al. [11] proved that for convex risk measures, the Fatou property [FA] automatically follows from the law invariance [LI]. Here we give a direct and shorter proof of this result (with a slightly weaker condition on the underlying probability space) although our method is somewhat similar to theirs. Let us recall that a set $A \in \Omega$ is called an *atom* of $\mathbf{P}$ if $\mathbf{P}(A) > 0$ and for every $B \subset A$ with $B \in \mathscr{F}$, one has either $\mathbf{P}(B) = 0$ or $\mathbf{P}(B) = \mathbf{P}(A)$. Then $(\Omega, \mathscr{F}, \mathbf{P})$ is called *atomless* if $\mathbf{P}$ does not have any atoms.

We first prove the following lemma, which may be of independent interest.

Lemma 2.1. *Suppose that $(\Omega, \mathscr{F}, \mathbf{P})$ is atomless. Let (X_n) be a sequence of random variables uniformly bounded in absolute value by 1, and $X_n \xrightarrow{\mathbf{P}} X$. Then one can find a triangular array of random variables Y_{nk}, $k = 1, \dots, N_n$ and $n \in \mathbb{N}$ on $(\Omega, \mathscr{F}, \mathbf{P})$ with the following two properties:*

(1) For each n, Y_{nk}, $k = 1, \dots, N_n$ has the same distribution as X_n.

(2) $\displaystyle\frac{1}{N_n}\sum_{k=1}^{N_n} Y_{nk} \to X$ in L^∞.

Proof (due to Delbaen). Fix any $m \in \mathbb{N}$ and set

$$A_j = \{\omega \in \Omega\colon j/m \le X(\omega) < (j+1)/m\}$$

for $j = -m, -m+1, \dots, -1, 0, 1, \dots, m-2$. For $j = m-1$, we define A_{mj} by the above equation with $<$ replaced by $\le$. Without loss of generality, we may assume $\mathbf{P}(A_j) > 0$ for all j (otherwise define everything to be 0 on such sets of measure 0). Now, for some n_m large enough, we have

$$\mathbf{P}\left(\{|X - X_n| > 1/m\} \cap A_j\right) \le \mathbf{P}(A_j)/m$$

for all $j = -m, -m+1, \ldots, -1, 0, 1, \ldots, m-1$ and $n \ge n_m$. We can take the sequence $(n_m)_{m\in\mathbb{N}}$ to be increasing. Let $C_{jn} = \{|X_n - j/m| > 2/m\} \cap A_j$. Then $\mathbf{P}(C_{jn}) \le \mathbf{P}(A_j)/m$. Using the assumption that $\mathbf{P}$ has no atoms, we can divide A_j into m sets $B_j^1, \ldots, B_j^m$ of equal $\mathbf{P}$-probability so that $C_{jn} \subset B_j^1$ and

$$\mathbf{P}(B_j^i \mid A_j) = 1/m, \quad i = 1, \ldots, m.$$

Applying Proposition 6.9 in [4] to the restrictions of $\mathbf{P}$ to the B_j^i, for each i and j, we can construct V_{nk} so that, for $k = 1, \ldots, m$,

$$\mathbf{P}\big(\{V_{nk} \le y\} \cap B_j^i\big) = \mathbf{P}\big(\{X_n \le y\} \cap B_j^{i+k-1}\big).$$

Here and in the rest of the proof, we use the convention "mod m" in the superscript of B. It then follows that

$$\begin{aligned}\mathbf{P}(V_{nk} \le y) &= \sum_{j=-m}^{m-1} \sum_{i=1}^{m} \mathbf{P}\big(\{V_{nk} \le y\} \cap B_j^i\big)\\ &= \sum_{j=-m}^{m-1} \sum_{i=1}^{m} \mathbf{P}\big(\{X_n \le y\} \cap B_j^{i+k-1}\big) = \mathbf{P}\big(X_n \le y\big).\end{aligned}$$

This shows that the V_{nk} have the same distribution as X_n under $\mathbf{P}$. Moreover, by construction, $\mathbf{P}$-a.s. on A_j

$$\left| V_{nk}(\omega) - \frac{j}{m} \right| \le \begin{cases} 2, & \text{if } \omega \in B_j^{m+2-k},\\ 2/m, & \text{otherwise.} \end{cases}$$

Therefore, $\mathbf{P}$-a.s. on A_j,

$$\left| X - \frac{1}{m}\sum_{k=1}^{m} V_{nk} \right| \le \left| X - \frac{j}{m} \right| + \left| \frac{j}{m} - \frac{1}{m}\sum_{k=1}^{m} V_{nk} \right| \le \frac{1}{m} + \frac{m-1}{m}\frac{2}{m} + \frac{2}{m} < \frac{5}{m}.$$

Note now that the V_{nk}'s in fact depend on m; thus write V_{nk}^m. What we have shown is that for each m, there exists an n_m such that for all $n \ge n_m$, we can construct random variables $V_{n1}^m, \ldots, V_{nm}^m$ satisfying that, for each n, V_{nk}^m, $k = 1, \ldots, m$ has the same distribution as X_n, and $\left|X - (1/m)\sum_{k=1}^m V_{nk}^m\right| \le$

$5/m$. For each n, there exists a unique m satisfying $n_m \leq n < n_{m+1}$. Let N_n be equal to this m and define $Y_{nk} = V_{nk}^m$. It is then clear that the Y_{nk} thus defined satisfy the required properties. □

Now we can easily prove the following theorem.

Theorem 2.2. *Assume that $(\Omega, \mathscr{F}, \mathbf{P})$ is atomless. Then every law invariant convex risk measure $\rho(X)$ satisfies the Fatou property.*

Proof. Let $|X_n| \leq 1$ for every n and ω, and $X_n \xrightarrow{\mathbf{P}} X$. Let Y_{nk} be a triangular array of random variables satisfying the properties stated in Lemma 2.1. Write

$$Y_n = \frac{1}{N_n} \sum_{k=1}^{N_n} Y_{nk}.$$

The convexity of ρ and the law invariance yield

$$\rho(Y_n) = \rho\Big(\frac{1}{N_n} \sum_{k=1}^{N_n} Y_{nk}\Big) \leq \frac{1}{N_n} \sum_{k=1}^{N_n} \rho(Y_{nk}) = \rho(X_n).$$

We use (1.1) and take limit inferior on both sides to get

$$\rho(X) = \lim_{n\to\infty} \rho(Y_n) \leq \liminf_{n\to\infty} \rho(X_n),$$

as required. □

3. Representation of law invariant, comonotonically additive coherent risk measures

Under the assumption that $(\Omega, \mathscr{F}, \mathbf{P})$ is a *standard* probability space, Kusuoka [12] showed that every law invariant, comonotonically additive coherent risk measure can be represented as the expectation of the risk under a convexly distorted distribution. Here we present his result in the form suitable for us and give an easy proof under a slightly weakened assumption of atomlessness, emphasizing the distorted expectation aspect of the risk measures. As a preparation, we recall the following results:

Proposition 3.1. *Let (X, Y) be random variables with a joint distribution function $H(x, y)$, and let F and G denote the marginal distribution functions of X and Y respectively:*

(1) Hoeffding's lemma: *Suppose* $\mathbf{E}|X|$, $\mathbf{E}|Y|$ *and* $\mathbf{E}|XY|$ *are all finite. Then*

$$\mathbf{E}(XY) - \mathbf{E}(X)\mathbf{E}(Y) = \int_{-\infty}^{\infty}\int_{-\infty}^{\infty}\big[H(x,y) - F(x)G(y)\big]\,dxdy.$$

(2) Frechét–Hoeffding bounds: *We have*

$$(F(x) + G(y) - 1) \vee 0 \leq H(x,y) \leq F(x) \wedge G(y),$$

where $a \vee b$ *and* $a \wedge b$ *denote the maximum and minimum of* a *and* b *respectively.*

For proofs of (1) and (2), see Lehmann [13], or Lemma 5.24 and Theorem 5.7 of McNeil et al. [15].

Next we give a definition of distortion function:

Definition 3.2. *Any distribution function* D *on* $[0,1]$ *is called a distortion function: Namely a distortion function* D *is a right-continuous increasing function on* $[0,1]$ *with values in* $[0,1]$ *such that* $D(0) = 0$ *and* $D(1) = 1$.

Given a distortion D and a distribution function F, $D \circ F$ is again a distribution function, which we will call the *distorted distribution* under D. And the expectation under the distorted distribution function $D \circ F$ will be called the *distorted expectation* under D.

Now we can give a streamlined proof of the following theorem due to Kusuoka [12].

Theorem 3.3. *Suppose that* $(\Omega, \mathscr{F}, \mathbf{P})$ *is atomless and that a coherent risk measure* $\rho(X)$ *satisfies [LI] and [CA]. For* $X \in L^\infty$, *let* F_X *be the distribution function of* X *under* $\mathbf{P}$ *and* F_X^{-1} *be its quantile. Then there exists a convex distortion* D *such that*

$$\rho(X) = \int_{[0,1]} F_X^{-1}(u)\,dD(u) = \int_{\mathbb{R}} x\,dD \circ F_X(x). \tag{3.1}$$

Conversely, ρ *given by* (3.1) *with a convex distortion* D *is a coherent risk measure satisfying [LI] and [CA].*

Proof. Let $\mathbf{Q} \ll \mathbf{P}$ and put $Y_{\mathbf{Q}} = d\mathbf{Q}/d\mathbf{P}$. We denote by $F_{Y_{\mathbf{Q}}}$ the distribution function of $Y_{\mathbf{Q}}$ under $\mathbf{P}$. Also let F be the joint distribution function of X and $Y_{\mathbf{Q}}$ under $\mathbf{P}$. Then, for $X \in L^\infty$, by Hoeffding's lemma (apply twice) and Frechét–Hoeffding upper bound in Proposition 3.1, we get

$$\begin{aligned}
\mathbf{E}^{\mathbf{Q}}(X) &= \mathbf{E}^{\mathbf{P}}(XY_{\mathbf{Q}}) \\
&= \int_{-\infty}^{\infty}\int_{-\infty}^{\infty} \left[F(x,y) - F_X(x)F_{Y_{\mathbf{Q}}}(y)\right] dxdy + \mathbf{E}^{\mathbf{P}}(X)\mathbf{E}^{\mathbf{P}}(Y_{\mathbf{Q}}) \\
&\le \int_{-\infty}^{\infty}\int_{-\infty}^{\infty} \left[F_X(x)\wedge F_{Y_{\mathbf{Q}}}(y) - F_X(x)F_{Y_{\mathbf{Q}}}(y)\right] dxdy + \mathbf{E}^{\mathbf{P}}(X)\mathbf{E}^{\mathbf{P}}(Y_{\mathbf{Q}}) \\
&= \int_{-\infty}^{\infty}\int_{-\infty}^{\infty} xy\, K(dx,dy) = \int_0^1 F_X^{-1}(u)F_{Y_{\mathbf{Q}}}^{-1}(u)\, du,
\end{aligned}$$

where $K(x,y) := F_X(x)\wedge F_{Y_{\mathbf{Q}}}(y)$ and $F_{Y_{\mathbf{Q}}}^{-1}$ is the quantile of the distribution function of $Y_{\mathbf{Q}}$. We have thus proved that for every $X \in L^\infty$ and $\mathbf{Q} \ll \mathbf{P}$,

$$\mathbf{E}^{\mathbf{Q}}(X) \le \int_0^1 F_X^{-1}(u)F_{Y_{\mathbf{Q}}}^{-1}(u)\, du \tag{3.2}$$

(with the equality when X and $Y_{\mathbf{Q}}$ are comonotone). In passing we remark that the same argument with the lower bound would yield a proof of *Hardy–Littlewood inequality*; see [9, Theorem 2.76].

Now let $\mathscr{P}_0 = \{\mathbf{Q}\colon \mathbf{Q} \ll \mathbf{P},\ \mathbf{E}^{\mathbf{Q}}(X) \le \rho(X) \text{ for all } X \in L^\infty\}$. It follows from Theorem 3.2 of [4] and (3.2) that

$$\rho(X) = \sup_{\mathbf{Q}\in\mathscr{P}_0} \mathbf{E}^{\mathbf{Q}}(X) \le \sup_{\mathbf{Q}\in\mathscr{P}_0} \int_0^1 F_X^{-1}(u)F_{Y_{\mathbf{Q}}}^{-1}(u)\, du. \tag{3.3}$$

On the other hand, since $(\Omega, \mathscr{F}, \mathbf{P})$ is atomless, for any $\mathbf{Q} \ll \mathbf{P}$ and $X \in L^\infty$, we can construct $\widetilde{X}$ which has the same distribution as X and is comonotone with $Y_{\mathbf{Q}}$. It then follows that for $\mathbf{Q} \in \mathscr{P}_0$,

$$\rho(X) = \rho(\widetilde{X}) \ge \mathbf{E}^{\mathbf{Q}}(\widetilde{X}) = \mathbf{E}^{\mathbf{P}}(\widetilde{X}Y_{\mathbf{Q}}) = \int_0^1 F_X^{-1}(u)F_{Y_{\mathbf{Q}}}^{-1}(u)\, du,$$

and hence

$$\rho(X) \ge \sup_{\mathbf{Q}\in\mathscr{P}_0} \int_0^1 F_X^{-1}(u)F_{Y_{\mathbf{Q}}}^{-1}(u)\, du.$$

But we have shown in (3.3) the reverse inequality, so the equality must hold in the above:

$$\rho(X) = \sup_{\mathbf{Q}\in\mathscr{P}_0} \int_0^1 F_X^{-1}(u)F_{Y_{\mathbf{Q}}}^{-1}(u)\, du. \tag{3.4}$$

Define

$$D(u) := \int_0^u F_{Y_{\mathbf{Q}}}^{-1}(v)\, dv. \tag{3.5}$$

Since $Y_{\mathbf{Q}}$ is positive, so is $F_{Y_{\mathbf{Q}}}^{-1}$, whence D is increasing. And D has an increasing density $F_{Y_{\mathbf{Q}}}^{-1}(v)$, so it is convex. Finally $D(1) = \mathbf{E}^{\mathbf{P}}(Y_{\mathbf{Q}}) = 1$. Thus D is a convex distortion.

Let $\mathscr{D}_{\text{cx}}$ denote the set of convex distortions. We shall prove the following two claims:

(1) $\mathscr{D}_{\text{cx}}$ is compact with respect to the topology of weak convergence.
(2) $D \mapsto \int_{\mathbb{R}} x \, dD \circ F(x)$ is continuous on $\mathscr{D}_{\text{cx}}$ for each distribution function F of $X \in L^{\infty}$.

Let $\mathscr{D}[0, 1]$ be the set of distribution functions on $[0, 1]$, which is compact. Since $\mathscr{D}_{\text{cx}} \subset \mathscr{D}[0, 1]$, we need only to show that $\mathscr{D}_{\text{cx}}$ is closed. Suppose that $D_n \in \mathscr{D}_{\text{cx}}$ and $D_n \stackrel{\text{d}}{\to} D$. Denoting by C the set of all continuity points of D, this means that $D_n(u) \to D(u)$ for every $u \in C$. If u and v belongs to C and if $0 < \lambda < 1$ is such that $\lambda u + (1 - \lambda)v \in C$, then we clearly have

$$D(\lambda u + (1 - \lambda)v) \leq \lambda D(u) + (1 - \lambda)D(v).$$

But C is dense in $[0, 1]$ (in fact, C^{C} is countable), so the right-continuity of D establishes the above inequality for all u, v in $[0, 1]$ and $0 < \lambda < 1$, i.e., $D \in \mathscr{D}_{\text{cx}}$. Note that $v = 1$ cannot be approached from the right, but we always have $D(1) = 1$. This shows the compactness of $\mathscr{D}_{\text{cx}}$.

For (2), note that $D \in \mathscr{D}_{\text{cx}}$ is continuous on $[0, 1)$ because it is convex and $D(0) = 0$. Thus the only possible discontinuity point of any $D \in \mathscr{D}_{\text{cx}}$ is $u = 1$. Now suppose $D_n \stackrel{\text{d}}{\to} D$ in $\mathscr{D}_{\text{cx}}$. Then for any x with $F(x) < 1$, one has $D_n \circ F(x) \to D \circ F(x)$. Also $D_n(1) = 1$ and $D(1) = 1$, so $D_n \circ F(x) \to D \circ F(x)$ holds for x with $F(x) = 1$ as well. Thus obviously $D_n \circ F \stackrel{\text{d}}{\to} D \circ F$. Since X is bounded a.s., this entails that

$$\int_{\mathbb{R}} x \, dD_n \circ F(x) \to \int_{\mathbb{R}} x \, dD \circ F(x),$$

which proves (2).

What we have shown in (3.4) can be rephrased as follows: there exist $\mathscr{D}_0 \subset \mathscr{D}_{\text{cx}}$ such that

$$\rho(X) = \sup_{D \in \mathscr{D}_0} \int_{[0,1]} F_X^{-1}(u) \, dD(u). \tag{3.6}$$

For the rest of the proof, we may argue as in Kusuoka [12] (see his Theorem 7 and Proposition 21). We include the proof for completeness. If we put

$$\mathscr{D}_\rho = \left\{ D \in \mathscr{D}_{\text{cx}} \colon \int_{[0,1]} F_X^{-1}(u)\, dD(u) \le \rho(X) \text{ for all } X \in L^\infty \right\},$$

$\mathscr{D}_0$ in (3.6) may clearly be replaced by $\mathscr{D}_\rho$. By (2) shown above, $\mathscr{D}_\rho$ is closed, and hence compact. Therefore for each fixed $X \in L^\infty$, one can find a $D_X \in \mathscr{D}_\rho$ for which one has $\rho(X) = \int_{[0,1]} F_X^{-1}(u)\, dD_X(u)$. Let

$$\mathscr{D}_\rho(F_X) = \left\{ D \in \mathscr{D}_\rho \colon \int_{[0,1]} F_X^{-1}(u)\, dD(u) = \rho(X) \right\}.$$

This is clearly closed, and what we have shown amounts to $\mathscr{D}_\rho(F_X) \neq \varnothing$.

Now we make the following assertion: For any finite number of distribution functions $F_1, \dots, F_k$ with bounded supports, $\mathscr{D}_\rho(F_1), \dots, \mathscr{D}_\rho(F_k)$ has a nonempty intersection. To prove this, let $X_1, \dots, X_k$ be comonotone random variables with distribution functions $F_1, \dots, F_k$ respectively (just let $X_i = F_i^{-1}(U)$ for a uniform random variable U). Put $X = \sum_{i=1}^k X_i$, and denote its distribution function by F. Then by [CA], we have $\rho(X) = \sum_{i=1}^k \rho(X_i)$.

Note that since $X_1, \dots, X_k$ are comonotone, we have $F^{-1} = \sum_{i=1}^k F_i^{-1}$ (see [6] or [7] for a proof). If we choose $D \in \mathscr{D}_\rho(F)$, then

$$\sum_{i=1}^k \int_{[0,1]} F_i^{-1}(u)\, dD(u) = \int_{[0,1]} F^{-1}(u)\, dD(u) = \rho(X) = \sum_{i=1}^k \rho(X_i).$$

On the other hand, we must have,

$$\int_{[0,1]} F_i^{-1}(u)\, dD(u) \le \rho(X_i), \quad i = 1, \dots, k.$$

Hence the equality must hold in each of the above inequalities, which implies $D \in \bigcap_{i=1}^k \mathscr{D}_\rho(F_i)$. We have proved that $\{\mathscr{D}_\rho(F) \colon F \text{ distribution function of } X \in L^\infty\}$ has the finite intersection property in $\mathscr{D}_{\text{cx}}$, which is compact, Thus there exists an element $\widehat{D} \in \mathscr{D}_{\text{cx}}$ which belongs to $\mathscr{D}_\rho(F)$ for every distribution function F of $X \in L^\infty$. Namely, for any $X \in L^\infty$,

$$\rho(X) = \int_{[0,1]} F_X^{-1}(u)\, d\widehat{D}(u).$$

This proves the first half of Theorem 3.3.

Finally, suppose that ρ is of the form (3.1). Then ρ is clearly a law invariant coherent risk measure. If X and Y are comonotone, then $F_{X+Y}^{-1} = F_X^{-1} + F_Y^{-1}$ as we noted above. Thus ρ is comonotonically additive. □

Theorem 3.3 suggests that we should look at risk measures of the form (3.1), i.e., the distorted expectation under D, if we are willing to accept the very plausible requirements of coherence, law invariance and comonotonic additivity. In fact, we know more from (3.5); the distortion function D has a density which is the quantile of the distribution function of the Radon–Nikodym density Y_Q.

The reason that we stick to the expression above and not the original form of Kusuoka representation is as follows: We can regard F_X^{-1} as the *rearrangement* of X in increasing order in the sense of Hardy et al. [10, §10.12]. Since X represents the loss, the larger values in the unit interval $(0, 1)$ correspond to unfavorable events. Thus if D in $\rho(X)$ above put much weight to the values near 1, it reveals decision maker's conservative attitude in assessing the risk X. In this way, intuitive interpretation of the distortion function D is possible.

Let us note that the renowned value at risk and the conditional tail expectation may be represented as a distorted expectation.

Example 3.4 (Value at risk). *Taking* $D(u) = \mathbf{1}_{[1-\alpha,1]}(u)$, $0 < \alpha < 1$ *produces the well-known value at risk (VaR), which is just the* $(1-\alpha)$*-th quantile* $F_X^{-1}(1-\alpha)$. *It is well known (see [2]) that the VaR is not a coherent risk measure. From the distortion point of view, it is because the corresponding distortion D is* not *convex.*

Example 3.5 (Expected shortfall). *For* $0 < \alpha < 1$, *let*

$$D_\alpha^{ES}(u) = \frac{1}{\alpha}\big[u - (1-\alpha)\big]_+,$$

where $a_+ = a \vee 0$. *Then the resulting risk measure is the renowned expected shortfall:*

$$ES_\alpha(X) = \frac{1}{\alpha}\int_{1-\alpha}^{1} F_X^{-1}(u)\,du.$$

This D_α^{ES} *is certainly convex, so the expected shortfall is a coherent risk measure, which is a well-known fact.*

4. Preservation of some stochastic orders

If D is a convex distortion, then, as a transformation on the space of distribution functions, it preserves some well-known stochastic orders. Recall the following definitions:

Definition 4.1. *Let* F *and* G *be distribution functions on* $\mathbb{R}$.

(1) G *is called stochastically larger than* F ($F \preceq_{st} G$) *if* $G(x) \le F(x)$ *for all* $x \in \mathbb{R}$.

For the next two stochastic orders, we assume that the means of F and G exist.

(2) *F is called less dangerous than G ($F \preceq_D G$) if there exists x_0 such that $F(x) \le G(x)$ for $x < x_0$ and $G(x) \le F(x)$ for $x \ge x_0$, and if $\int x\,dF(x) \le \int x\,dG(x)$.*

(3) *G is called larger than F in increasing convex order ($F \preceq_{icx} G$) if $\int h(x)\,dF(x) \le \int h(x)\,dG(x)$ for every increasing convex function h on $\mathbb{R}$ for which the integrals exist.*

Note that the increasing convex order is also known as *stop loss order* in actuarial mathematics. See Müller and Stoyan [16] for properties of these stochastic orders.

Theorem 4.2. *Let $D \in \mathscr{D}_{cx}$. Then we have:*

(1) *If $F \preceq_{st} G$, then $D \circ F \preceq_{st} D \circ G$.*
(2) *If $F \preceq_D G$, then $D \circ F \preceq_D D \circ G$.*
(3) *If $F \preceq_{icx} G$, then $D \circ F \preceq_{icx} D \circ G$.*

For (2) and (3), we assume that the means of F, G, $D \circ F$ and $D \circ G$ all exist.

Proof. (1) is trivial (we do not need convexity for (1)).

(2) Let $F \preceq_D G$, and x_0 be a point such that $F(x) \le G(x)$ for $x < x_0$ and $G(x) \le F(x)$ for $x \ge x_0$. Then clearly $D \circ F(x) \le D \circ G(x)$ for $x < x_0$, and $D \circ G(x) \le D \circ F(x)$ for $x \ge x_0$. So we need only prove $\int x\,dD \circ F(x) \le \int x\,dD \circ G(x)$. First suppose that $0 < G(x_0) < 1$. Note that

$$\int_{-\infty}^{\infty} x\,dD\circ G(x) - \int_{-\infty}^{\infty} x\,dD\circ F(x) = \int_{-\infty}^{\infty} [D\circ F(x) - D\circ G(x)]\,dx =: I_1 + I_2,$$

where

$$I_1 := \int_{-\infty}^{x_0} [D\circ F(x) - D\circ G(x)]\,dx, \quad I_2 := \int_{x_0}^{\infty} [D\circ F(x) - D\circ G(x)]\,dx.$$

Since $F(x) \le G(x)$ for $x \in (-\infty, x_0)$, we have $D \circ G(x) - D \circ F(x) \le d(G(x))(G(x) - F(x))$, where d is the left derivative of D. Then

$$I_1 \ge -d(G(x_0)) \int_{-\infty}^{x_0} [G(x) - F(x)]\,dx.$$

One can show in a similar manner that

$$I_2 \ge d(G(x_0)) \int_{x_0}^{\infty} [F(x) - G(x)]\,dx.$$

Hence,

$$I_1 + I_2 \geq d(G(x_0)) \int_{-\infty}^{\infty} [F(x) - G(x)]\,dx \geq 0$$

because d is positive and $\int_{-\infty}^{\infty}[F(x) - G(x)]\,dx = \int x\,dG(x) - \int x\,dF(x) \geq 0$.

If $G(x_0) = 1$, then we must have $F(x) \leq G(x)$ for all $x \in \mathbb{R}$. On the other hand, $0 \leq \int x\,dG(x) - \int x\,dF(x) = \int_{-\infty}^{\infty}[F(x) - G(x)]\,dx$ implies that $F \equiv G$.

Finally, if $G(x_0) = 0$, then $F = G \equiv 0$ on $(-\infty, x_0)$. This means $F(x) \geq G(x)$ for all $x \in \mathbb{R}$, i.e., $F \preceq_{\mathrm{st}} G$. By (1), $D \circ F \preceq_{\mathrm{st}} D \circ G$ then holds, and so we get $\int x\,dD \circ F(x) \leq \int x\,dD \circ G(x)$.

(3) Define the dual D^* of D by $D^*(u) = 1 - D(1-u)$. The survivor function $\overline{F}$ of a given distribution function F is defined by $\overline{F} = 1 - F$. Then the survivor function of the distorted distribution function $D \circ F$ is given by $D^* \circ \overline{F}$. By Theorem 1.5.7 of Müller and Stoyan [16], to prove $D \circ F \preceq_{\mathrm{icx}} D \circ G$, it is enough to show that

$$\int_t^{\infty} D^* \circ \overline{F}(x)\,dx \leq \int_t^{\infty} D^* \circ \overline{G}(x)\,dx$$

holds for each $t \in \mathbb{R}$.

Convexity of D implies that D^* is concave, so there exists a sequence of piecewise linear concave distortions D_n^* such that $D_n^* \uparrow D^*$ pointwise. Such a D_n^* can be written as a convex combination of functions having the form $(u/\alpha) \wedge 1$, $0 < \alpha \leq 1$ (In fact, this is precisely the dual of the distortion associated with the expected shortfall in Example 3.5. Therefore, in view of monotone convergence theorem, we have only to show, for a fixed $t \in \mathbb{R}$ and $0 < \alpha \leq 1$,

$$\int_t^{\infty} \left(\frac{\overline{F}(x)}{\alpha} \wedge 1\right) dx \leq \int_t^{\infty} \left(\frac{\overline{G}(x)}{\alpha} \wedge 1\right) dx. \tag{4.1}$$

Note that $\overline{G}(x) \leq \alpha$ iff $x \geq G^{-1}(1-\alpha)$. So we separate two cases: When $t \geq G^{-1}(1-\alpha)$, (4.1) follows easily. Using the assumption $F \preceq_{\mathrm{icx}} G$, we get

$$\int_t^{\infty} \left(\frac{\overline{G}(x)}{\alpha} \wedge 1\right) dx = \int_t^{\infty} \frac{\overline{G}(x)}{\alpha}\,dx \geq \int_t^{\infty} \frac{\overline{F}(x)}{\alpha}\,dx \geq \int_t^{\infty} \left(\frac{\overline{F}(x)}{\alpha} \wedge 1\right) dx.$$

When $t < G^{-1}(1-\alpha)$, splitting the range of the integral at $G^{-1}(1-\alpha)$ yields

$$\begin{aligned}
\int_t^\infty \left(\frac{\overline{G}(x)}{\alpha} \wedge 1 \right) dx &= \int_t^{G^{-1}(1-\alpha)} 1\, dx + \int_{G^{-1}(1-\alpha)}^\infty \frac{\overline{G}(x)}{\alpha}\, dx \\
&\geq \int_t^{G^{-1}(1-\alpha)} \left(\frac{\overline{F}(x)}{\alpha} \wedge 1 \right) dx + \int_{G^{-1}(1-\alpha)}^\infty \left(\frac{\overline{F}(x)}{\alpha} \wedge 1 \right) dx \\
&= \int_t^\infty \left(\frac{\overline{F}(x)}{\alpha} \wedge 1 \right) dx,
\end{aligned}$$

as required. □

Remark 4.3. Another way of proving (3) would be to apply Theorem 1.5.19 in Müller and Stoyan [16], together with (2) although a careful treatment of the step involving limits is necessary.

When X and Y have distribution functions F and G respectively, we write $X \preceq_{\mathrm{st}} Y$ when $F \preceq_{\mathrm{st}} G$; and similarly for $X \preceq_{\mathrm{D}} Y$ and $X \preceq_{\mathrm{icx}} Y$. Since $X \preceq_{\mathrm{st}} Y$ implies $X \preceq_{\mathrm{D}} Y$, which in turn implies $X \preceq_{\mathrm{icx}} Y$, we have the following corollary.

Corollary 4.4. *Any of $X \preceq_{st} Y$, $X \preceq_{D} Y$ or $X \preceq_{icx} Y$ implies $\rho_D(X) \leq \rho_D(Y)$.*

Remark 4.5. A proof of the above corollary in Wang [18, Theorem 1] contains an error. One can find a similar statement in Yaari [20]. A simple proof of a part of the Corollary 4.4 is also given in Leitner [14]. In the literature, this is a common statement concerning the preservation of stochastic order by risk measures. Note, however, that Theorem 4.2 is a stronger result in that if $D \in \mathscr{D}_{\mathrm{cx}}$, then $F \preceq_{\mathrm{icx}} G$ implies $\int h(x)\, dD \circ F(x) \leq \int h(x)\, dD \circ G(x)$ for all convex increasing h, not just for $h(x) = x$.

5. Concluding remarks

We note that many premium principles in actuarial mathematics can be written as a distorted expectation. Wang [18] is considered to be the first to propose the distortion approach to premium principles although Denneberg [5] had already indicated possible generalization using distorted probabilities. He also showed that for a convex D, the distortion premium principle possesses many desirable properties as a premium principle. Wang et al. [19] take the axiomatic approach similar to that given above and prove the analogous representation theorem for premium principles.

In Tsukahara [17], the present author introduces parametric families of convex distortions, and several examples of distortion risk measure can be found therein.

References

1. Acerbi, C.: Spectral measures of risk: A coherent representation of subjective risk aversion. J. Banking Finance **26**, 1505–1518 (2002)
2. Artzner, P., Delbaen, F., Eber, J.-M., Heath, D.: Thinking coherently. RISK Mag. **10** (November), 68–71 (1997)
3. Artzner, P., Delbaen, F., Eber, J.-M., Heath, D.: Coherent measures of risk. Math. Finance **9**, 203–228 (1999)
4. Delbaen, F.: Coherent risk measures on general probability spaces. In: Sandmann, K., Schönbucher, P.J. (eds.): Advances in finance and stochastics. Berlin: Springer 2002, pp. 1–37
5. Denneberg, D.: Premium calculation: Why standard deviation should be replaced by absolute deviation. ASTIN Bull. **20**, 181–190 (1990)
6. Denneberg, D.: Non-additive measures and integral. Dordrecht: Kluwer 1994
7. Dhaene, J., Denuit, M., Goovaerts, M.J., Kaas, R., Vyncke, D.: The concept of comonotonicity in actuarial science and finance: theory. Insur. Math. Econ. **31**, 3–33 (2002)
8. Föllmer, H., Schied, A.: Robust preferences and convex measures of risk. In: Sandmann, K., Schönbucher, P.J. (eds.): Advances in finance and stochastics. Berlin: Springer 2002, pp. 39–56.
9. Föllmer, H., Schied, A.: Stochastic finance: An introduction in discrete time. Berlin: Walter de Gruyter 2002
10. Hardy, G.H., Littlewood, J.E., Pólya, G.: Inequalities, 2nd edn. Cambridge: Cambridge University Press 1952
11. Jouini, E., Schachermayer, W., Touzi, N.: Law invariant risk measures have the Fatou property. Adv. Math. Econ. **9**, 49–71 (2006)
12. Kusuoka, S.: On law invariant coherent risk measures. Adv. Math. Econ. **3**, 83–95 (2001)
13. Lehmann, E.L.: Some concepts of dependence. Ann. Math. Statist. **37**, 1137–1153 (1966)
14. Leitner, J.: A short note on second-order stochastic dominance preserving coherent risk measures. Math. Finance **15**, 649–651 (2005)
15. McNeil, A.J., Frey, R., Embrechts, P.: Quantitative risk management: concepts, techniques, and tools. Princeton, NJ: Princeton University Press 2005
16. Müller, A., Stoyan, D.: Comparison methods for stochastic models and risks. Chichester: Wiley 2002
17. Tsukahara, H.: One-parameter families of distortion risk measures. Math. Fin. (2009) (to appear)
18. Wang, S.S.: Premium calculation by transforming the layer premium density. ASTIN Bull. **26**, 71–92 (1996)
19. Wang, S.S., Young, V.R., Panjer, H.H.: Axiomatic characterization of insurance prices. Insur. Math. Econ. **21**, 173–183 (1997)
20. Yaari, M.E.: The dual theory of choice under risk. Econometrica **55**, 95–115 (1987)

Subject Index

Instructions for Authors

A. General

1. Papers submitted for publication will be considered only if they have not been and will not be published elsewhere without permission from the publisher and the Research Center for Mathematical Economics.

2. Every submitted paper will be subject to review. The names of reviewers will not be disclosed to the authors or to anybody not involved in the editorial process.

3. The authors are asked to transfer the copyright to their articles to Springer-Verlag if and when these are accepted for publication.

The copyright covers the exclusive and unlimited rights to reproduce and distribute the article in any form of reproduction. It also covers translation rights for all languages and countries.

4. Manuscript must be written in English. Its pdf file should be submitted to:

Office of Advances in
Mathematical Economics
c/o Professor Toru Maruyama
Department of Economics
Keio University
maruyama@econ.keio.ac.jp

5. **Offprints**: Twenty-five (25) **offprints** of each paper will be supplied free of charge. Additional offprints can be ordered at cost price.

B. Preparation of Manuscript

1. Manuscripts must be double-spaced (not 1.5), with wide margins (at least 25 mm), and large type (at least 12 point) on one side of A4 paper. Any manuscript that does not meet these requirements will be returned to the author immediately for retyping.

2. All manuscripts would finally be composed using our Springer LaTeX macro package. The Springer macros use standard LaTeX packages - if you do not have these packages refer to `http://www.ctan.org` or `http://www.dante.de/tex`. If authors make manuscripts by word-processing software other than TeX, please follow our styles as possible. For authors who prepare their manuscripts by TeX, we strongly recommend to visit our homepage, `http://www.springeronline.com/economics/`. You can download all the necessary macro packages with instructions for LaTeX2e from `ftp://ftp.springer.de/pub/tex/latex/svjour/global/`. For support, please contact `texhelp@springer.de`.

3. **The title page** must include: title; short (running) title of up to 60/85 characters; first names and surnames of all coauthors with superscript numerals indicating their affiliations; full street addresses of all affiliations; address to which proofs should be sent; fax number; and any footnotes referring to the title (indicated by asterisks*).

4. **Summary/abstract**: Each paper must be preceded by a summary/an abstract, which should not exceed 100 words.

5. **The Journal of Economic Literature index number (JEL classification)** should be indicated and the statement of the **2000 Mathematics Subject Classification (MSC) numbers** is desirable. You can check JEL classification with Internet at `http://ideas.repec.org/JEL/` as well as 2000 MSC numbers at `http://www.ams.org/msc`.

6. **Main text**: All tables and figures must be cited in the text and

numbered consecutively with Arabic numerals according to the sequence in which they are cited. Please mark the desired position of tables and figures in the left margin of the manuscript.

Do not italicize, underscore, or use boldface for headings and subheadings. Words that are to be italicized should be underscored in pencil.

Abbreviations must be spelled out at first mention in summary/abstract and main text. Abbreviations should also be spelled out at first mention in figure legends and table footnotes.

Short equations can be run in with the text. Equations that are displayed on a separate line should be numbered.

7. **References**: The list of references should be in alphabetical order and include the names and initials of all authors (see examples below). Whenever possible, please update all references to papers accepted for publication, preprints or technical reports, giving the exact name of the journal, as well as the volume, first and last page numbers and year, if the article has already been published or accepted for publication.

When styling the references, the following examples should be observed:

Journal article:
1. or [F-M] Freed, D.S., Melrose, R.B.: A mod k index theorem. Invent. Math. **107**, 283-299 (1992)

Complete book:
2. or [C-S] Conway, J.H., Sloane, N.J.: Sphere packings, lattices, and groups (Grundlehren Math. Wiss. Bd. 290) Berlin Heidelberg New York: Springer 1988

Single contribution in a book:
3. or [B] Border, K.C.: Functional analytic tools for expected utility theory. In: Aliprantis, C.D. et al. (eds.): Positive operators, Riesz spaces and economics. Berlin Heidelberg New York: Springer 1991, pp. 69-88

8. **Citations in the text** should be either by numbers in square brackets, e.g. [1], referring to an alphabetically ordered and numbered list, or by the author's initials in square brackets, e.g. [F-M], or by author and year in parentheses, e.g. Freed and Melrose (1992). Any of these styles is acceptable if used consistently throughout the paper. In the third system, if a work with more than two authors is cited, only the first author's name plus "et al." need be given and if there is more than one reference by the same author or team of authors in the same year, then a, b, c should be added after the year both in the text and in the list of references.

9. **Tables** are to be numbered separately from the illustrations. Each table should have a brief and informative title. All abbreviations used in a table must be defined in a table footnote on first use, even if already defined in the text. In subsequent tables abbreviations need not be redefined. Individual footnotes should be indicated by superscript lowercase a, b, c, etc. Permission forms must be provided for any tables from previously published sources (same procedure as with figures; see below).

10. **Figures**: If you have access to suitable software, you can design your figures directly on a computer, but creation by other means is of course also possible. In any case the originals should be pasted into the camera-ready copy at the appropriate places and with the correct orientation. If necessary, the figures may be drawn overscale, but in this case suitably reduced copies should be pasted into the script.

If a figure has been published previously, acknowledge its source and submit written permission signed by author and publisher. The source must be included in the reference list. If a permission fee is required, it must be paid by the author. Responsibility for meeting this requirement lies entirely with the author.

GPSR Compliance

The European Union's (EU) General Product Safety Regulation (GPSR) is a set of rules that requires consumer products to be safe and our obligations to ensure this.

If you have any concerns about our products, you can contact us on ProductSafety@springernature.com

In case Publisher is established outside the EU, the EU authorized representative is:

Springer Nature Customer Service Center GmbH
Europaplatz 3
69115 Heidelberg, Germany

Batch number: 10755053

Printed by Printforce, the Netherlands